GLOBAL RECESSION AND ECONOMIC RECOVERY

GLOBAL RECESSION AND ECONOMIC RECOVERY

Edited by

ANIL KUMAR THAKUR

and

ARUN PRABHA CHOUDHARY

Published on behalf of
THE INDIAN ECONOMIC ASSOCIATION

DEEP & DEEP PUBLICATIONS PVT. LTD.
F-159, RAJOURI GARDEN, NEW DELHI-110027

GLOBAL RECESSION AND ECONOMIC RECOVERY

ISBN 978-81-8450-356-2

Typeset by S.S. COMPOSERS
3190, Mohindra Park, Shakur Basti, Delhi-110034.

Printed in India at MAYUR ENTERPRISES
WZ Plot No. 3, Gujjar Market, Tihar Village, New Delhi-110018.

Published by DEEP & DEEP PUBLICATIONS PVT. LTD.
F-159, Rajouri Garden, New Delhi-110027.
Phones: 25435369, 25440916
E-mail: ddpbooks@yahoo.co.in • ddpubs@gmail.com
Showroom:
2/13, Ansari Road, Daryaganj, New Delhi-110002 • Telefax: 23245122

Contents

Preface

The challenges of Global recession confronted the Indian economy from 2008-10. The major challenges include the short-term macroeconomic challenges of monetary and fiscal policy and the medium-term challenges of returning to high growth path. The former covers issues such as the tradeoff between inflation and growth, the use of monetary *versus* fiscal policy and their relative effectiveness and coordination between the two. The latter includes the tension between short and long-term fiscal policy, the immediate longer-term imperatives of monetary policy and institutional reforms necessary for restoring high growth. To counter the negative fallout of the global recession on the Indian economy, the Government responded by providing a substantial fiscal expansion in the form of tax relief to boost demand and increased expenditure on public projects to create employment and public assets. Simultaneously, the Reserve Bank of India took a number of monetary easing and liquidity-enhancing measures including reduction in cash reserve ratio, statutory liquidity ratio and key policy rates. Luckily, the Indian economy recovered soon and came out of the trap of global recession in early 2010.

The present book is an edited volume comprising the research papers contributed to 92nd Annual Conference of Indian Economic Conference held at KIIT, Bhubaneswar, Orissa during December 27-29, 2009. The volume includes those papers which have been presented during the technical session on the theme "Global Economic Crisis and its Impact on Indian Economy" under the chairmanship of Prof. Manoj Panda.

We acknowledge our sincere gratitude and thanks to Indian Economic Association and President (2009) Prof. C.H. Hanumanta Rao for giving us the opportunity to edit this volume. We express our thanks to learned chairman Prof. Manoj Panda and all the paper contributors of this volume who have analysed all the aspects of global recession and economic recovery. Special thanks are due to Prof. Sudhakar Panda, Dr. Prashant Panda and KIIT University for holding the 92nd Conference very successfully. Our deep appreciation goes to Mr. G.S. Bhatia, Managing Director, Deep and Deep Publications and his team for bringing this volume in an excellent manner.

ANIL KUMAR THAKUR
ARUN PRABHA CHOUDHARY

List of Contributors

A.C. Jha, Lecturer, Department of History, G.S. College, Chapra.

A.K. Khan, Lecturer in Commerce, Gaya College, Gaya (Bihar).

Anil Kumar Thakur, Department of Commerce, College of Commerce, Patna.

Anup Kumar, Research Scholar, Department of Economics, University of Allahabad, Allahabad.

Arun Prabha Choudhary, Assistant Professor, Department of Economics, U.C.S.S.H., M.L. Sukhadia University, Udaipur, Rajasthan.

C.K. Shahi, Department of Economics, B.R.A. Bihar University, Muzaffarpur.

Elizabeth Joey Henriques, Associate Professor, Department of Economics, Government College of Arts, Science and Commerce, Quepem, Goa.

K. Hari Haran, Flat No. 153-D, Kamaraj St., Rama Krishna Nagar, Chennai.

Kamesh Kumar, University Professor and Head, P.G. Department of Economics, A.N. College, Patna.

Kamna, Jawahar Navoday Vidyalay, Vaishali.

Kishore Kumar Roy Choudhury, Reader in Economics, D.N College, P.O. Aurangabad, Dist. Murshidabad.

Manindra Kumar Singh, Department of Economics, M.A.M. College, Naughachia, Bhagalpur.

Md. Qaiser Alam, Sr. Assistant Professor, Department of Eonomics, M.P.P.G. College, Mau, Chitrakoot (U.P.).

Md. Reyazuddin, Reader in Commerce, Vanijya Mahavidyalaya, Patna University, Patna.

Md. Shabbir Alam, Research Scholar, Department of Economics, A.M.U., Aligarh.

N. Sudhakara Rao, Professor of Economics and Applied Economics, Acharya Nagarjuna University, Guntur, A.P.

Niraj Kumar Verma, Reader in Economics, H.D. Jain College, Veer Kunwar Singh University, Ara.

Niraj Kumar, Lecturer, Department of Pol. Science, R.P.S. College, Patna.

P.C. Panda, Associate Professor of Economics, School of Management, KIIT University, Bhubaneswar.

P.K. Bhargava, Emeritus Fellow—UGC and former Head, Dean, Faculty of Social Sciences and Director, IRD Centre, Banaras Hindu University, Varanasi, U.P.

P.S.K. Sudheer, Research Scholar, School of Economics, Andhra University, Visakhapatnam.

Pradeep Kumar Singh, Doctoral Research Fellow—UNCTAD, Department of Economics, University of Allahabad, Allahabad.

Purabi Borthakur, Department of Economics, C.K.B. Commerce College, Jorhat, Assam.

Puspa Tarafdar, Reader in Economics, Sarojini Naidu College for Women, Kolkata.

Rekha Ramesh Gaonkar, Associate Professor and Head of Department of Economics, M.E.S. College of Arts and Commerce, Zuarinagar, Goa.

S. Narayanan, Department of Economics, IDE, University of Madras. Chennai, Tamil Nadu.

S. Natchathira Jothi, Reader in Economics, Lady Doak College, Madurai, Tamil Nadu.

S. Pati, Adjunct Professor of Economics, School of Management, KIIT University, Bhubaneswar.

S.S. Choudhary, Professor and Head, Department of Business Administration, J.R.N. Rajasthan Vidyapeeth University, Udaipur, Rajasthan.

Saroj Sinha, Head, Department of Economics, Patna Women's College, Patna University, Patna.

Shatyaki, Project Manager, Thomson Digital, Noida (U.P.).

Shrawan Kumar Singh, Professor of Economics, IGNOU, (Retd.), B-2/71-A, DDA Flats, Keshavpuram, Delhi.

Sudhakar Panda, Professor of Economics (Retd.), Utkal University, Bhubaneswar

T.G. Gite, Chairman of BOS in Business Economics, University of Pune, H.R. College, Rajgurunagar, Dist. Pune.

U.S. Rai, Professor, Department of Economics, University of Allahabad, Allahabad.

V.B. Chaurasia, Senior Lecturer, Department of Economics, D.A.V. (P.G.) College, Dehradun (Uttarakhand).

Vinod Kumar Singh, Professor and Head, Department of Economics, Veer Kunwar Singh University, Ara (Bihar).

Yogendra Kumar Singh, Department of L.S.W., A.N. College, Patna.

Introduction

The Global Financial Crisis was started in August 2007 in United States. It originated due to creation of structured investment instruments out of sub-prime mortgage lending in U.S. The securitization process, however, was not backed by due diligence and led to large-scale default. The complexity of the instruments and the credit rating agencies assignment of high rating played a contributory role in creation of panic situation among investors. The initial effect on the crisis was profound on the US financial institutions, and less serious on emerging economies like India.

In the initial stages, the capital flows to the emerging economies actually increased, giving rise to what is termed as 'positive shock' and the 'decoupling debate'. The net FII inflows in India were increased to US $ 22.5 billion from Sept. 2007-Jan. 2008, as against a FII inflow of US $ 11.8 billion during April-July 2007. After January 2008, the effect of global recession on Indian economy was aggravated and casted adverse effects on the economy, e.g. fall in exports, increase in unemployment, stock market crash, reduction in demand and so on. The Government of India and Reserve Bank of India announced specific fiscal and monetary measures to address the impacts of global recession on Indian economy.

We are thankful to Indian Economic Association for selecting such an important issue as one of themes of 92nd Annual Conference of the Association. We extend our hearty gratitude to the contributors who have touched and analysed every dimension of global recession and economic recovery and made the session very vibrant with their deliberations and discussions. The book will be very useful for economists, teachers, researchers, students, policy-makers, bankers and for all those who are having their interest in current socio-economic and political issues. A brief introduction of the papers included in this volume, is given below:

P.C. Panda, S. Pati and Sudhakar Panda, in their joint paper, "Globalisaton, Global Meltdown and the Indian Economy: Challenges Ahead", have analysed global meltdown and bursting of bubble in globalized era. They have, very comprehensively, discussed state intervention and crisis management at global and at India's level and observed that financial crisis occurred on account of our failure to manage the crisis efficiently. They believe that the biggest challenge is to avoid the happenings of such events in future. It requires to bring into existence an international order that prevents such major turmoil's in future.

S. Narayanan, in his paper entitled, "The Global Economic Crisis and its Impact on India", has observed that Indian economy was partially hit by global crisis through Financial Channel, Real Channel and Confidence Channel. He has assessed the impact of global crisis on Indian economy in terms of slow growth rate, increased job losses and fall in the wealth. He has also described several measures taken by the Reserve Bank of India to mitigate the adverse effects of the global financial crisis on the Indian economy.

The paper entitled "Impact of the Global Economic Crisis on the Indian Economy" is contributed by Niraj Kumar and A.C. Jha. They have very well elaborated Global Economic Crisis and its impact on various sectors of the Indian economy. After analysing monetary and fiscal measures, the authors conclude to avoid such crisis, India should focus on development of domestic market.

Shrawan Kumar Singh, in his paper, "Global Economic Crisis and the Indian Economy: An Analysis" has analysed the impact on the Indian Economy in terms of employment and growth rate parameters. He has also analysed the policy response of India and concluded that for smooth functioning of free market economy, strong governmental regulations, closer oversight, greater transparency and accountability is required.

N. Sudhakara Rao, in his paper, "Impact of the Global Economic Crisis on SMEs in India", has estimated impact of global economic crisis on Indian exports, labour market and on

Micro, Small and Medium Enterprises (MSMEs) and unorganized sector and concluded that globalisation has adversely affected India's real economy. To correct the disequilibrium requires various fiscal and monetary measures with stimulai packages to revive domestic demand, diversification of markets and enhance competitiveness of Indian exports.

P.K. Bhargava has deliberated upon, "Global Meltdown: Its Impact on Fiscal Scenario of the Central Government". He has analysed fiscal health of the Government of India and observed that the fiscal situation of the Central Government is not satisfactory. The problem of fiscal imbalance is structural not cyclical. The global financial crisis did affect the financial liabilities of the centre but it is not the sole cause for dismal fiscal situation.

Mohammed Qaiser Alam and Mohammed Shabbir Alam's paper "Global Financial Crisis and the Indian Economy: Myth and Reality" analyses macroeconomic performance of Indian economy and fiscal situation of central government. The authors conclude that global financial crisis has reduced the world GDP growth rate and shaken the business confidence. It also reduced FDI inflows in India. They suggest that interests of the poor people should be protected along with job security.

S.S. Choudhary and Arun Prabha Choudhary, in their paper "Global Economic Crisis and Growth: Dynamics of the Indian Economy", have analysed global economic crisis and its impact on overall GDP growth of India, on financial sector, on balance of payments, on money and capital markets, etc. The policy measures to counter economic crisis have also been discussed. The paper also focuses on recent growth dynamics and future prospects and challenges of Indian economy. The paper concludes that Indian economy is fastly recovering. To attain the growth momentum, policy measures to be adopted, should be focused on short and long-term challenges and ensure the sustainability of growth and progress.

Pradeep Kumar Singh, Anup Kumar and U.S. Rai have focused on growth of service sector in their paper "Strategic Importance of Business Process Outsourcing in India's Service Sector". They have dealt upon growth trends and share of service sector in GDP. They have also analysed growth problems and prospects of BPOs in India, in the context of global economic crisis. They have also made SWOT analysis of BPO sector and observed that in order to compete with global market, India needs to build a full spectrum BPO industry as it is emerging as an important sector in the world.

A.K. Khan, in his paper entitled "Impact of Global Recession on Indian Economy" has analysed impact of global crisis on Indian economy. He has observed the impact on various sectors of the economy and concluded that due to global crisis, India is facing the problems of declining growth rate, increasing fiscal and revenue deficit, increasing unemployment, crash of share market, etc.

Kamesh Kumar and Shatyaki have analysed impact of global meltdown on Indian Economy, in their paper "A Study Identifying Factors Considered for Evaluating the Global Economic Crisis". They have considered NREGS Act as ray of hope, for Indian poors, in global meltdown. They, very optimistically, remark that Global Financial Crisis may be an opportunity for India if the country anticipate and assess the needs of the world correctly and transform herself accordingly.

The paper entitled "Is India Really Immune to the Global Meltdown?" is authored by Purabi Borthakur. She has analysed different macroeconomic indicators with the help of secondary data and concluded that global meltdown has affected Indian economy partially and very soon India will recover from the global crisis.

S. Natchathira Jothi, in his paper "Global Economic Crisis and its impact on India", has dealt with causes and impact of the crisis on Indian economy. He has also made suggestions to minimize the negative impact of the crisis and observed that despite the severity of the global crisis, Indian economy has shown considerable resilience.

In her paper "Impact of the Global Financial Crisis on the Indian Economy", Puspa Tarafdar has focused on the optimistic approach based on endorsement of decoupling theory. The decoupling theory asserted that growth in Asian Economies were decoupled from growth trends in west and the growth process in Asia would not only be continuous but also may help the western economies to pull them out of the recession. She has also dealt upon global inflation. She concludes that this crisis has affected weaker sections adversely and in India very little have done to relieve the distress, caused by the crisis to the vulnerable sections of the society.

Anil Kumar Thakur, Manindra Kumar Singh and P.S.K. Sudheer, in their paper, titled "Global Meltdown and Indian Economy" have specifically analysed the impact of global recession on trade, agriculture and employment. They have suggested to break supply side bottlenecks to come out of the crisis.

V.B. Chaurasia, in his paper "Global Economic Crisis and its impact on the Indian Economy" has observed that the effect of global recession, on Indian economy, has been indirect through trade and investment channels. To come out of the recession both monetary and fiscal measures have adopted. He has suggested that efforts should be made to keep prices at low level to generate and maintain demand.

K. Hari Haran has focused on various impacts of financial crisis in his paper "Financial Meltdown and its Impact on the Indian Economy". He observed that global recession had adversely affected the unorganized workers especially in construction industry and the poor section of the society. He believes that youngsters and upwardly mobile masses will rebuild the nation and keep the heads of Indians high.

Mohammed Reyazuddin and Yogendra Kumar Singh have very comprehensively analysed global crisis and its affects on Indian Economy. Their paper entitled "International Economic Crisis and the Indian Economy" has been focused on dynamics of international trade, competitiveness and reasons for economic crisis in India. To overcome the problem, Indian policy-makers need to maintain vigilance and be proactive.

Vinod Kumar Singh and Niraj Kumar Verma, in their paper entitled "Housing Bubble and Credit Derivatives as Factors Behind the Financial Crisis", have analysed housing bubble and related issues in detail as the factors behind the financial crisis. They believe that the widespread use of financial instruments should be checked and supervised.

T.G. Gite, in his paper "The Global Economic Crisis and the Indian Economy", has dealt upon the causes of crisis and policy measures adopted to correct global crisis.

He believes that Indian economy does not require any

further fiscal stimulus to combat the crisis as the Government of India is seriously concerned over this issue and has already initiated several measures.

Kishore Kumar Roy Choudhury has focused on linkages between employment and global recession, in his paper "The Global Economic Crisis and the Impact of the Indian Job Market". He has discussed Neo-Liberal theory of Globalisation. While analysing the impact of crisis on Indian job market, he observed both private and public employment have adversely affected by the crisis.

Kamna, in her paper "The Global Economic Crisis and the Indian Economy" has elaborated global economic crisis and Indian situation of slump. She has focused upon 'Social impact' of global recession. While discussing several domestic policies, she suggests expansion of the NREGS, public health care and education, universal access to the PDS to protect poorest of the poors.

Rekha Ramesh Gaonkar and Elizabeth Joey Henriques, in their paper "Tackling Unemployment Problem under Global Recession: Can Self-Help Groups be the Solution?" have made quantitative analysis to analyse the role of SHGs in employment generation. The results show that SHGs give the employment to their members and generate additional employment opportunities in informal sector for unskilled and semi-skilled workers.

Saroj Sinha and C.K. Shahi, in their paper "Can the Present Post-Crisis Recovery be Sustained?" have observed that India is at satisfactory position in terms of recovery due to aggressive fiscal expansion and appropriate monetary measures adopted by the Government and Reserve Bank of India. Inspite of several positive signs shown by the Indian economy, a sustained turnaround is not assured.

ANIL KUMAR THAKUR
ARUN PRABHA CHOUDHARY

Globalisation, Global Meltdown and the Indian Economy: Challenges Ahead

P.C. Panda, S. Pati and Sudhakar Panda

GLOBALISATION

Years of steady and sustained efforts aimed at reforming the Indian economy since July 1991 when the present Prime Minister was the Finance Minister could reverse the path of India's slow growth and declining opportunities to a period of high growth and expanding opportunities. When Dr. Manmohan Singh assumed office as India's Prime Minister on 22nd May 2004, the economy was growing fast on an average, at 7 percent per annum. It was the result of sound macroeconomic policies that created a business friendly and pro-growth environment in India. Once the barriers to growth were removed, foreign investors found India an attractive destination and the country could gain immensely from the entry of foreign capital and technology. India got the benefits of fiscal reforms, public sector reforms, financial deregulations and world trade. Its economic fundamentals became strong. Savings could rise from 23.5% of GDP to 34% of GDP between 2001 to 2006. Gross capital formation increased from 22.8% to 35.9% of GDP during the same period. Foreign exchange reserves could reach US$ 151.6 billion by the end of March 2006. The state though committed to reforms and liberalization could, however, make the right interventions in market operations and in the functioning of the economy to save it from risks and regulatory failures. The economy became competitive. Prices of goods and services, as per the market forces, were rationalized and found their own levels. Indian stock market could attract global finance for its superior investment opportunities, not to speak of the funds from the Indian mutual funds and insurance companies.

The economy from 1991 onwards moved on in an assured way. It was virtually a period of smooth development. Banks, financial institutions and industrial houses performed better, became bigger and entered international markets to play a bigger role. There were mergers and acquisitions. Tata acquired Corus, the Anglo-Dutch Steel unit. Two important brands namely Jaguar and Land Rover in the passenger car segment were also acquired by the Tatas at a cost of $ 1.5 billion. Indian software industry became global and India emerged as a leader in Information Technology. TCS, WIPRO, SATYAM AND INFOSYSIS became international brands and were much sought after in USA, UK and in the EU countries for their professional efficiency and excellent delivery of services. Globalisation created new business opportunities. Overseas investments by India increased significantly from $ 0.7 billion in 2000-01 to $2.7billion in 2005-06 and then rose to $ 11 billion in 2006-07 after Tata's acquisition of Corus [Majumdar: 2007]. Indian companies acquired an international status. They could face global competition successfully by improving their operational efficiencies. "India's two-way trade [merchandise exports plus imports], as a proportion of GDP grew from 21.2 per cent in 1997-98 the year of the Asian crisis to 34.7 per cent in 2007-08 [Subbarao: 2009]. New products and new services appeared in the market. A larger and wider choice was available to the Indian consumers. What is more important to note was the change in the attitude and aspirations of the people.

Our business environment, because of high returns on companies' equity could attract more and more capital from abroad. Foreign Institutional Investors (FIIs) brought in by the end of November, 2007 as much as $68 billion by way of equity ($65.18 bn.) and debt ($2.72 bn.). FIIs could become the largest investors in India with holdings valued at over US $751.14 billions as on December 31, 2008 (Gautam Chand: 2009). Foreign Direct Investment (FDI) started coming to India. Cumulative amount of FDI inflows to India (from August 1991 to March 2009) stood at Rs. 4,53,647 crore (GoI: 2009). International finance found India a safe place for business. FIIs from US, UK, Canada, France, Ireland, Australia and Switzerland came to India. More than 1000 FIIs are working in India. Financial integration with the world increased. By taking advantage of new and emerging international business and trade developments Indian companies became global companies with global operations and global strategies. A challenging environment was also created at home by the entry of Multi National Companies (MNCs) to the Indian market threatening the home companies as they offered better products at competitive prices. They brought in capital, new technology and professional and managerial expertise which no Indian companies could ignore for their survival. In fact the Indian economy experienced increasing specialization in production and exchange as never before. Retail business, estate business, car makers, manufacturing and investments in infrastructure along with rising consumption spending contributed to the growth of the economy. India experienced expansion in its trade and commerce, IT business, property business, hospitality and infrastructure. It was a period of good performance for the economy. All this could also result in opportunities for self-employment, self-improvement and created linkages—both forward and backward—for the development of the economy. India, China and many other developing countries became steady beneficiaries of the process of globalization. A sense of robust optimism prevailed in the entire economy. With an economist as India's Prime Minister guiding reforms and development, no doubts were ever expressed about the sustainability of India's growth process until the sub-prime crisis hit the American economy.

GLOBAL MELTDOWN

The sub-prime crisis in the housing mortgage sector in America "the result of long periods of excessively loose monetary policy in the major advanced economies" [Rakesh Mohan: 2009] "turned successively into a global banking crisis, global financial crisis" and then into a "global economic crisis" (Subbarao: 2009) and cast its shadow on the world economy. World-wide fears about its adverse impact on money market, finance, trade, capital movement and particularly on income and employment were expressed. The crisis that originated in America soon spread to Europe, to Asia and then to the entire world. The emerging economies like India which was fast moving towards global integration in terms of trade, finance and business acquisitions abroad were adversely affected by such developments. Developed countries like USA, UK and the EU countries got exposed to its negative impact. Companies like Boeing, Microsoft, Caterpillar, ING, Nortel, DHL and Philips started shedding labour. Downsizing became the mantra in the global management of companies. The IMF revised downwards its forecast of growth rates for US, UK, EU, Japan and even for India for 2009. Growth rate of the world economy was also projected to decline to 2.2 per cent in 2009.

Slow growth in the advanced economies affected India's exports to these countries. India's IT and IT-enabled services, finance and share market operations, aviation, garment manufacturing, engineering, mining, jewellery and handicraft sectors came under the impact of global recession. This consequently had its negative impact on our imports which, in turn, contributed to the slow-down in the growth of the developed countries. India's merchandise trade received a setback. Value of merchandise exports which stood at $15.5 billion in May 2008 declined to $11 billion in May 2009.Our imports were also affected. It shrank by 39.2 per cent to $16.21 billion in May 2009 compared to performance a year ago. [Business Standard, 2nd July, 2009] Not only that FIIs which brought funds from abroad for investment in India's equity market started withdrawing the funds. India faced a crisis in maintaining capital flows from abroad.

Critics of globalization look at the crisis more as the failure of the state to regulate and manage the process and contents of global businesses which change their course so rapidly and unpredictably and generate uncertainties for the entire world. In America financial regulation was slack. Because of continuous developments and innovations in the financial system including the use of derivatives and securitization of diverse types of financial papers, it was really a very difficult job for the banking and financial regulators to exercise any effective control over the system and prevent gross violation of financial norms and regulations. Absence of regulation and too much greed on the part of banks and mortgage houses to make as much money as quickly as possible generated a sort of market condition that virtually lured people to borrow money beyond their paying capacity. Presence of 'shadow banking system' made large and flexible funds available in the market. Funds could be borrowed easily for buying houses even by the people who had a poor record of payments. People indulged in speculative borrowing to buy house, sale it and make money. Banks and financial outfits could securities the mortgaged properties/documents and get finance from other institutions that would repackage them and then raise finance against them to pump in more money into the housing sector where the housing prices were seen rising and rising. The mechanism of Collateralized-Debt Obligations (CDOs) were used to convert "mortgage securities and corporate bonds from huge, illiquid assets owned by local investors into liquid financial instruments that could be flogged across the world" (Rajan, R.: 2009) Financial markets were too willing to lend and there seemed to be prosperity for everybody who could borrow and invest in houses. Financiers grew rich and billions of dollars were injected into the market. A sort of wild animal spirit seized the market. And the market went on feeding itself till the bubble burst and house prices crashed sending shock waves throughout the economy.

The financial market failed. Financial services became totally disorganized. The shock waves originating from the housing sector spread to other sectors and to other economies. Countries that had parked their savings in American banks and Mutual Funds (MFs) suffered as the fund managers had used the money to finance housing booms. It is estimated that between 2000 and 2008 American market received more than $5.7trillion from abroad to invest, which was over 40% of its 2007 GDP. Britain and Ireland received as much as 20% of their GDP. The corresponding share for Spain stood at 50% (The Economist, January, 2009). And all this money coming from abroad was used to finance credit operations in these countries. It is not surprising that loans became cheap and everybody had easy access to credit. There prevailed strong competition in the financial market to woo the borrowers. Borrowers' creditworthiness was not the prime consideration for the lenders. They had their ambitious plans to capture the market and borrowers were too willing to take more debts and become richer by investing in houses.

It is where the financial regulation failed. In fact, given the spread of financial innovations and the development of shadow banking network of hedge funds and money-market funds, etc. the regulatory system that was in vogue was not equipped enough to deal with the system which, over the years, had grown more complex and intractable. Besides, the banks and fund managers would always find some ways to circumscribe the operational effectiveness of the regulatory system. This went on till the bubble burst and the financial system in America plunged into chaos.

House owners failed to make their mortgage payments and the lenders, in turn, failed to meet their obligations and that caused not only uncertainty but also panic in the financial market. American International Group (AIG), one of the biggest insurance companies of the world and Fannie Mae and Freddie Mac, America's mortgage houses were to be rescued at great cost to the shareholders and tax payers. The collapse of Lehman Brothers in September, 2008 created world-wide fears and exposed the vulnerability of the banking industry. Attempts to save collapsing financial institutions would reveal the size, magnitude, extent and depth of the financial crisis and the loss to the stkeholders. Companies and individuals lost their net-worth in no time.

The crisis deepened and spread fast to different sectors of the economy. Housing, banking, finance, automobile, manufacturing and aviation activities declined. Asset prices tumbled. Share prices crashed. Goods were offered at reduced rates. Global operations of companies were affected. Companies filed for bankruptcies. Even the General Motors had to declare bankruptcy. People lost jobs. Top executives accepted reduced pay packets. Spending in the economy declined. Liquidity in the economy shrank. Borrowing became difficult. Optimism in the market was lost. Gloom and uncertainty marred the confidence of the investors. It became imperative that given the magnitude of the crisis, the state must intervene to save the economy from a total collapse.

BUBBLES, BURSTS AND THE FREE MARKET IDEOLOGY

Failure of finance created chaos and disrupted banking and financial services in the world. Ideology of deregulation and free market operations came under attack. It also called for state intervention and enactment of laws to deal with the delinquent financial institutions. But then free markets have a history of living with such disturbances—the bubbles and bursts—and then recovering from them to move on to growth till they get into market failure and instability.

Galbraith J.K. who in his book "A Short History of Financial Euphoria" (1990) examines the recurring episodes of major speculative events in free enterprise economies and their consequences says, "beyond a better perception of these speculative tendency and process itself, there probably is not a great deal that can be done" (Chapter 8, p. 108). Krugman, Paul (2008) referring to the "global credit system" which he finds to be "in a state of paralysis" recommends two things: "get credit flowing and prop up spending" (Chapter 10, p. 184). Alan Greenspan [2009] the former chairman of America's Federal Reserve terms such erratic behaviour of the economy experiencing booms and busts "a once-in-a-half century type of event" (*The Economist*, January, 2009). Kindleberger, Charles finds that once an economy gets into financial instability, such instability tends to become an in-built process going deeper into the economy. Keynes J.M. pointed out long ago to the behaviour of the investors who seized with an animal spirit would herd together in a period of boom and become overconfident investors and run into difficulties. In a free market economy, investors play an important role. They bring in funds for investment, finance new ventures and create new business. They bring in technologies and create opportunities for further growth. But sometimes they make mistakes. Their attempts to produce wealth become counterproductive. People, instead of becoming rich, become poor. Capitalist market behaves the way it has been behaving. Its flawed functioning makes it unstable and unpredictable. Galbraith in his study of the causes and consequences of the great economic crash in America makes an appropriate remark that "...throughout history, financial capacity and political perspicacity are inversely related.....It is what causes men who know that things are going wrong to say that things are fundamentally sound" (The Great Crash 1929: Chapter X, p. 210). What happened in America, in UK and in the EU countries that is in the capitalist world was a part of the historical pattern.

STATE INTERVENTION AND CRISIS MANAGEMENT

Financial markets have not recovered from the shock as yet. Economies in advanced countries continue to suffer from the effects of recession. This is impacting the developing economies including India. Economic stimulus that is the use of fiscal policy—government taxing and spending—is advocated throughout to revive the economies. Sometimes this is called the "recovery package". In February 2009 a stimulus package for $789 billion which includes $282 billion of tax relief was announced to revive the American economy from recession. The Obama administration also sanctioned $ 2.5 trillion as the rescue package for the financial system—"a combination of loans to banks and incentives to bring private capital into the banking system" (*The New York Times*, July 3, 2009).

State intervention to manage the crisis became the top most priority of the governments in the world. Mervin King, the Governor of Bank of England warned of "a sharp and prolonged slowdown in domestic demand" (Swan: 2009). Government in UK not only bailed out the banks and insured depositors' savings, but also increased public spending to fight the effects of recession. Bank of England reduced "its base rate to a record low rate of 0.5% and purchased securities mainly government bonds worth $206 billion equal to 9% of GDP to increase money flow into the economy. (*The Economist*, July 4, 2009). Corporate tax rates in Germany were cut to 30% from 39% earlier. German government provided a rescue package of 500 billion euro to its banking sector. Tax cuts and subsidies amounting to 64 billion euro has also been offered. A German fund with 115 billion euro has been set-up to assist non-financial companies hurt by recession [*The Economist*, June 27 2009]. Russia extended a bail out package of $220 billion to support its financial services industry. Italy provided for tax cuts to promote investments. Asian economies affected by the recession have been taking both fiscal and monetary measures to take care of recession and provide for growth. South Korea stood by its banking industry and guaranteed banks debts. China offered subsidies to its people to buy consumer durables including televisions and refrigerators to boost up consumption spending.

INDIA'S RESPONSE TO THE CRISIS

Indian economy has been adversely affected by the crisis. Its GDP growth rate in 2008-09 has been lowered to 6.8% compared to 9% in 2007-08.

The impact has been felt more deeply in the financial markets. India's equity market crashed. Corporate sector found it difficult to raise funds in the overseas market. There was a reverse flow of capital as the FIIs withdrew their fund invested in India's share market. As pointed out earlier, India's exports declined. The threat of unemployment and loss of income loomed larger.

The economy would have suffered a serious decline had it not been given the fiscal support by the government. Reserve Bank of India on its part maintained a close watch on the developments in money and foreign exchange markets and was quick enough to initiate suitable changes in monetary policies to keep bank credit flowing into the economy to facilitate spending and investments. In fact, ... "the measures put in place since mid-September 2008 have ensured that the Indian financial markets continue to function in orderly fashion" (Subbarao: 2009). The union government relaxed the provisions of the FRBM Act to raise public spending and move beyond the prescribed fiscal limit. It implemented the recommendations of the Sixth Pay Commission Report, gave relief to the farmers by waiving their loans and provided a larger safety-net for the rural poor. The fiscal stimulus in 2008-09 came to Rs. 1,86,000 crore to counter the impact of recession. Its budget 2009-10,which has projected an expenditure of Rs. 10,28,838 crore and announced tax cuts and plans to implement a number of schemes that would enhance investment and consumption spending in the economy to boost demand and encourage production activities. Higher government spending on infrastructure, housing and social sector has also been provided for in the budget. India has combined a policy of fiscal enlargement with a supportive monetary policy, that is, provision of credit at lower rates to the business sector to raise investment spending to fight recession and sustain growth.

CHALLENGES AHEAD

The crisis is far from over. It calls for a co-ordinated and long-term approach to prevent the recurrence of bubbles and then the bursts. The developing economies suffered for no fault of their own but for the unethical conduct of banks, mortgage houses and financial outfits in the advanced economies. Emergence of shadow banking and innovative financial instruments in the world market had a dramatic effect on the size and magniude of Collateral Damage and Response. Reserve Bank or international financial transactions. Regulatory authorities failed to exercise any effective power over the activities of these institutions.

Failure of the "parallel banking system" or the 'shadow banking system' which include institutions of regulatory authorities to regulate the financial markets, particularly the activities like money market funds, hedge funds and exchange-traded funds contributed to a large extent to the severity of financial instability in the international market. They need to be brought under the control of the financial authorities. Governments in the developed countries need to amend existing rules and regulations to empower their regulatory bodies to monitor financial activities and take punitive action against the erring financial institutions.

It is time that Central Bankers of the world meet to review the existing norms of lending for the commercial banks and suggest appropriate changes. Global financial integration and liberalization of markets which facilitated faster movement of money and capital made competition more intense. The banks took bigger risks than what was warranted by their financial strength and capital adequacies. They, in fact, compromised dangerously with rules and regulations to the extent that they not only sacrificed depositors' interests but they themselves collapsed and dragged the entire world into the financial storm.

The financial crisis and the global melt down exposed our inability to manage success that with globalization and brought closer integrity and interdependence among the nations of the world. The task today before the international authorities is to initiate changes and bring into existence an international order that prevents such major financial turmoils in future and ensures growth and stability and protects the interests of the developing countries.

This, in fact, is the biggest challenge.

2

The Global Economic Crisis and its Impact on India

S. NARAYANAN

INTRODUCTION

It is often said that when the US sneezes the rest of the world catches cold. The financial crisis in the US, the worst since the Great Depression of 1929, is reaching perilous proportions. The collapse of the big five financial giants on Wall Street, Fannie Mac, Freddie Mac, AIG, Lehmman Brothers and Merrill Lynch—with revenues totaling nearly $ 322 billion in 2007, followed by two of the largest banks—Washington Mutual (Wa Mu) and Wachovia—has sent shock waves through global financial markets. It was transmitted internationally through trade flows, capital flows and commodity prices. Banking and financial crisis have been a common phenomenon under capitalism. The world has witnessed hundred of such crises and the frequency of the crises has increased over time. According to a World Bank study of 2001, there were as many as 112 systematic Banking crises from the late 1970's to until 2001.

THE INDIAN ECONOMY BEFORE THE GLOBAL CRISIS

India had emerged as a leading emerging market economy (EME) by the time when the sub-prime crises started. The average GDP growth of 8.8 per cent during the 5 year period 2003- 08 was not only one of the highest in the world in the recent period, but it has also permanently raised India's growth trajectory to a higher level. There was a clear structural transformation, driven by reforms, globalization and significant increase in domestic savings and investment rates, which helped in boosting both investments and productivity driven growth in the system.

Why has India been Hit by the Crisis?

We may examine to what extent India was affected by the global Economic Crisis: (i) The Indian Banking system has no direct exposure to the sub-prime mortgage assets, (ii) Indian financial sector has only limited off-balance sheet activities, (iii) Indian banks continue to remain sound and healthy. Therefore, India does not have much to do with any of the maladies that are at the core of the crisis. And the second argument is that India's recent growth has been driven predominantly by domestic consumption and domestic investment. External demand as measured by merchandize exports, account for less than 15 per cent of our GDP; to this extent there is some impact.

India's integration into the world economy over the last decade has been remarkably rapid. Integration into the world implies more than just exports. Going by the common measure of globalization, India's two way trade (Merchandize exports plus imports), as a proportion of GDP, increased from 21.2 per cent in 1997-98, the year of the Asian Crisis to 34.7 per cent in 2007-08. So the reason India has been hit by the crisis, despite mitigating factors, is clearly India's rapid and growing integration into the global economy. The main reason is India is more closely integrated with the rest of the world and also financial integration as deep as trade integration.

How India has been Hit by the Crisis?

The main reason for the crisis has spread to India through these channels: (i) Financial Channel, (ii) Real Channel, and (iii) Confidence Channel.

(i) Financial Channel

India's financial markets—equity market, money market, forex market and credit market—had all come under pressure from a number of directions. First as a consequence of the global liquidity squeeze, Indian corporates found their overseas financing drying up, forcing corporates to shift their credit demand to the domestic banking sector. Second, the forex market came under pressure because of reversal of capital flows. Both these factors put downward pressure on the rupee. Third, the Reserve Bank's intervention in the forex market to manage the volatility in the rupee further added to liquidity tightening. Rupee-US $ rate moved up from 40.25 during 2007-08 to 45.92 during 2008-09 and 48.65 during April 01-July 2009, a few months later.

(ii) Real Channel

As for as the real sector is concerned, the transmission of the global national economy has been quite straight forward—through the slump in demand for exports. The United States, European Union and the Middle East, which account for the three quarters of Indian goods and services trade, are in a synchronized downturn. Export in India experienced negative growth from October 2008, and service export decelerated. Remittances from migrant workers also declined. These are the important reasons.

(iii) Confidence Channel

Indian crisis spreads through the confidence channel. In sharp contrast to global financial market, which went into a seizure on account of a crisis of confidence, Indian financial markets continued to function in an orderly manner. However, the tightened global liquidity situation in the period immediately following the Lehman failure in mid-September 2008, increased the risk aversion of the financial system and made some banks cautious about lending. The credit growth during 2008-09 decelerated to 17.3 per cent from 22.3 per cent in the pervious year.

IMPACT ON THE INDIAN ECONOMY

India had a dream run of five years during 2003-08 as the GDP growth averaged nearly 9 per cent annually. But the economy began to slow down from the middle of 2007-08. As economic growth contracts, demand for labour has fallen. The unemployment estimates for the first quarter of the fiscal year beginning April 2009 were not optimistic. The Labour Bureau estimated that hundreds of thousands of people lost their jobs in the period. The worst affected sector was the textile industry which has shed 1,54,000 jobs followed by IT/BPO sectors (34,000) jobs and the gems and jewellery sector (20,000) job losses. Employment was the worst hit in exporting companies across all sectors with losses touching 1,67,000 jobs. In the period October-December 2008, the hit was the highest across India affecting 5,00,000 workers.

The global financial crisis made many financial institutions bankrupt. It has left India's top 40 billionaires poorer by $212 billion. According to Forbes Report dated 12 Nov. 2008, the total wealth of India's top 40 billionaires fell from $212 billion to $139 billion, it was $351 a year ago.

Outlook for India

India faced the problem of declining economic activity during Oct. 2008-Jan. 2009. Services sector decelerated, investment demand declined and corporate margin was dented, several positive features are declining inflation, lower crude prices as modest current account deficit. Banks are healthy, well-capitalized, comfortable in foreign exchange reserves, agriculture credit was not affected.

POLICY RESPONSE TO THE CRISIS

The, policy responses in India since September 2008 have been designed largly to mitigate the adverse impact of the global financial crisis on the Indian Economy. The Reserve Bank's policy stance will continue to maintain comfortable rupee and forex liquidity positions. The Reserve Bank has multiple instruments at its command such as repo and reserve repo rates, cash reserve ratio (CRR), statutory liquidity ratio (SLR), open market operations including the market stabilization scheme

(MSS), Special market operations and sector specific liquidity facilities. In addition, the Reserve Bank also uses prudential tools to modulate flow of credit to certain sectors consistent with financial stability. Within less than a month, it announced a second fiscal stimulus packages. India's two fiscal packages together accounted for USD 8.1 billion which represent 0.7%share of the country's GDP in 2008.

The Reserve Bank of India has been actively engaged in policy action to minimize the impact of the global crisis on India. The policy response of the Reserve Bank has helped in keeping India's financial market functioning in a normal manner.

References

Ben S. Bernake, "The Crisis and the Policy Response at the Stamp Lecture, London School of Economic, London, Jan. 13, 2009.

C.R.L. Narashimhnan, What caused the global economic crisis, *The Hindu*, dated 16-03-09.

How the global financial crisis affects India, *Business Standard*, 19 Sept. 2008.

Prime Minister Dr. Manmohan Speech, *CNN-IBN*.

Rakesh Mohan, "Global Financial Crisis: Causes, Impact, Policy, Responses and Lessons", *RBI Monthly Bulletin*, May 2009 (879-904).

Subbareo, D. (2009), "Global financial crisis" at the Confederation of Indian Industry, New Delhi, 26 March 2009.

3

Impact of the Global Economic Crisis on the Indian Economy

NIRAJ KUMAR AND A.C. JHA

With the Collapse of Lehman Brothers and other Wall Street icons, there was growing recession reach affected the US, the European Union (EU) and Japan. This was the result of large scale default in the US housing market as the banks went on providing risky loans without adequate security and the repaying capacity of the borrower. The principal source of transmission of the crisis has been the real sector, generally referred to as the 'Main Street'. This crisis engulfed the United States in the form of creeping recession and this worsened the situation. As a consequence, US demand for import from other countries indicate a decline. The basic causes of crisis were largely an unregulated environment, mortgage lending to sub-prime borrowers. Since the borrowers did not have adequate repaying capacity and also because sub-prime borrowing had to pay two-to-three percentage point's higher rate of interest and they have a history of default, the situation became worse. But once the housing market collapsed, the Lender institutions show their balance-sheets go into red. Although at one time it was thought that this crisis would not affected the Indian economy, later it was found that the Foreign Direct Investment (FDI) started drying un nab this affected investment in the Indian economy. It was, therefore, felt that the Indian economy will grow at about 7% in 2008-09 and at 6% in 2009-10. This lesson of this experience is that India must exercise caution while liberalizing its financial sector. A redeeming feature of the current crisis in that its magnitude is much lesser than that of the Great Depression of the 1930s when unemployment rate in the United State exceeded 25%. Currently, it stands at 6.5% and is predicate to remain around 8% in 2009.

There was a full-blown meltdown of the global financial market. It created a crisis of confidence that led to the seizure of enter-bank market and had trickle-down affected on trade financing in the emerging economics. Together with slacking global demand and declining commodity trice, it led to fall in exports, thereby transmitting financial sector crisis to the real economy. Countries with export-led model of growth, as in many South East Asian countries, and that dependent upon commodity exports, where more severely affected. The impact on Indian economy was less segere because of lower dependence of the economy on export market and the fact that sizeable contribution to GDP is from domestic's sources. India's trade reforms since 1991 have moved progressively towards neutral regime for exports and imports, eschewing tax and other incentives for exports.

The global financial crisis surface around August 2007. Its origin lay in structure investment instrument (Collateralized Debt Obligations, Synthetic CDO's) created out of subprime mortgage lending in the United States. The securitization process, however, was not backed by due diligence and led to large scale default. The complexity of the instruments and role of credit rating agency played a contributory role. The high rating assigned to certain CDO trenches, which were than with quickly reserved with the onset of the crisis, created a panic situation among investor and participated the crisis.

While the initial effect of crisis was profound on the US financial institution and to a lesser extent on European institutions, the effect on emerging economies was less serious. In the initial stage, the capital flow of the emerging economies actually increased, giving rise to what is termed as "positive shock" and the "decoupling" debate. In the case of India, for example, the net Fill flows during the five-month period from September 2007 to January 2008 was US$ 22.5 billion as against an inflow of US$ 11.8 billion during April-July 2007, which were the four months immediately preceding the onset of crisis.

The effect of the financial crisis on emerging economies thereafter was mainly through reversal of portfolio flows due to unwinding of stock positions by Fills to replenish cash balance abroad. Withdrawal of Fill investment led to stock market crash in many emerging economies and decline in the value of local currency *vis-à-vis* US dollar as a result of supply-demand balances in domestic market. In the case of India, the extent of reversal of capital flows was US$ 15.8 billion during five months (February-June 2008) following the end of "positive shock" period in January 2008.

The direct impact of the crisis on financial sector was primarily through exposure to the toxic financial assets and the linkage with the money and foreign exchange markets. Indian bank however had very limited exposure to the US mortgage market, directly or through derivatives, and to the fail and stressed international financial institutions. The deeping of the global crisis and subsequent deliberating and risk aversion however affected the Indian economy leading to slowing of growth momentum.

The government advice the sector of wreakening demand to reduce price. It provided some relief by cutting down excise duties, but such simplistic solution was domed to failure. Weakening demand led to producer cutting production. To reduce the impact of the crisis, firms reduce their workforce, to reduce cost. This led to increase the unemployment but the total impact on the economy was not very large. Industrial production and manufacturing output decline to five per cent in the last quarter of 2008-09. Consequently, a vicious cycle of weak demand and falling output developed in the Indian economy. A weakening of demand in the US affected our IT and Business Process Outsourcing (BPO) sector and the loss of opportunities for young person seeking employment at lucrative salaries abroad. India's famous IT sector, ethic earned about $50 billion as annual revenue, is expected to fall by 50 percent of its total revenues. This would reduce the cushion to set off the deficit in balance of trade and thus enlarge our balance of payments deficit. It has now been estimated what sluggish demand for export would result in a loss of 10 million jobs in the export sector alone.

There was a view among global market analyst, that growth in emerging markets and developing countries was driven by the global excess liquidity/monetization, the associated capital flows from develop countries and the demand for commodities. Consequently, with the bursting of the bubble of the initial impact would be a growth collapse, followed by a return in the medium term to growth rates that prevailed before 2004-05, because of the painful process of the de-leveraging and collapse of capital flows. It was therefore concluded by some of these analysts that India's growth would collapse to around 4 per cent during the subsequent four to six quarters and thereafter it may revert to around 5 to 5.5 per cent over the medium-term. An analysis of the growth history of India suggests that this superficial generalization of a plausible global analysis to India is erroneous.

Money and credit markets have been affected indirectly through the dynamic linkages. The drying up of liquidity, a fallout of repetition of portfolio investment by fills, affected credit markets in second half of 2008-09. This was compounded by the risk aversion of banks to extend credit in the face of general downturn. The extent of the external financial and monetary shock on the Indian monetary financial is best captured by the precipitous contraction in reverse money by more than 15 per cent between August 2008 and November 2008 (compared to 0.5% increase in the corresponding period of the previous year). Reverse money growth (y-0-y) collapsed from 26.9% in August 2008 to 10.3% in November 2008 and further to 6.4% in March 2009. The various monetary policy measures taken by RBI kept narrow money M1 and broad money M3 from falling as precipitously. Despite these, however, M1 growth decelerated from 19.4% in August 2008 to 10.3% in November 2008 and further to 8.2% in March 2009, while M3 growth decelerated from 21% in August 2008 to 18.7% in March 2009. A series of unconventional measures actually helped to push up the rate of growth of bank credit from 25.4% in August 2008 to 26.9% in November 2008. However, this only partly offset the effects on short- and long-term credit to Indian companies in the United States and EU markets, because of the freezing of financial markets. Subsequently, credit growth decelerated sharply to 17.1% in March 2009, partly because of transmission of OECD recession effects to Indian exporters and organized manufacturing.

GROWTH OF PRIVATE CONSUMPTION LEVEL

The first half (H1) of 2008-09 saw the Indian economy recording a growth of 7.8% in GDP, despite the built-up of uncertainty in the international commodity and fiscal markets. Among the domestic growth drivers, gross fixed capital formation (GFCF) retained some of its momentum from the preceding years with a growth of nearly 11%. Consumption—both private and government—however, declined significantly. The growth in private consumption expenditure (PFCE) in H1 2008-09 was 3.3%, which was less than half of the corresponding period in 2007-08. Similarly, government's final consumption expenditure (GFCE) grew at less than 1%, or just one-third of the growth of the H1 of 2007-08.

In the second half (H2) of 2008-09, GDP growth decline to 5.8%, with a further decline in private consumption growth to 2.5% and a significant moderation in growth rate GFCF to about 6% over the corresponding period of 2007-08. However, with the roll-out of the fiscal stimulus, primarily in the ship of implementation of the Sixth Pay Commission recommendations in Q3, as well as second round of fiscal expansion announced in Q4, the growth of government's final consumption expenditure short up to nearly 36%, partly making up for the shortfall in other components of the domestic aggregate demand. The overall GDP growth of the fiscal 2008-09 at 6.7% surpassed all estimates and forecast, mostly ranging from 5.5% to 6.5%, made by international agencies and analysts.

GROWTH OF GDP COMPONENTS

It is useful to compare the till 2008-09 growth slowdown to earlier slowdowns in 2002-03, 1997-98 and 1991-92. If we use the difference between the five-year moving average growth rate and growth rate of the last of the five years. As a measure of the slowdown, the 1991-92 slowdowns was the sharpest, while the other three whereof similar orders of magnitude. The growth rate of GDP at factor cost (GDP_{SC}) is about 65% higher than the average of last two slowdown. On all other previous occasions, agriculture GDP declined significantly and barring 2002-03 the decline in manufacturing GDP in earlier slowdown years was also sharper than in 2008-09. The deceleration of private consumption growth in 2008-09 is of concern, but it can be seem that growth rate is higher than in earlier years. The GDCF growth rate has however fallen to about half of what it was in the last two slowdown. This is perhaps an indication or how strongly the heightened global uncertainty, risk perception and risk aversion have impact Indian entrepreneurs. Despite the collapse in exports in second half of 2008-09, export growth for the year as a whole was fairly robust, while import growth was the highest among these slowdown years.

POLICY FORWARD TO THE SLOWDOWN

To counter the negative fallout of the global slowdown on the Indian economy, the government responded by providing a substantial facial extension in the form of tax relief to boost demand and increase expenditure on public project to create employment and public assets. The net result was an increase in facial deficit from 2.7% in 2007-08 to 6.2% of GDP in 2008-09. The differences between the actual 2007-08 and 2008-09 constituted the total facial stimulus, notwithstanding the fact that some expenditure was on account of the implementation of Sixth Pay Commission award and the agriculture debt relies scheme (small farmer debt wager) announced in the union budget 2008-09. Together about 0.5% of GDP was committed prior to the dramatic deterioration of the international financial market in September 2008.

In incrementing the facial stimulus, the government increase it's spending on the plan, both central sector as well as central assistance to the state and union territories plans, by nearly 1% of the GDP. There was an increase of nearly 2.5% of GDP on non-plan expenditure that included increased spending on fertilizer and food subsidies, agriculture debt waiver, defense, salaries and pension. The government renewed its effort to the increase infrastructure investment in telecommunication, power generation, airport, port, road and railways.

The RBI took a number of monetary easing liquidity enhancing measures including reduction in cash reverse ratio, statutory liquidity ratio and keys policy rate. The objective was to facilitate the flow of fund from the financial system to meet the need of productivity sector. In well developed financial market like the United States, monetary policy instruments and their effectiveness in meeting the objectives is well known. However, the financial crisis in the US market had the effect of fragmenting these markets, so that conventional instrument was no longer effective. There was partly an issue of this was only and partly an issue of the Keynesian liquidity trap. In relatively less developed financial markets like India's the effectiveness of instrument is constrained by missing and imperfect financial market. The global crises accentuated the non-integrated nature of the markets, requiring more careful attention to the different channels, namely interest rate, money supply and credit and the instrument appropriate to each. Further it became imperative to use both traditional (considered by some) and unconventional instruments. The breadth and depth of global crisis and the uncertainty and the fear surrounding it, required use of fiscal policy to supplement monetary policy. It was therefore necessary to ensure adequate coordination between the two, so that they did not work at cross-purpose. Though it would be far from the return to claim perfection, by and large the conceptually sound approach was eventually implemented.

FISCAL PACKAGE TO MINIMISE THE PAIN

In short, the fiscal package is aimed at boosting growth in exports, real estate, auto textile and small and medium enterprises. The aim is to encourage growth and boost employment which have been threatened by the recession in the world economic, more especially in the United State. Just within a month, the government announced another package to bail out the Indian economic. Dr. Montek Singh Ahluwalia said: "We should expect, from all global projection that the next year (2009) is going to be very difficult year for the global economy." The purpose of the new package announce on January 1, 2009 was to minimize the pain. With this end view, the new package include the following measures:

1. To boost investment and spending to revive growth, the RBI cut the repo rate, which it charges on short-term loans to bank from 6.5% to 5.5% and also reduce the Cash Reserve Ratio (CRR)—the share of deposits which has to be kept with the RBI from 5.5.% to 5%.
2. To revive export which has resulted in a contraction of industrial output, drawback benefits have been enhance for some exporters. Export-Import Bank also gets Rs. 5000 crores as credit from the RBI.
3. To help the realty sector, realty companies have been allowed to borrow from oversea to develop "integrated township".
4. To boost infrastructure the India Infrastructure Finance Company Ltd. (IIFCL) has been allowed to raise Rs. 30,000 crores from tax free bonds. Besides, Non-Banking Finance Companies (NBFCs) need no government approval to borrow from overseas for infrastructure projects. This will sustain the growth momentum on infrastructure.
5. To make more funds available, ceiling on foreign institutional investments (FIIs) in corporate bonds has been increased to $15 billion from $6 billion. The purpose is to seek much bigger FII investment.
6. To stimulate the Commercial Vehicle (CVs) sector, deprecation benefit on commercial vehicle has been increased from 15% to 50% on purchases. Besides, the States will get one-time funding from the Center to buy buses for urban transport. In additions, public sector banks would provide finance firms fund for commercial vehicles. It is hoped that Tata Motors and Ashok Leyland's sales would revive. On February 24, 2009, the government announced a slashing down of excise duty from 10% to 8%—reduction by 2%. Since 90% of the manufactured goods attract 10% excise duty, this measure is

designed to reduce the prices of color TV sets, washing machine, refrigerators, soaps, detergent, colas, cars and commercial vehicles. Cement prices are likely to drop Rs. 4-5 per bag of 50 kg while steel prices may cost Rs. 500-600 per tone less. In addition to this, the government decided to cut service tax from 12% to 10%—a reduction by 2%. As a consequence, phone bills, airline tickets, credit card charges, tour package, etc., would cost less. A 2% reduction in service tax will directly touch the lives of over 500 million persons by reducing monthly expenses. The entire stimulus package of Rs. 30,000 crores to boost demand in the economy and thus reduce the impact of recession. Commerce and Industries Minister Kamal Nath announced a small relief package of Rs. 325 crores for leather, textile, gems, and jewellery on February 26, 2009.

CONCLUDING REMARKS

The government also announced specific measures to address impact of global slowdown on India's exports. These included extension of export credit for labour-intensive exports, improving the pre- and post-shipment credit availability, additional allocation for refund of terminal excise duty/CST and export-intensive scheme, and removal of export duty and export can on certain items. Though it is not possible to substitute for the dramatic fall in foreign demand, these measures would be helpful in facilitating the adjustment of companies and workers to the new reality and to survive the temporary setback.

There is no doubt that government is motivated with good intension and is and thus aiming to spend a huge amount of Rs. 1,00,000 crores for developing intrastate in road, ports, etc. which pose a serious handicap to growth. Besides, the aim of others measure is to boost export and help sector like textile and small and medium industries which are labour-intensive and generate more payment. But the success of fiscal package will be depend on the equality and speed of implementation so that delays in implementation may not aggravate the economic recession to move into the dangerous zone of depression. One of the major stumbling block which may neutralize the positive effect of large expenditure on intrastate is corruption. In case corruption is not simultaneously curbed to reasonably low levels, it may delay and reduce the much-desired effect in enlarging infrastructure. It may result in the Indian infrastructure network being geared into a temporary employment generation program with much smaller impact on the economy as against the intended objectives. For reducing corruption, two things need to be ensured—transparency and avoidance of arbitrariness. By cutting arbitrariness in decision-making, corruption can be curbed to a great extent. Transparencies instills confidence in the government. Secondly, there is a need to orient the fiscal package towards inclusive growth so that the weaker section benefit. This would required special emphasis, for instance, on rural infrastructure—rural road and housing, instead on only highways and urban housing. Similarly, a much larger expenditure on primary and secondary education, health and sanitation can also result in a more inclusive growth process. Thirdly, the chances of our export in increasing are very limited unless the G-3 economy, namely, the US, EU and Japan, are able to bring about positive shift in their growth in near future for which the prediction at present are not very optimistic. The world bank has projected the world output to grow at 0.9 per cent in 2009 as against 2.5% in 2008. In this prediction come out to true, there is a fear of recession in 2008 turning into a depression into 2009. But the Indian economy is predicted to grow at about 7% in 2008 and about 6% in 2009. Since the G-3 economics of the US, EU and Japan are affected seriously by the present recession, the chance of Indian export in increasing in this county appear to be very dim. The mature conclusion is that the Indian economy should concentrate on developing the domestic market. Thus, inward looking policies should be preferred as against the outwards looking approach of integrating the Indian economy to the world economic is followed during the last decade. It is heartening that the Prime Minister intend to insult the Indian economy from the world economy. Fourthly, although there is a demand for much larger Fiscal Package to bail out the Indian economy, there are serious faced by the government because it has fight terrorism on the one hand and financial melt down on the other. The government has to undertaken a huge expenditure at the Central as well as State levels to enhance security. It is difficult to precisely estimate this expenditure at this stage since it entails larger recruitment of police and paramilitary forces along with equipping them with the most up-to-date weapons. But there is massive increase in expenditure to combat terrorism, along with a facial package to boost the Indian economy; there is also likely to be shortfall in tax revenues. Cosequently, the Budget deficit is bound to increase.The government will not be able to reduce the fiscal deficit to 2.5% of GDP, it may increase three to 3.5% during 2008-09. But this is inevitable and the target of reducing it according to the schedule prescribed by the Fiscal Responsibility and Budget Management Act, has to be postponed. But the Finance Minister has not agreed to the abolition of the FRBM is like a chasity belt, but don't loosen it without a better alternative." It may, however, be mentioned that the quasi fiscal deficit(the deficit left out of the Budget) is presently estimated as 6% of the GDP. A comprehensive view of the fiscal deficit (as shown in the Budget and kept outside the Budget) would be in the range of 9 to 9.5% of the GDP, though it may now be lower due to very sharp decline in international crude oil prices from $140 per barrel to about $40 per barrel at present. This is a welcome relief. If the government is also able to push the fertilizer prices to lower levels which is possible in the changed circumstances, eventually the total fiscal deficit (shown as well as kept outside the Budget) may come down to 6.5 to 7% of the GDP. This is quite large but it is inevitable in the present situation. To conclude: As againt the US package of $800 billion to bail out the US economy and the Chinese package to $580 billion to salvage its economy, the Indian economy. It is due to this reason that the chieftains of industry want a much bigger package to bail out the Indian economy, as against the minuscule announced by the government. But the plan to spend more on housing is commendable if it can be implemented in a short time and an effective manner. The government should have transparency and avoid arbitrariness in the implementation so that corruption can be kept within reasonable limits. The government has been provide relief with the sharp fall in the international price of crude oil and this should be taken advantage of in reducing expenditure to subsidise oil imports.

Additional employment generation by helping SMEs will be a step towards inclusive growth since they are labour-intensive. The intention to create infrastructure by expanding highways and ports and to spend Rs. 1,00,000 crores through the IIFCL is commendable. However, it may be more prudent to expand rural roads and rural so as to promote more inclusive growth. This would required proper planning which may take more time and does not provide immediate befefit. It may not be possible to reduce the fiscal deficit during 2008-09 since much larger expenditure are needed to combat terrorism and as there is recession in the Indian economy, but the international factors will influence the process. As the G-3 economies of the US, EU and Japan peek up, the Indian economy will also benefit from their reversal of recessionary trends. In this situation, the expectation of 7% growth of the GDP in 2008-09 and 6% in 2009-10 reflect a fairly good performance of the Indian economy.

References

Bhardwaj, R. (1962), "Factor Proportion and the Structure of India-US Trade", *Indian Economy*.

Bihar Economy Survey, 2007-08.

Economic Survey, Government of India Publication.

Indian Economy, Mishra and Puri.

Indian Economy, Rudra Dutta and Sundram, S. Chand.

Journal, October.

Leontief, W.W. (1956), "Factor Proportion and the Structure of American Trade: Further Theoretical and Empirical Analysis", Restat.

Mithani, D.M. (2000), International Economics, Himalaya Publication House.

Global Economic Crisis and the Indian Economy: An Analysis

SHRAWAN KUMAR SINGH

INTRODUCTION

The global financial crisis is now the staple of front page news. Banks around the world, including those in India, are in the forefront of managing the challenge of crisis resolution. The global financial situation continues to be uncertain and unsettled. This crisis is also the first of a kind in the sense that it is the first financial crisis since the Great Depression that originated in the advanced economies and rapidly engulfed the whole world, such is the depth and sweep of financial globalisation. By far, the most frequently asked questions (FAQ) today is whether the worst—in terms of the financial sector meltdown and in particular, failure of financial institutions—is behind us. No one is really willing to take a definitive call on this, which is a sign of the increasing number of unknown/unknowns (D. Subbarao, 2009). Crises feed uncertainty and uncertainty affects behaviour, which feeds the crisis.

It may be said that the current crisis was shaped in the U.S. by its unique complex financing structures—structures generally not found in emerging countries. It was once believed that the crisis of "subprime" mortgages—loans to weaker borrowers—would be limited, because these loans represent only 12 per cent of all home mortgages. Subprime mortgage losses triggered a full-blown financial crisis. Confidence evaporated, because subprime loans were embedded in complex securities whose values and ownership were hard to determine.

The bankruptcy of the investment bank Lehman Brothers (with $639 billion in assets—the biggest bank failure in U.S. history) on 15 September 2008 marked a crucial turning point—it took the financial markets from a period of turmoil to a major crisis. That has resulted in a breakdown of trust in interbank and inter-institutional lending. These include the Lehman Brothers (Investment bank), Freddie Mac and Fannie Mac (Mortgage Govt. Sponsored enterprise), AIG, Merrill Lynch (Investment bank), Bear Stearns (Investment bank), Wachova Group, Goldman Sachs, Northern Rock, Barclays Capital (Investment bank), Deutsche Bank (Bank), Citigroup (Investment bank), HSBC (Bank), UBS AG (Investment bank), Morgan Stanley (Investment bank) and many many more. Uncertainty stemming from this situation gave rise to the risk of a domino effect, affecting one financial institution after the next. The crisis has spread through two channels: reduced money flows and reduced trade. Global financial markets are interconnected. The sub-prime crisis has tended to be contagious with the contagion spreading from the credit market to the money market affecting the liquidity and the foreign exchange market; spreading from the U.S. to the Euro Area and to the rest of the world. The world economy is entering a major slowdown, driven by the worst financial crisis in 75 years. The crisis has gone global; economic growth in 2009 will be the lowest since at least 1980. The question that is being asked is whether this recession will be longer, wider and deeper than previous economic downturns that took place a generation ago. Frankly, no one knows the answer. There is much pessimism on how long this recession would last as well.

IMPACT ON THE INDIAN ECONOMY

Prime Minister Dr. Manmohan Singh had stated as early

as October 24, 2008 that "we cannot remain totally unaffected...our stock markets and the exchange rate of the rupee are under pressure due to capital outflow of foreign institutional investors". He had further admitted the rate of growth in India would slow down because of the international ambience. India's exports have declined because of the economic crisis faced by the developed capitalist countries. We are certainly more integrated into the world economy today than ten years ago at the time of the Asian crisis.

The Indian economy is now a relatively open economy, despite the capital account not being fully open. While encouraging foreign investment flows, especially direct investment inflows, a more cautious, nuanced approach has been adopted in regard to debt flows. The major sectors in India that would be affected out to a certain extent due to the current crisis are, the Banking Industry, IT and IT enabled services, Real Estate, Oil and Gas; and FMCG. The adverse effects have so far been mainly in the equity markets because of reversal of portfolio equity flows, and the concomitant effects on the domestic forex market and liquidity conditions.

The main impact of the global financial turmoil in India has emanated from the significant change experienced in the capital account. Portfolio investments by foreign institutional investors (FIIs) witnessed a net outflow. The combined impact of the reversal of portfolio equity flows, the reduced availability of international capital both debt and equity, the perceived increase in the price of equity with lower equity valuations, and pressure on the exchange rate, growth in the Indian corporate sector is likely to feel some impact of the global financial turmoil.

Employment

The financial crisis in the advanced economies and the likely slowdown in these economies could have some impact on the IT sector. About 15 per cent to 18 per cent of the business coming to Indian outsourcers includes projects from banking, insurance, and the financial services sector which is now uncertain. The country's diamond-capital, Surat, where the economic melt-down in America has had a direct, lethal impact. The processing units there, and adjoining areas in Maharashtra, are likely to terminate the services of 125,000 workers. There are just no orders to execute, indeed unsold items are being returned as people in the US struggle to retain their jobs and homes. Experts see no sparkle in business prospects until the US economy revives. That could take quite a few years. Another example of an Indian industry failing to grow beyond servicing a specific market? It is easier to say that the decline in growth has adverse effects on employment than to comprehend the real shock such a scenario implies. Using macro-employment elasticities, a drop in GDP growth from 9 per cent to 5 per cent means six million jobs lost. That's a huge shock, with a severe social impact. India's employment data is not only unsatisfactory, there is also a time lag.

Rate of Growth

"How bad will 2009-10 be? Dr. Montek Singh Ahluwalia said the Planning Commission reviewed assorted econometric models and decided global slowdown would shave-off between 1.5% and 2.5% from baseline growth. On a base of 7.5%, after netting out the effects of tight monetary policy, which reduced growth before the global crisis, this means GDP growth of between 5% and 6%. The range of forecasts by assorted institutions (Assocham, Allianz, Morgan Stanley, Citibank, Goldman Sachs, Merrill Lynch, Nomura, World Bank and IMF) is between 5.3% and 6.5%, with IMF also having reduced its forecast for calendar year 2009 to the 5% range. On the eve of its quarterly monetary policy announcement, the RBI said "the balance of risks on the growth outlook is tilted towards downside". The central bank based its contention on further moderation in economic activity for 2008-09 by pointing to the Survey of 13 Professional Forecasters.

The macro effects have so far been muted due to the overall strength of domestic demand, the healthy balance sheets of the Indian corporate sector and the predominant domestic financing of investment. Questions marks are greater for investments. Investments have been driven by the public and private corporate sectors. There are no signs yet that monetary policy changes have had the desired impact and there is a time lag of around eight months. While there is demand for working capital, there does not seem to be demand for investments—political uncertainty also contributing to postponements. CMIE's capital expenditure database also shows this" (The Financial Express, January 28, 2009). Risk aversion, deliveraging and frozen money markets have not only raised the cost of funds for Indian corporates but also its availability in the international markets. This will mean additional demand for domestic bank credit in the near term. Reduced investor interest in emerging economies could impact capital flows significantly.

And yet little of this storm has touched the Indian banking system. Not only is there no sign yet of any bank failure, three private banks have reported impressive earnings growth for the third quarter. It is not that the Indian economy has been spared in the present crisis. The Indian situation is different from that in the western world. In the US and Europe, the housing market collapsed and dragged down banks. The two together have dragged down the real economy. In India, it is the real economy that got impacted first – on account of exports and the drying up of overseas finance for many firms. Banks are affected indirectly by the slowing down of the economy. The direct impact of the crisis on the Indian banking system has been small because Indian banks do not have big exposures to the subprime market. Indian banks are well placed to weather this impact. This is not a contrarian view (T.T. Ram Mohan, 2009). The RBI itself exudes optimism about the outlook for Indian banking in its latest Report on Trend and Progress in Banking. The Report says: "At a time when the financial system across the globe is engulfed in a deep crisis, the Indian banking system continues to show resilience. The underlying fundamentals of the Indian economy would continue to underpin the robust performance of the banking sector which remains profitable and well capitalized". There are good reasons for such optimism. There is always the danger of one or two weak players having serious problems. But we do have the capacity to contain systemic risk arising from such a situation.

The broader lesson of the Indian banking system emerging relatively unscathed in the present crisis should not be ignored. Our unique approach to the issues of bank ownership and regulation, our reliance on home-grown solutions, has served us well. The Report underlines the need for caution on several fronts. However, according to Prof. T.T. Ram Mohan there are two areas that do not receive the attention they merit. One of the need to improve the quality and performance of public sector bank boards. Another is the sharp rise in off-balance-sheet (OBS) assets in the banking system in recent years. For banks as a whole, OBS assets are 333% of balance sheets assets. The biggest exposures are among foreign banks (2,803%) and new private banks (302%). OBS items have proved the undoing of banks in the recent crisis. The RBI needs to keep its eyes and ears peeled. The Indian financial system is not directly exposed to the toxic or distressed assets of the developed world. This is not surprising since Indian banks have very few branches abroad.

The indirect impact on the economy because of the recession abroad is very much there. The decoupling theory does not hold good. The indirect impact is felt both through trade and capital flows. The fall in international commodity prices and more particularly crude oil will reduce the import bill from previous estimates. The import growth rate this year may be around 20 per cent. The recession abroad will have an adverse effect on our exports of goods and services. The overall effect will be to take the current account deficit in 2008-09 to around 2.5 per cent of GDP. The decline in growth rate in exports will affect strongly some sectors where exports constitute a significant proportion of the total production.

There has been significant pressure on the Indian exchange rate in recent months. In contrast, to the strong inflow of over $100 billion last year, this year may not see any net increase in capital flows. Portfolio capital has earlier turned negative with a significant impact on the stock market. However, there has been a gradual revival in the stock market. Indian firms may also experience difficulties in raising money abroad. All this will impact the exchange rate. However, draw down of reserves would moderate the impact. However, there is the impact of the drying up of liquidity because of the fall in reserves. The inability of Indian firms to raise funds abroad, including trade credit, puts pressure on the domestic banking system for more credit. It is, in this context, one must view the actions of the Reserve Bank in expanding liquidity.

The Reserve Bank of India has warned of a 'second-order' impact of the economic slowdown on the real sector. Unlike in the advanced countries where the contagion spread from the financial to the real sector, in India, the slowdown in the real sector is affecting the financial sector, which in turn, has a second-order impact in the real sector. "If the recession is deeper and the recovery is long drawn, as is the current expectation, emerging economies have also to contend with second round effects in the form of potential terms of trade losses, erosion of export competitiveness and restricted external financing". Industrial activity, particularly in the manufacturing and infrastructure sectors, is decelerating. In the coming months, the services sector too, which has been the prime engine of growth for the last five years, will slow, mainly in the construction, transport and communication, trade, hotels and restaurants sub-sectors.

In sum, "India has by-and-large been spared of global financial contagion due to the sub-prime turmoil for a variety of reasons. India's growth process has been largely domestic demand driven and its reliance on foreign savings has remained around 1.5 per cent in recent period. It also has a very comfortable level of forex reserves. The credit derivatives market is in an embryonic stage; the originate-to-distribute model in India is not comparable to the ones prevailing in advanced markets; there are restrictions on investments by residents in such products issued abroad; and regulatory guidelines on securitisation do not permit immediate profit recognition. Financial stability in India has been achieved through perseverance of prudential policies which prevent institutions from excessive risk taking, and financial markets from becoming extremely volatile and turbulent" (Rakesh Mohan, 2008).

India, with its strong internal drivers for growth, may escape the worst consequences of the global financial crisis. Indian banks have very limited exposure to the US mortgage market, directly or through derivatives, and to the failed and stressed financial institutions. The equity and the forex markets provide the channels through which the global crisis can spread to the Indian system. The other three segments of the financial markets—money, debt and credit markets—could be impacted indirectly. The impending recession will also impact on Indian exports.

INDIA'S POLICY RESPONSE

Since September 2008, the Reserve Bank of India (RBI) has been in overdrive on monetary policy relaxation. Reduction of the CRR and repo and reverse repo rates are steps in the right direction. The role of the Reserve Bank of India is to create an environment in which additional credit can be made available. These measures were, ostensibly, in the context of distinct signs of slowdown in the global economy and the financial meltdown in the industrial countries. It was increasingly felt that unless quick steps were taken to relax monetary policy and also provide a strong fiscal stimulus, the economies of these countries would hurdle down into deep depression. The crucial issue is whether it was the right policy for India to keep matching the industrial countries in easing monetary policy. The problem in India is that expectations are always unidirectional but with asymmetry. On the downtrend all economic agents and policymakers argue for more and more relaxation

Our fiscal actions to stimulate the economy have taken two forms. One is to cut excise duty and the second is to enlarge government expenditure. Both should lead to stimulating aggregate demand. It depends finally on whether the additional expenditures planned are actually incurred. Also we need to look at the composition of expenditure and effectiveness of expenditures. Digging holes and filling them up is not a right prescription. Expenditures should be biased towards investment so that capacities can be created which can facilitate growth later. That public spending should remain at a high level in a situation like the present one is not a matter for dispute. With the two Supplementary Grants approved by the Parliament perhaps the fiscal deficit in the current year will exceed 5 per cent of GDP, at least 2 percentage points above the FRBM target. (S.S. Tarapore, 2009) has emphasised that when there is a sharp downturn, the major instrument has to be fiscal policy but since there is no fiscal space in India to prove a stimulus, monetary policy should hold up the rear. The policy has a 12-18 months lag and it is meaningless to expect instant results. The paradox is that those to whom are banks wish to lend do not wish to borrow, while those who wish to borrow are not deemed to be creditworthy. Using a dirigiste approach to credit disbursement is dangerous.

The Real Effective Exchange Rate (REER) on the six-country model (1993-94=100) is virtually at the neutral rate. The RBI deserves kudos for managing the exchange skillfully. Small and medium enterprises (SMEs) are relatively export-oriented while large industry is generally import-intensive. Keeping up the momentum of exports is vital and as SMEs have been severely affected by the global crisis, and further loss of export orders will be more intensely felt in the January-March, 2009 quarter, it would be appropriate to work towards a 5 per cent depreciation in REER terms, which would provide more relief to SMEs than a large interest rate reduction.

However, while the downside risks would be extending to the future, the fall in commodity, including oil prices, and the coordinated fiscal and monetary stimulus are expected to revive the growth momentum. The central bank has also identified positive factors including an expected increase in consumption demand mainly reflecting rise in basic exemption limits and tax slabs, the Sixth Pay Commission awards, debt waiver for farmers and pre-election expenditure. The consumption expenditure is also expected to improve in the medium-run due to changing pattern of demographic profile in India.

CONCLUSION

It was first described as the subprime crisis, then it became known as the credit crisis, and after that the financial crisis. Now it is time for a new nomenclature: the global economic crisis. According to Nobel laureate Joseph Stiglitz globalisation had failed primarily because it was based on a flawed economic ideology. Globalization requires a larger role for the state in providing social protection...Making out a case for a global regulatory authority, he said there was a need to design a new global system to develop immunity or at least limit the consequences of failure. Failure was contagious in the present brand of globalisation as a result of which the U.S. was exporting its recession to the rest of the world. While there was recognition of the importance of a coordinated global fiscal and monetary response, the required reforms went deeper, and include creating a new global reserve system and a new global financial regulatory authority. A global reserve currency (what

Keynes called Bancor, or the IMF calls SDRs) could help fuel global aggregate demand and be used to promote development (Joseph E. Stiglitz, 2009). And he underlined globalisation had to ensure the maximum good for the maximum numbers and not just the privileged few who got richer under the existing regime. About bailout packages, he likened it to giving mass blood transfusion to a patient who was haemorrhaging from internal bleeding. Worse, he added, there was still no change in the mindset. As for American banks' refrain on self-regulation, Prof. Stiglitz said: "Self-regulation is an oxymoron. Banks said they knew how to manage risk and needed no regulation. What they knew was how to create risk. There is so much of blame to go around that they can all lay claim to it."

If we are to maintain global financial liberalization, with financial products moving easily across borders, we must be sure that these products are safe and that the financial institutions who are selling them can stand behind the products they create. Economy is going to be in difficulties. The US is going to get worse before it gets better. And that's why in the new world of globalization it makes so much sense to have a global currency. The rapid slowdown of the global economy consequent on the intensification of the financial crisis since has posed extraordinary challenges for economic policy-makers everywhere. Fiscal measures to stimulate the slowing economies are the flavour of the season. United Nations economists have called for deep reforms of the global financial system to prevent a recurrence of the current crisis, including stronger regulation of financial institutions, adequate international liquidity provisioning, an overhaul of the international reserve system and a more inclusive global economic governance. They wanted coordinated global economic stimulus packages, linked with sustainable development measures, beyond liquidity and recapitalization steps already taken, to counter the world-wide economic meltdown.

The invisible hand of the market works best only when there is the very visible hand of the government to restrain it. This means better regulation, closer oversight, greater transparency and accountability. The fundamental rule is, if an institution is systemically large enough or important enough to warrant bailing out with taxpayer money when it fails, it must be seen as important enough to be subjected to thorough public scrutiny means tight regulation.

The great relearning is about the perils of standalone investment banks with their penchant for taking absurd risks. It is important they are not resurrected under some other guise. There is a strong case for financial conglomerates with walls separating different activities. The relearning is about credit rating agencies and their feet of clay. Rating agencies must be regulated and their wings clipped so that they cannot hold the world to ransom again.

The events rocking the world are a consequence of imbalances in the global economy. The US twin deficits, budget and the current account deficit, and the corresponding Chinese surpluses are only a symptom of this deeper malaise. Unless these are addressed, nothing that all other central banks or their government do, will be able to save the world from a similar convulsion a few years hence. Globalisation is a two-way street. The US needs the rest of the world as much as the latter needs the US. The US recognizes this but is loath to follow through with any action that entails ceding the dollar's preeminent position, such as the acceptance of an alternate international reserve currency. It's not going to be easy; UK's Prime Minister Gordon Brown is right to emphasise the importance of an early-warning system for financial crises. He is also spot on in his call for standard rules for transparency of banks, and standard rules for global supervision and write-offs that are similar for all countries. Recognizing the importance of international coordination to achieve these goals, he has issued a call for the establishment of a 'New Bretton Woods'.

A locally customized global governance model is imperative. All support structures such as rating agencies, SEC rules, external auditors and boards must function transparently to restore trust. As the financial system has become extremely global, complex, volatile and interdependent, we must go beyond mathematical models such as value at risk (VaR) to a deeper understanding of their underlying assumptions. We have to move from understanding trends to understanding discontinuities. Economically, the world is more connected. But political rivalry is still intense. The political mentality must be changed to meet the changing realities. Otherwise, this cold war mentality will produce a mess for the world. Policymakers need to shed received wisdom and forget useless dichotomies such as "markets versus government" or "nation-state versus globalization". They need to come to grips with the reality that national regulations and international markets are inextricably linked with—and in need of—each other. The more pragmatically and creatively they act, the more quickly the world economy will recover (Dani Rodrik, 2009).

Coherent financial, fiscal and monetary measures are all needed. All three will have direct effects on demand. But, as importantly, they will help reduce uncertainty, lower risk spreads, and get consumers and firms spending again. If policy-makers act decisively, private demand will recover sooner rather than later. And, within a year or less, we can be on the path to recovery. Fortunately, the financial system in India has escaped relatively unscathed, thanks in part to state ownership that gives the public a high degree of confidence in domestic banks and prudent regulation by the RBI. So we must focus on international cooperation in designing a common framework for financial policies and the need for short-run policies to be consistent with the long-term viability of the financial system.

References

—— (2009): Banking remains a bright spot, *The Economic Times*, January 22.

—— (2008 'b'): Who killed Wall Street?, *Business Standard*, October 14.

—— (2008 'c'): Let Developing Country Rule, *Business Standard*, December 16.

—— (2009): A time to experiment, *Business Line*, January 13.

—— (2009): Mitigating spillovers and contagion—Lessons from the Global Financial Crisis, *RBI Monthly Bulletin*, January.

——(2009): The Global financial Turmoil and Challenges for the Indian Economy, *RBI Monthly Bulletin*, January.

—— (2009): Well-modulated Monetary Policy, *The Hindu Business Line*, January 30.

Acharya, Shankar (2008): Crisis and response, *Business Standard*, September 25.

Araghi, Farhad (2008): Political economy of the financial crisis: A world historical perspective, *The Economic and Political Weekly*, November 8.

Babu, Tapan (2008): Six characters in search of the crisis, *The Economic and Political Weekly*, November 8.

Baker, Dean (2008): The Housing Bubble and the financial crisis, *Real World Economics Review*, No. 46.

Chitale, Rajendra (2008): Seven triggers of the US financial crisis, *The Economic and Political Weekly*, November 1.

Desai, Nitin (2008): The Market for Credit, *Business Standard*, November 11.

Ghosh, D.N. (2008): Navigating the future in the midst of global Uncertainty, *The Economic and Political Weekly*, October 11.

Greenspan, Alan (2008): We will never have a perfect model of risk, *The Financial Times*, March 16.

Herman, Barry (2008): United Nations as a Forum for Reform of Global Institutions, *The Economic and Political Weekly*, November 8.

Kapadia, Anush and Arjun: The Credit Crisis: Where it came from, Jayadev (2008): What happened, and how it might end; *The Economic and Political Weekly*, December 6.

Khor Hoe Ee and Kee Rui Xiong Asia: A perspective on the subprime crisis, (2008): *Finance and Development*, June.

Mattoo, Aditya and Arvind: India and Bretton Woods II, The Subramanian (2008), *Economicand Political Weekly*, November 8.

Mohan, Rakesh (2008): Global Financial Crisis and Key Risks: Impact on India and Asia, *RBI Bulletin*, November.

Mohan, T.T. Ram (2008): From the Subprime to the Ridiculous, *The Economic and Political Weekly*, November 8.

Rixtel (2008): Turmoil of 2007-08: An Introductory Overview; Banco de Espana, Documentos Occasionales No. 0808.

Rodrik, Dani (2008 'a'): The globalisation consensus is dead, *Business Standard*, July 15.

Stiglitz, Joseph E. (2009): The rocky road to recovery, *The EconomicTimes*, January 12.

Subbarao, D. (2008): Lessons from the Global Financial Crisis with special reference to Emerging Market Economies and India, *RBI Bulletin*, November.

Tarapore, S.S. (2008): '...We all, fall down', *The Hindu Business Line*, November 21.

The Economist (2008): A special report on the world economy, October 11.

Impact of the Global Economic Crisis on SMEs in India

N. Sudhakara Rao

INTRODUCTION

India is one of the fast growing economies in the world but with low industrial base. The level of industrialization in the country is very low as compared to many other developed as well developing countries in the world. Though India has made rapid strides in over all development but it could not make rapid progress in industrialization and technological development. The slow progress in industrialization could be attributed many factors including the Governmental Policy. There is no serious concern about industrialization during the first five-year plan period. The second five-year plan period gave lot of importance to basic and heavy industries. Because gestation period of these industries is very long and hence they could not make the desired results, the country remained as one of the low industrialized countries only.[1]

The planners in India shifted their emphasis from heavy industries to small-scale industries. Accordingly small and medium scale industries have shown and continue to show, strong signs of adaptability, innovation and competitiveness providing an important source of income opportunities, and entrepreneurial skills.[2] Planners had felt that for a developing country such as India, the growth of small-scale industries is of great significance.[3] and hence the role of small industry was emphasized in successive Industrial Policy Resolutions, Five Year Plans and Reports of Expert Bodies. Small-scale industries are expected to help the nation in different ways. Apart from increased production, the growth of small-scale industries will help in the better utilization of local resources both men and materials, correcting regional imbalances, thereby improving the standard of living of the people, especially deprived sections of the society. Further, Small and Medium sector industries expected to contribute significantly to the strengthening of the industrial structure, which is very poor at present in India. SMEs are expected to serve as seedbeds of entrepreneurship and serve not only by their output of goods but also promoting necessary entrepreneurial and managerial talent in the economy. Thus, the small-scale industries play a decisive role in Indian economy. The development of small-scale sector has been felt important in India because the small-scale unit requires less capital outlay and at the same time they provide more employment than the large-scale sector in view of their labour intensify nature. A small-scale unit does not require highly sophisticated technology. It can therefore, be located in backward areas where workers can be trained to meet the challenge of sophisticated technology.

Objective

The main objective of the present paper is be examine the impact of Global Economic Crisis on various factors including SMEs in India based on secondary data.

GLOBAL ECONOMIC CRISIS—AN OUTLOOK

Present Global economic crisis is of recent origin and there is hardly any country on the World untouched by this phenomenon. However, its intensity varied from country to country and region to region. The main factors associated with the crisis situation were inflation and falling interest rates the world has witnessed relatively low inflationary levels and low short-term interest rates and high growth of EMEs.

The global financial situation continues to be uncertain and unsettled. In the rapidly globalizing world, the decoupling theory was never totally persuasive; the decoupling theory has almost completely lost credibility. The recent date stemming from sources such as IMF and other International organizations as well as national resources is seriously at variance with the decoupling thesis.

The global economy is set to decline during 2009. Global output would be lower by 2.9 percent, and the world trade by as much as 10 per cent. Private capital flows will drop sharply from $707 billion in 2009.

There has been a sharp fall in the production of manufactured goods, and in global trade in manufactures. The bank makes an interesting point that much of the growth in the developing world is coming from India and China. If these two are excluded, the developing countries too would post-negative growth.

IMPACT ON THE INDIAN ECONOMY

The impact of the global economic crisis on the Indian economy has been different from that of the developed G3 countries (USA, European Union and Japan), in the sense that in the context of India, the strain through slowdown in the real economy got transmitted to the financial sector, including banks from October 2008, unlike the other countries, where it was the other way round from August 2007.

Increasing gradual integration of India into the world economy over the last decade has resulted in the fast spread of the slowdown in economic activity, despite the strong fundamentals of the economy, and high level of regulation in the financial and other sectors. They are four major potential channels of contagion viz. trade, foreign capital, financial assets and interdependence of assets. The downturn of the Indian real economy, can be observed in respect of index of industrial production, and the external economy, particularly merchandise exports and imports, and invisibles.

IMPACT ON INVESTMENT

India too has been made to weather the negative impact of

the crisis. Even as consumption and domestic investment continue to be the key drivers of our growth, India's integration into the world economy has been on the increase. Going by the common measure of globalization, India's to-way trade (merchandise exports plus imports), as a proportion of GDP, grew from 21.2 per cent in 1997-98 to 34.7 percent in 2007-08. If we take the expanded measure of globalization, that is the ratio of gross current account and gross capital flows to GDP, this ratio has increased from 46.8 per cent in 1997-98 to 117.0 per cent in 2007-08. This is a clear evidence of India's increasing integration into the world economy over the last ten years.

India has undoubtedly benefited from integrating into the world. By corollary, we also need to manage the downsize ramifications of integrating into the world. The fundamentals of our economy continue to be strong.

The Indian economy is presently faced with a severe downturn or recession that has already been seen through a year-on-year GDP (real gross domestic product at factor cost at 1999-2000 prices) growth during 2008-09 compared to the growth rates of 2007-08. Economic activity in terms of GDP growth rate slowed down in quarters, Q1 and Q2 of 2008-09 as compared with over 9.0 per cent in the previous three years.

The Indian economy which was on a robust GDP growth path up to 2007-08, averaging 9.0 per cent during the period 2003-04 to 2007-08, witnessed moderation in 2008-09.

Industrial growth experienced a significant downturn; and the loss of growth momentum was evident in all categories, viz., the basic capital, intermediate, and consumer goods, a few of the categories showing negative growth in the recent times. The downturn was noticed in particular in the manufacturing sector (2.3% in 2008-2009 as compared to 9.0% in 2007-08). On the whole, the performance is still weak, and the domestic demand is not rising, and the recovery will take some time.

IMPACT ON TRADE

World merchandise exports in US$ terms, which grew on an average at 22.6 percent during January-September 2008, declined by 1.1 percent in October 2008, and the declining trend continued in the subsequent months of 2008 and 2009 as well.

Accordingly, the world's merchandise exports, showed a sharp decline of 29.1 per cent in January 2009 as against a growth of 24.4 percent during January 2008.

This sharp deceleration was on account of decline in the export of textiles, and textile products, gems and jewellery, leather products, agriculture and allied products, and iron ore and minerals, as these sectors have been adversely affected under the impact of demand recession, mainly in developed countries.

The slowdown in the Indian economy during 2008-09 has been associated with a deceleration in investment demand, which has been an important driver of growth in the recent years. The adverse conditions for access to external capital, and the depressing effects of the global crisis on domestic business confidence contributed to moderation in investments demand. The deceleration in private consumption expenditure was partly offset by a sharp increase in government consumption expenditure in the third and the fourth quarters. External demand conditions weakened, particularly since October 2008, with the decline in exports, and turning negative growth; and growth of imports turning negative from November 2008; resulting in a sharp widening of the merchandise trade deficit. Savings and investment rates which had peaked in 2007-08, are likely to be affected adversely by the slowdown in economic growth during 2008-09.

Exports in 2008-09 recorded $168.7 billion, compared to $163.13 billion in 2007-08 (3.4% growth rate in 2008-09 compared to 29.1% in 2007-08). Accordingly trade deficit for 2008-09 was pegged at $119.05 billion as compared to the trade gap of $88.52 billion in 2007-08, and lower still in earlier years. The gap widened substantially.

Gross invisibles receipts witnessed a lower growth of 18.8 percent during April-December 2008 (30.2% in the corresponding period of the previous year), mainly due to the slow pace of growth in travel, business services, and investment income receipts. Indian exports cannot remain unaffected in a situation where external demands are dwindling globally. Exports are also facing new challenges due to the present financial crisis.

SUGGESTIONS ON INCENTIVES FOR EXPORTS

While India announced measures for exporters to counter the global slowdown through interest subvention, reduction in excise duties (to stimulate demand), and reduction in service tax, countries in the neighbourhoods are announcing such measures on a much larger scale as compared to India. Exporters are asked to improve their competitiveness, besides pushing up sales in the domestic markets.

The measures announced so far should be supplemented by a few more steps as listed here, as suggested by the Federation of Indian Export Organization (FIEO)—

1. SMEs are provided marketing support by most of the developing and developed countries. The government should give incentives to exports diversifying their exports to new and unexplored destinations.
2. Unless a scheme to neutralize the local taxes/level is evolved, the government should factor in 'Drawback/DEPB' and other instruments, and increases their rates by 3-5 percent.
3. The post-shipment credit now available up to 180 days should be extended up to 365 days.
4. The government should provide a moratorium on term loans to exporters for two years in view of the present difficult position.
5. Interest rate subvention of 2 per cent available up to end-September 2009 should be extended up to further one year.
6. The pre-shipment and post-shipment credits in foreign currencies are virtually not available particularly to MSMEs, should be made
7. Insurances companies should adopt a flexible stand on single buyer policy, and adopt case by case approach rather than taking a rigid stand not to give single buyer policy to exporters as the same will be detrimental to the cause of diversification of exports in the present scenario.
8. Government should exempt exporters from fringe benefit tax (FBT). Exemption should also be given to exporters from service tax at least on services exclusively used for exports.

IMPACT ON EMPLOYMENT

The major social costs of a recession are those associated with the enforcement of job cuts, lay-offs, and upheavals in labour markets.

The Indian Government's official survey of the unemployment impact of the global crisis was conducted by the Labour Bureau[4], with focus on eight sectors mining, metals and metal products, textiles and garments, automobiles, gems and jewellery, construction, transport, and information technology/ business process outsourcing. The survey estimated a total job loss of 50,000 over the quarter September-December 2008. The official growth projections of the Economic Advisory Council to the Prime Minister (EAC) (2009), the estimated job losses would be about 1.5 million over the entire recessionary phase (September 2008 to December 2009).

The ILO Report recognizes the need to look beyond unemployment rates *per se* to get a more accurate assessment of the social distress dimension of the crisis.

Under the Union Ministry of Micro, Small and Medium Enterprises (MSMEs), the National Commission for Enterprises in the Unorganized Sector (NCEUS) has made a monumental contribution to the creation of a safety net for persons engaged in the unorganized sector. According to the NCEUS, about 45 per cent of the labour in the organized sector would be denied access to basic workers' rights, and would thus come under the ILO classification of vulnerable employment (in the unorganized sector, this proportion would be nearly 99%).

In a memorandum submitted to the Government of India, the NCEUS has given several pointers as to how the crisis could affected this segment of workers (NCEUS, 2008). Small producers and traders and traders dependent upon export markets have already been badly affected in industries such as handlooms, textiles, apparel, leather products, gems and jewellery, metal products, carpets, oil meal, marine products, and handicrafts. The NCEUS estimates that prior to the onset of the crisism enterprises with investment in plant and machinery up to Rs.25 lakh used to get a mere 5 per cent of the formal sector credit, whereas those with investment up to Rs.5 lakh investment got less than 2 per cent of the formal credit.

The commission has proposed the establishment of 'growth poles' in different parts of the country with a view to integrating with in a geographical location, a number of clusters of production units engaged in manufacturing, services, and non-farm activities, and facilitating the expansion of production and employment in micro and small enterprises.

National Minimum Social Security Scheme has been recommended by the NCEUS. Two bills proposed by the Commission, one for agriculture workers, and another for unorganized non-agricultural workers have been passed by the Parliament. These bills relate to conditions of work, promotion of livelihoods, and social security measures for those engaged in unorganized enterprises. An inter-ministerial group has been set-up to facilitate processing of the wide ranging recommendations of NCEUS in its various reports. Several categories of unorganized workers have been identified, and the recommendations proposed specific benefits to them in the short- and long-run.

IMPACT ON MSMEs

Wider implications of the widespread slowdown on micro, small and medium enterprises (MSMEs) and unorganized sector enterprises have been observed with varying employment intensities, investment, output, and exports and imports. Enhancing competitiveness of Micro, Small and Medium. Enterprises to withstand pressures in the global economy has been presented as an important strategy for the revival of the economy.

Many MSMEs reported business slowdown in July 2007. The major centres and the product groups affected are Ahmedabad (pharmaceuticals and textiles), Chennai (leather), Coimbatore (textiles/textile and other machinery), Girgaon (auto components), Ichalkaranji (cotton), Ludhiana (engineering), Pune (auto components), Rajkot (engineering/machine tools), Surat/Mumbai (diamonds), and Tirupur (garments-hosiery). While the impacts as above are visible in several other centers, such impacts are more pronounced in some traditional centers of crafts and non-farm activities. Because of the downturn, many enterprises in most places have laid off workers in different degrees. In sectors such as auto ancillaries, hosiery, and gem and jewellery, with the decline in demand as a result of the overall postponement of consumption decisions in developed countries, the industry has been badly hit in many parts of the country.

The recent study carried out by the Institute of Small Enterprise and Development (ISED), Kochi (Kerala), published in its India Micro, Small and Medium Enterprises Report Series 2007 and 2008, has captured the major trends in the Small and Medium Enterprise (SME) sector of recent months from various angles. An important aspect of economic recession relating to SMEs, is their strong linkage with the agriculture sector. A slowdown in agriculture will also lead to a decline in demand from other sectors such as industrial goods, consumer goods, housing, and production of construction materials.

POLICY SUGGESTIONS

1. Despite the implementation of cluster development programmes for over a decade to promote moderation, and export promotion, the programmes has not focused on social objectives in many locations. Despite significant public investment, employment and balanced regional development it remains as an unfulfilled objective.
2. Steps taken by the Union Government including RBI need reexamination to evolve an SME-specific package to overcome the crisis. Credit including guarantee cover is an important pointer in this direction.
3. Export promotion is another crucial area. It includes diversification of markets also.
4. Building confidence among SMEs by reducing panic through intelligence sharing is another direction for SMEs. The SME intelligence unit at different levels should act as a monitoring agency by involving professional consultants from time to time.
5. The firm level strategies can focus on enhancing competitiveness among the enterprises, with focus on modernization, greater productivity, and export promotion to cater to diversified markets.
6. Encouraging the adoption of innovative schemes like

SMECARE and SMEHELP (initiated by State Bank of India) by other banks on an extensive scale.

7. More provisions for special treatment of risk weights on loans to MSMEs under Basel II norms.
8. Loans above a certain limit to manufacturing and services enterprises in sensitive sectors can be tied to employment protection guarantees.
9. NCEUS (National Commission for Enterprises in the Unorganized Sector) has suggested in one of its reports an effective safety net for unorganized sector entrepreneurs and workers.

CONCLUSION

With the increasing trend of globalization in emerging economies and India, in particular, the impact of global economic crisis has adversely affected India's real economy from October 2008; and as a result of it balance of payments. India's banking sector has been largely left unaffected in view of the high level of regulation, and appropriate timely steps taken by the Reserve Bank of India. The real economy has to be brought back on the rails with fiscal and monetary policy instruments in the near future, with stimulai packages to revive demand domestically, facilitate diversification of markets, and enhance competitiveness of Indian exports *vis-à-vis* competitors from Asia as well. Developments in the real economy, financial markets, and global commodity prices point to a period of moderation in growth with declining inflation.

Notes and References

1. Institute of Small Enterprise and Development (ISED) (2008), India Micro, Small and Medium Enterprises Report, 2008, ISED, Kochi (Kerala).
2. Nachane, Dilip M. (2009), "The Fact of India Unincorporated", *Economical and Political Weekly*, March 28, Vol. 44, No. 13, special issue on Global Economic and Financial Crisis, pp. 115-22.
3. Rakesh Mohan (2009), "Global Financial Crisis: Impact, Policy Responses, and Lessons", *Reserve Bank of India Bulletin*, May, Vol. 63, No. 5, pp. 879-904.
4. Reserve Bank of India (2009), "Macroeconomic and Monetary Developments in 2008-09, issued with the Annual Policy Statement, 2009-10", *Reserve Bank of India Bulletin*, May, Vol. 63, No. 5, pp. 741-865.

6

Global Meltdown: Its Impact on Fiscal Scenario of the Central Government

P.K. Bhargava

During recent past, Indian economy achieved spectacular growth; the economy grew at an average rate of 8.8 per cent during the five year period from 2003-04 to 2007-08. In fact, during the three year period from 2005-06 to 2007-08, the economy witnessed a growth rate of 9 per cent or above in each of the years, not experienced ever before. The period of higher growth rate was also accompanied with an improvement in the fiscal situation of the Central Government. The tax-GDP ratio of the Central Government improved from 9.23 (2003-04) to 12.5 (2007-08). Further, during this period the revenue deficit as a percentage of GDP declined from 3.6 to 1.1 and the fiscal deficit also came down from 4.5 to 2.7. It may be noted that Centre's fiscal deficit at 2.7 per cent of GDP in 2007-08 signified the attainment of the target a year earlier as was envisaged in the Fiscal Responsibility and Budget Management Act, 2003. This was a healthy situation but could not be continued as there was a great set-back to the process of growth as also to the fiscal position in 2008-09 owing largely to global commodity price rise and financial meltdown. Although, initially the emerging market economies, including India, felt that they could decouple themselves from the global financial meltdown but it was soon realized that it was simply not possible. This is confirmed by the fact that the growth rate of the Indian economy in 2008-09 declined to 6.7 per cent as against the growth rate of 9 per cent attained in the preceding year 2007-08. The decline in growth rate would have been greater but for the various safety measures adopted by the Government.

To counter the negative fall out of the global meltdown and to bring about an economic revival of the Indian economy, the Government provided three focused fiscal stimulus packages in the form of tax relief (6 percentage points in Union excise duties and 2 percentage points in service tax) to boost demand and increased expenditure on public projects to generate employment and create public assets. In addition, the Reserve Bank of India also took a number of monetary measures to enhance liquidity so as to facilitate flow of funds from the financial system to meet the needs of the productive sectors of the economy.

The fiscal expansion/accommodation has led to an increase in revenue deficit as also fiscal deficit. The Union Finance Minister in his budget speech for 2009-10 observed that "This fiscal accommodation led to an increase in fiscal deficit from 2.7 per cent in 2007-08 to 6.2 per cent of GDP in 2008-09. The difference between the actuals of 2007-08 and 2008-09 constituted the total fiscal stimulus. This fiscal stimulus at 3.5 per cent of GDP at current market prices for 2008-09 amounts to Rs. 1,86,000 crore." Needless to say, the Government efforts have continued to push the economy through increased expenditure on various schemes and the quantum of fiscal stimulus is reported to be of the order of Rs. 2,14,000 crores. However, some of the important questions that arise in this context, need to be examined. Whether the fiscal stimulus provided by the Government is responsible for the deteriorating situation in regard to revenue and fiscal deficits of the Government in the years 2008-09 and 2009-10. More importantly, how much of the fiscal imbalance is cyclical and how much of it is structural in nature? In examining these questions, it is relevant to look at some of the fiscal indicators of the Central Government as contained in Table 1.

If one examines the data contained in Table 1, one would come across the following conclusions:

Total expenditure as also revenue expenditure of the Central Government have continued to increase but revenue expenditure constitutes a significant portion of the total expenditure and that in all the years (excepting the years 2003-04 and 2004-05) such expenditure constituted over 80 per cent of the total expenditure. Even during the period of improved fiscal situation, capital expenditure as a percentage of GDP declined from 4.0 (2003-04) to 2.5 (2007-08) and constituted 1.8 per cent of the GDP in 2008-09 (Revised). Further, revenue receipts have not kept pace with increase in expenditure on revenue account. In the process, therefore, the problem in regard to quantum of revenue deficit has persisted and varied in quantum even during the era of improved fiscal situation (2003-04 to 2007-08). The problem of revenue deficit has aggravated in the years 2008-09 (Revised) and 2009-10 (Budget) in view of resource compression due to tax relief measures and expenditure expansion.

It is also clear from Table 1 that capital expenditure, over the years, as a proportion of total expenditure has declined which means required capital formation and creation of productive assets is not taking place in the economy. This is also evidenced by the fact that only a small portion of the capital receipts are used to finance capital expenditure. It is also clear from the Table that Plan expenditure constitutes a small portion of the total expenditure and non-plan expenditure, though essential and desirable, absorbs a major portion of the total expenditure.

Table 1 also shows that three items, namely interest payments, major subsidies and defence expenditure account for a significant portion of the expenditure on revenue account. In the year 2001-02, these three items constituted 58 per cent of the expenditure on revenue account. Even while their share has gradually declined, they constituted as much as 47 per cent of the expenditure on revenue account in 2009-10 (Budget). Further, amongst these three items of expenditure, interest payments have continued to be the most significant in view of the increasing reliance on debt finance by the Central Government.

The Table shows that the Government has considerably depended on market borrowings and the same have also been used to finance current expenditure of the Government. In the process, therefore, the liabilities of the Government as also interest payments have continued to increase. Table 1 shows that quantum of interest payments has continued to increase throughout and such payments constituted 30 per cent or more of the revenue expenditure upto the year 2005-06 and thereafter, though the absolute amount of interest payments considerably increased but as a percentage© of revenue expenditure, the share of interest payments declined from 29 per cent in 2006-07 to 25 per cent in 2009-10 (Budget). It is also clear from the Table that interest payments consume a significant portion of the receipts on revenue account. In the year 2001-02, interest payments constituted 53 per cent of the revenue receipts. This percentage gradually came down but was still as high as 41% in 2004-05 and stood at 37% in 2009-10 (Budget).

Table 2 shows the situation regarding revenue and fiscal deficits of the Central Government. In the year 2001-02, the revenue deficit and fiscal deficits of the Central Government were as high as 4.4 per cent and 6.2 per cent of the GDP, respectively. This was primarily due to the deteriorating fiscal situation in the later half of the nineties on account of the implementation of the recommendations of the Central Fifth Pay Commission. In order to improve the fiscal situation, the Government of India enacted the Fiscal Responsibility and Budget Management Act (FRBMA), 2003. The data in Table 2 show that revenue deficit as also fiscal deficit as a percentage of GDP declined and in the year 2007-08, fiscal deficit at 2.7 per cent of the GDP was not only lower but a year ahead of the target of 3 per cent envisaged to be achieved by the year 2008-09 as per the FRBMA, 2003. The target towards zero revenue deficit was sought to be achieved a year later by 2009-10 when entire revenue expenditure was to be financed out of revenue receipts. But that was not to be so, in view of the global financial meltdown, as referred to above. As of today, the fiscal situation is almost the same as that existed in the year 2001-02, rather in some sense it has worsened; for the year 2009-10 (Budget), the revenue and fiscal deficits are estimated at 4.8 per cent and 6.8 per cent of the GDP, respectively.

TABLE I

Selected Fiscal Indicators of the Central Government

(Rs. in crores)

		2001-02	2002-03	2003-04	2004-05	2005-06	2006-07	2007-08#	2008-09 (Budget)	2008-09 (Revised)	2009-10 (Budget)
1.	Revenue receipts...	201306	230834	263813	305991	347077	434387	541925	602935	562173	614497
	Of which:										
	(a) Tax revenue (net of States' Share)	133532	158544	186982	224798	270264	351182	439547	507150	465970	474218
2.	Revenue Expenditure...	301468	338713	362074	384329	439376	514609	594494	658118	803446	897232
	Of which:										
	(a) Interest payments	107460	117804	124088	126934	132630	150272	171030	190807	192694	225511
	(b) Major Subsidies	30447	40716	43535	44753	44480	53494	67498	67037	122728	106004
	(c) Defence Expenditure...	38059	40709	43203	43862	48211	51682	54219	57593	73600	86879
3.	Capital Receipts ...	161004	182414	207390	192261	158661	149000	170807	147949	338780	406341
	Of which:										
	(a) Borrowings & Other Liabilities*	140955	145072	123272	125794	145435	142573	126913	133287	326615	400996
4.	Capital Expenditure	60842	74535	109129	113923+	66362	68778	118238	92766	97507	123606
5.	Total Expenditure	362310	413248	471203	498252	505738	583387	712732	750884	900953	1020838
	Of which										
	(a) Plan expenditure	101194	111470	122280	132292	140638	169860	205082	243386	282957	325149
	(b) Non-plan Expenditure	261116	301778	348923	365960	365100	413527	507650	507498	617996	695689

Based on Provisional Actuals for 2007-08.

* Does not include receipts in respect of Market Stabilization Scheme which will remain in the cash balance of the Central Government and will not be used for expenditure.

+ Includes repayment to National Small Savings Fund.

Source: 1. Economic Survey, 2006-07 (p.21), 2007-08 (p. 33) and 2008-09 (p. 37). Ministry of Finance. Government of India.
2. Union Budget, 2009-10.

TABLE 2

Revenue and Fiscal Deficits of the Central Government

(Rs. Crore)

	Revenue Deficit	*Fiscal Deficit*	*(1) as % of (2)*
	(1)	*(2)*	*(3)*
2001-02	1,00,162 (4.4)	1,40,955 (6.2)	71.05
2002-03	1,07,879 (4.4)	1,45,072 (5.9)	74.36
2003-04	98,261 (3.6)	1,23,272 (4.5)	79.71
2004-05	78,338 (2.5)	1,25,794 (4.0)	62.27
2005-06	92,299 (2.6)	1,46,435 (4.1)	63.03
2006-07	80,222 (1.9)	1,42,573 (3.5)	56.26
2007-08*	52,569 (1.1)	1,26,913 (2.7)	41.42
2008-09 (Budget)	55,183 (1.0)	1,33,287 (2.5)	41.40
2008-09 (Revised)	2,41,273 (4.5)	3,26,515 (6.2)	73.89
2009-10 (Budget)	2,82,735 (4.8)	4,00,996 (6.8)	70.50

*Based on Provisional Actuals for 2007-08.

Source: 1. Economic Survey, 2006-07 (p. 21), 2007-08 (p. 33) and 2008-09, (p. 37), Ministry of Finance, Government of India.

2. Union Budget, 2009-10.

Increasing revenue deficits not only pose a challenge but disclose the poor quality of the deficits. Revenue deficit can be financed only by any one of the three sources: domestic borrowing, borrowing overseas or printing money (monetization). Each of these have its effect on the economy: the first two have the impact in terms of rising interest rate, crowding out private investment and increasing debt liabilities for the posterity. The worst aspect of the revenue deficit is that it does not create any assets directly but adds to the liabilities for its financing. It is for this reason that it should be brought down to the zero level.

The past experience shows that the Government has continued to borrow heavily and a large part of such receipts are also used to finance revenue expenditure. In the process, the internal liabilities of the Government have a tendency to increase: the internal liabilities of the Central Government were as high as 61.4 per cent of the GDP in 2003-04 and stood at 56.6 per cent in 2008-09 (Revised). As the Government in the current year has an ambitious programme of borrowing over Rs. 4 lakh crores, it is desirable that a detailed information regarding the overall public sector borrowing requirements (PSBR) should be disclosed/available so that it may be possible to have an idea of public sector's draft on savings. This is desirable as both the public and private sectors compete for same pool of savings and too large a PSBR eats into the share of the private sector.

Further, at present the Reserve Bank of India (RBI) carries out both the debt management and the monetary policy implementation functions for the Central Government. In the process, the RBI is conflicted when it acts both as the Government's banker trying to borrow as cheap as possible, and also as the private authority responsible to enforce the monetary policy with the prevalent interest rates. Hence, there is need for a sound public debt management strategy so as to lower the cost of borrowing and at the same time balancing it with extant monetary policy initiatives and refinancing risks inherent in any government borrowing plan. It is a happy situation that the Government plans to bring about structural reform in the financial sector by creating an independent office to manage debt. An independent Debt Management Office (DMO) will also absolve the RBI from its responsibility of debt management function and it will also be in line with the practice of having a separate authority for debt management as is prevalent in a number of countries such as U.K., U.S.A., Sweden and Brazil, etc.

It may also be pointed out that fiscal situation is distorted due to off-budget items and in the process the fiscal deficit is augmented but not reflected in the budget. As part of the consumer subsidy towards petroleum products, fertilizer and food, companies selling them are given bonds but the same are not accounted for in the budget. In the budget for 2008-09, the Government disclosed the amount of bonds issued, as a foot note and not directly under the head 'expenditure'. The Prime

Minister's Economic Advisory Council (EAC) in its economic outlook for 2008-09 reported that together with certain 'unbudgeted' expenses, these off-budget subsidies could amount to 5 per cent of the GDP, over and above the budgeted fiscal deficit of 2.5 per cent. Needless to say, the quantum of subsidies tends to be substantial; for instance the fertilizer subsidy bill was estimated to surge to Rs. 1,02,000 crores from only Rs. 45,659 crores in 2007-08.

Additionally, the Government has a number of social welfare programmes which would involve huge outlays/ expenditure. The Government proposes to enlarge the scope of NAREGA by providing employment even beyond 100 days in some drought affected areas as also incorporate foodgrains component in the scheme to insulate the rural poor from inflation and drought. Further, to realize the vision of a slum-free India, the Government proposes to build 50 lakh dwelling units in five years for 6 crores slum-dwellers across 400 towns and cities. The Food Security Act, though kept in abeyance for the time being, and the Right to Education are some of the very ambitious programmes which will require enormous quantum of expenditure. Needless to say, the various on-going programmes, such as Bharat Nirman, programmes/schemes for socio-economic infrastructure development are already heavily drawing upon the resources of the Government. Under such a situation, it is therefore necessary that the Government should, in a transparent manner, provide item-wise details of each expenditure together with the resources that will be available for the purpose. To ensure fiscal transparency, nothing should be left to chance. It may be relevant to add here that the fiscal situation that improved during the five year period from 2003-04 to 2007-08 was largely due to Centre's tax-GDP ratio rising from 9.23 to 12.5 and at the same time there was compression of capital expenditure from 4 per cent of GDP in 2003-04 to 2.5 per cent in 2007-08, as referred to above.

From the above discussion, it is clear that the fiscal situation of the Central Government has been far from satisfactory; it remains doubtful whether the improvement in the fiscal situation of the Centre during the five-year period 2003-04 to 2007-08 was primarily due to the enactment of Fiscal Responsibility and Budget Management Act, 2003. Further the problem of fiscal imbalance, to a considerable extent, is structural rather than cyclical, in view of the fact that the Centre has not been transparent in presenting its expenditure requirements. The off-budget items, such as the large quantum of subsidies, being met through issue of bonds/securities, have tended to distort the fiscal situation. The global financial meltdown did affect the growth of the economy and in consequence the finances of the Centre but the entire blame for dismal fiscal situation cannot be attributed to it. The fiscal stimulus packages did impact the Centre's fiscal situation and helped in revival of the economy but the need for fiscal consolidation and fiscal restructuring cannot be over-emphasised to achieve the objective of fiscal discipline.

Global Financial Crisis and the Indian Economy: Myth and Reality

MD. QAISER ALAM AND MD. SHABBIR ALAM

INTRODUCTION

The global financial crisis has started around mid-2007 and become exacerbated since August 2008. This has led to the collapse of the major financial institution of the world and also started to deteriorate the real economy in the developed economies. The global financial crisis impacted the world economy by affecting the GDP rate of growth, contraction in world trade and a rising unemployment in the advanced economies, etc.

In the recent past, IMF reviewed that the global economy is expected to remain in recession, with a GDP growth rate of (-) 1.4 per cent measured in terms of Purchasing Power Parity (PPP) weights during the year 2009. World Bank 2009, projected that global GDP (at market exchange rates) would decline by a record of 2.9 per cent in the year 2009. It is estimated that financial turmoil has declined the value of world financial assets by about US$ 20 trillion. The world trade volume has declined from 7.2 per cent in 2007 to 2.9 per cent in 2008, however, it is projected that world trade volume is expected to shrink by (-) 12.2 per cent in the year 2009 (IMF June 2009).

In the year 2008, world wide FDI flows declined by 20 per cent on account of firstly, the weakened capacity of the companies and secondly, due to a fall in the growth prospects of the companies. This has also altered MNCs decisions to invest abroad and it has also led to the suspension of the cross border Merger and Acquisitions (M&A) projects across the world.

The emerging economies in Asia are facing the financial turmoil problems through transmission of stock markets turbulence and domestic credit problems due to sudden pull out of funds by FIIs. The global downturn has affected the real sectors in India and other Asian developing countries by declining the trade GDP ratio. On the financial side, it resulted in a fall in the prices of shares and corporate bonds similar to those in the other countries.

The Indian economy is the second fastest growing economy after China on the globe with a GDP growth rate of 6.7 per cent during 2008-09. The global financial crisis has affected the basic fundamental of the economy. It has created a sudden panic situation in the stock market and also to a sharp depreciation of the rupee against the US dollar. This has resulted in a decrease in demand, deceleration in manufacturing output growth, rising unemployment, lowering exports and created credit squeeze problems. It is also said that slowdown is the core of the financial turmoil which suppresses demand everywhere on the globe. In this reference, this paper aims to review the impact of the global financial crisis and its impact on India. For this purpose, the paper is divided into four sections accompanied by conclusions and suggestions.

LITERATURE REVIEW

There is a large number of growing literatures on the issue of financial crisis. One such study is put forward by Wray 2009, who stated that there is a wide ranging historical analysis of what went wrong and why financial crisis has erupted. He examined the historical antecedents of today's money managers, capitalism through the lines of works of Veblen, Hilferdind, Keynes, Scheupmpter and of Minsky. He has analyzed the rise and fall of the contemporary money manager's capitalism from the 1970s throughout the current crisis. Wade 2009, exerts the financial crisis from the historical perspective. He stated the importance of structural, macroeconomic imbalances in the global economy and requires the need for any appropriate measures.

D. Arista, 2009, in her studies brought a series of measures which include among others such as international monetary system reform including the public investment fund for emerging economies, reform proposals for international payment system and a new structure for revising SDR issuances. Pagano and Rossi, 2009, provides an imaginative and thought provoking explanation of the role of the new knowledge economy and intellectual property rights in bringing about the crisis. Furthermore, Gene Ma, was of the view that the US and EU economies suffer and while international capital will put off the emerging markets and go back to their home countries.

HISTORICAL BACKGROUND

There is no unanimity among the economists about the occurrence of the global financial crisis across the globe. But governments and central governments across the countries have responded to the crisis through the big aggressive and unconventional measures. In spite of this there is no unanimity among the economists about how much deeper it will be and how much time it will take to recover.

The financial crisis which has been erupted in the global economy after mid-2007 is worst since the great depression of 1930s. This is said to be a 'V'-shaped type of recession which created panic situation in Japan during 1990s. Similar type of recession erupted in Indonesia in 1997 and in Korea in 1997-98.

The present financial crisis has invalidated the so called "decoupling theory" which states that even if advanced economies went to a downturn, emerging economies will remain unscattered because of their substantial foreign exchange reserves, improved policy framework, robust corporate balance sheets and healthy banking sector. Given the evidence of the last few months, capital flows reversals, sharp widening of spreads on sovereign and corporate debt and abrupt currency depreciation suggests that "decoupling theory" is on the verge of loosing its existence. This raises a question on the validity of the "decoupling theory" that in a globalizing world can any country be remain isolated?

IMPACTS ON INDIA

The impact of the financial crisis on Indian economy is mixed. The real GDP growth rate of the economy has slow down. The prime growth sector that is the service sector is slowing. The construction, communication, trade hotels and restaurants and sub-sectors are also showing signs of slow down. Industrial growth is declining, current account deficit is widening, foreign exchange reserves are depleting.

India's growing internationalization is evident from the fact that a sum of the current receipts and payments increased from 19 per cent of GDP in 1990-91 to 53 per cent in 2007-08. Similarly, the sum of the gross capital inflows and outflows increased from 12 per cent of GDP in 1990-91 to around 64 per cent in 2007-08. This increasing financial globalization of the Indian economy clearly reflects the fact that any developments across the world will affect the Indian economy.

The financial turmoil in the global economy is transmitted in the Indian economy through two distinct channels namely, capital flows and trade flows. The global financial crisis has put a break on FIIs and banks to access Indian markets thereby bringing a downfall in the stock market. Moreover, net capital flows to India's has also declined. There is a fall in the foreign exchange reserves with a loss in the business confidence in the economy. Similarly, the exports of goods and services have gone down. This decline in the export sector brings down the GDP rate of growth. This is also attributed to the decline in the export to the USA, EU and Japan, etc.

India's GDP growth rate has decreased from 9.0 per cent in the financial year 2007-08 to 6.7 per cent in the financial year 2008-09, which was even lower than the average growth of 8.8 per cent per year during 2003-08. This is largely due to a sharp decline in the industrial growth and also due to the slow down in the growth of agriculture and service sectors.

FIGURE I

Macroeconomic Performance of the Indian Economy during 2001-02 to 2007-08

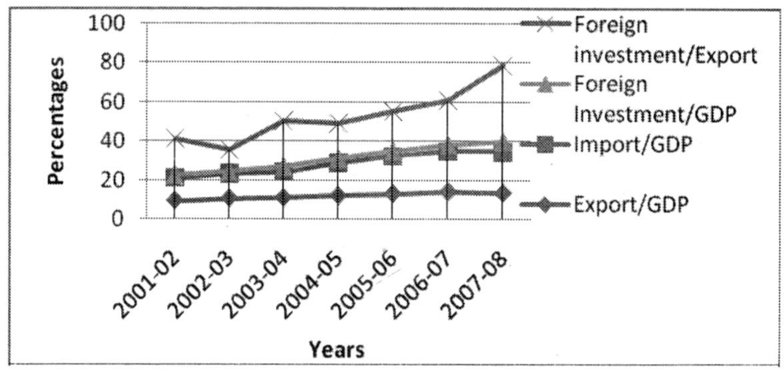

Source: Economic Survey (Various issues), Government of India and www.rbi.org.

The growth in the service sector declines from 10.8 per cent in 2007-08 to 9.4 per cent in the financial year 2008 - 09. The slow growth of service sectors during the first quarter of the financial year 2009-10 is due to decline in the foreign tourist arrivals, production of commercial vehicles, cargo handled at major ports, etc.

The Figure 1, depicts the macroeconomic performance of the economy during last seven years. This is evident from the figure that export as a percentage of GDP increased from 9.4 per cent in 2001-02 to 13.5 per cent during 2008 - 09. Likewise, export as a percentage of GDP increased from 11.8 to 21.2 per cent during the above mentioned period. It can be stated that on the external front, our export growth has fallen, but import growth has fallen more sharply. This has resulted in an improvement in the net exports of goods and services in the last quarter of 2008-09 and which continued during first few months of financial year 2009-10. Similarly, foreign investment as a percentage of GDP and export growth shows a positive sign from 1.7 per cent and 18.2 per cent during 2001-02 to 5.2 per cent and 38.8 per cent during the financial year 2007-08. Moreover, revenue and fiscal deficit as a percentage of GDP is all time high and gross fiscal deficits would be the highest since 1993-94 (Table 1).

TABLE I

Key Fiscal Indicators of Central Government during 2007-08 to 2009-10

Year	*Primary Deficit*	*Revenue Deficit*	*Gross Fiscal Deficit*
2007-08	-0.9	1.1	2.7
2008-09*	2.5	4.4	6.0
2009-10**	3.0	4.8	6.8

*Revised Estimates, **Budget Estimates.

Source: Macroeconomic and Monetary Developments, *First Quarter Review*, 2009-10, RBI.

This however signifies the fact that inspite of the widened financial indicators economic growth of the country has not been affected badly due to the strong fundamentals of the economy. The saving rate as a percentage of GDP to 38 per cent and investments as a percentage of GDP to 40 per cent is enough to finance the economic growth of the country. This relatively favourable position of the country is also due to the government favourable policy, sufficient amount of foreign exchange reserves, and increasing FDI inflows, required levels of employment, strong banking system and good business prospects of the companies.

The eruption of the financial crisis has created panic situation in the equity market due to sudden pull out of funds by the FIIS. In the financial year 2007-08, FIIs have invested around US$ 20.3 billion, but outbreak of financial crisis in September 2007 has led the FIIs to withdraw US$ 11.1 billion during just first 9 months of the year 2008 and to withdraw around US$ 8.1 billion during a short span of the financial year 2008-09. Similarly, net capital flows has decreased from US$ 108.0 billion in 2007-08 to US$ 9.1 billion during 2008-09.

The heavy pull out of funds by FIIs has also led to a sharp depreciation of the rupee by 25 per cent by RBI from Rs. 39.2 to a US dollar to Rs. 48.96 between January to October 2008. In spite of this fall in the value of the rupee our exports growth have also decreased. In spite of the downturn, there is an indication about the revival in the capital flows to India during the financial year 2009-10. This is attributed to the strong macroeconomic performance and resistance of the India economy during 2008-09, various fiscal and monetary measures and the growing interests of the global investors about India's growth potential. Meanwhile, India's foreign exchange reserve has declined by US$ 58.0 billion down from US$ 309.7 billion by the end of the march 2008 to US$ 251.7 billion by the end of the march 2009. However, this has increased subsequently to US 266.2 billion by mid of July 2009.

In the light of the above circumstances the present challenge is to preserve the economy relatively on the favourable position and to adopt the economic measures not only to minimize the loss but also to put the economy on the rapid and sustained growth path.

CONCLUSIONS AND SUGGESTIONS

The global financial turbulence in the world economy has reduced the world GDP growth rate and brought a loss of business confidence. The emerging economies in Asia have to face the financial turmoil problems more severely due to stock market turbulence and domestic credit problems. It has also reduced the world wide FDI flows by 20 per cent during the year.

The world economic situation has deteriorated and global downturn is projected to shrink by 0.6 per cent. The growth rate of the Indian economy has come down from 9.0 per cent in 2007 to 6.7 per cent in the financial year 2008-09. Moreover, the sudden pull out of funds by FIIs from the equity markets created panic situation among the investors and also brought a fall in the value of the rupee by 25 per cent in a very short period. This has also brought a decline in the FDI flows in India by US $35.0 billion a year.

This requires on the part of the policy-makers to launch a programme not only to reduce the negative impact of the financial crisis but also put the economy on the rapid growth path. There is an urgent need to protect the interests of the poor people, securing employment opportunities and income of the majority of the people. There is also a need to boost and strengthen the consumer's and investor confidence.

References

ADB (2009): Key Indicators of Developing Asia and the Pacific Countries, Manila.

ADB (2009): Asian Development Outlook, 2009, Manila.

Crotly, J. (2009): Structural Causes of the Global Financial Crisis: A Critical assessment of the New Financial Architecture; *Cambridge Journal of Economics*, Vol. 33, No. 4, pp. 563-80.

D. Arista (2009): The Evolving International Monetary System, *Cambridge Journal of Economics*, Vol. 33, No. 4, pp. 533-52.

Gosh, J and Chandrashekhar, C.P. (2009): The cost of coupling the global crisis and the Indian Economy, *Cambridge Journal of Economics*, Vol. 33, No. 4, pp. 685-702.

Goverbment of India (2008-09): Economic Survey, Ministry of Finance, New Delhi.

IMF (2009): World Economic Outlook, Crisis and Recovery, *World Economic and Financial Surveys*, Washington, DC, April.

Mohan Rakesh (2008): Global Financial Crisis and Key Risk: Impact on India and Asia, RBI, Oct.

OECD (2009): Economic Outlook, June

RBI (2009): Macroeconomic and Monetary Developments, *First Quarter Review*, 2009-10.

World Bank (2009): Global Development Finance, 2009.

Global Economic Crisis and Growth: Dynamics of the Indian Economy

S.S. Choudhary and Arun Prabha Choudhary

The global economic crisis began with the bursting of the United States housing bubble and high default rates on 'subprime' and adjustable rate mortgages (ARM) approximately in 2005-06. Due to fall in home prices and increase in interest rates, defaults and foreclosures accelerated in United States in late 2006 and further intensified the crisis in 2007 and 2008. During 2007, there have been 79 per cent increase in foreclosures as compared to 2006. This subprime crisis had affected financial institutions in the United States and Europe including the shadow banking system-comprising inter alia investment banks, hedge funds, private equity and structured investment vehicles. The collapse of the Lehman Brothers, in mid-September 2008, further aggravated the situation leading to a crisis of confidence in financial markets.

This global financial meltdown and consequent economic recession in developed economies have clearly been major factor in India's economic slowdown. India could not insulate itself from the adverse developments in the international markets despite having a banking and financial system that had little to do with investments in structured financial instruments (like subprime mortgage).

This paper is focused on global economic crisis and its impact on Indian economy. It also discusses the absorbers which protected the economy from the worst effects of global economic crisis. The paper has been divided into five sections: Section I gives the brief history of present recession and focuses on the reasons of global crisis. Section II analyses the impact of global economic crisis on Indian economy. Section III highlights policy measures adopted to counter this crisis. Section IV discusses growth dynamics and prospects of Indian economy. Section V concludes the study.

SECTION I

The reasons behind global economic crisis, that originated from United States, are many. The main reasons are inability of homeowners to make their mortgage payments, poor judgement by the borrower or the lender, speculation and over building of houses during the boom period, risky mortgage products, high personal and corporate debt levels, complex financial innovations, faulty central bank policies and government regulations, etc.

Low interest rates and large inflow of foreign funds created easy credit conditions in United States. This also increased demand for housing and thereby housing prices and consumer spending. Home prices, in America, increased by 124 per cent between 1997-2006. Due to prevailing culture of consumerism, Americans spent 800 billion per year more than they earned. This led to over construction of houses, causing home prices to decline in summer of 2006. Easy credit, combined with the assumption that housing prices would continue to appreciate, had encouraged many subprime borrowers to obtain adjustable rate mortgages they could not afford after the initial incentive period. Once housing prices started depreciating moderately in U.S., refinancing became more difficult. Some homeowners were unable to re-finance and began to default on loans as their loans reset to higher interest rates and payment amounts. As a result of this, nearly 10.8 per cent of total homeowners had the worth of their homes less than their mortgage. This compelled them to walk away from the home, which further gave rise to foreclosure and increased inventory of houses. This excess supply of home inventory placed significant downward pressure on prices. As price declined, more homeowners were at risk of default and foreclosure.

Another reason for this economic crisis was speculation in real estate. The role of speculative borrowing has been dominating in subprime mortgage crisis. During 2006, nearly 40 per cent of home purchases were for investment purposes, which indicate towards speculative borrowing. Securitization of home loans for people with poor credit is also blamed for the current global credit crisis. Due to securitization, investor's appetite for mortgage backed securities (MBS), and the tendency of rating agencies to assign investment grade ratings of MBS, loans with a high risk of default could be originated, packed and the risk readily transferred to others. In securitization, credit risk is transferred to investors through MBS. The securitized share of subprime mortgages increased from 54 per cent in 2001 to 75 per cent in 2006. The securitization process was not backed by due diligence and led to large-scale default.

Faulty credit rating process, over ambitious government and central bank's policies, financial institutional debt levels and incentives and credit default swaps were also responsible for global economic crisis, which surfaced around August 2007 in United States.

SECTION II

IMPACT OF GLOBAL ECONOMIC CRISIS ON OVERALL GDP GROWTH OF INDIA

The financial institutions across the world began to feel the consequences of subprime crisis in February 2007. The global financial meltdown and consequent economic recession in developed economies have also affected Indian economy. India could not remain immune to the global economic shock. In the beginning, the effect was not significant. After a few months, recession has decelerated economic growth in 2008-09 to 6.7 per cent from 9.0 per cent in 2007-08 and 9.7 per cent in 2006-07. The deceleration of growth in 2008-09 was spread across all sectors except mining and quarrying and community, social and personal services. The following table presents rate of growth at factor cost at 1999-2000 prices.

TABLE I

Rate of Growth at Factor Cost at 1999-2000

Prices (per cent)

	2003-04	2004-05	2005-06	2006-07	2007-08	2008-09
Agriculture, forestry and fishing	10.0	0.0	5.8	4.0	4.9	1.6
Mining and quarrying	3.1	8.2	4.9	8.8	3.3	3.6
Manufacturing	6.6	8.7	9.1	11.8	8.2	2.4
Electricity, gas and water supply	4.8	7.9	5.1	5.3	5.3	3.4
Construction	12.0	16.1	16.2	11.8	10.1	7.2
Trade, hotels and restaurants	10.1	7.7	10.3	10.4	10.1	*
Transport, storage and communication	15.3	15.6	14.9	16.3	15.5	*
Financing, insurance, real estate and business services	5.6	8.7	11.4	13.8	11.7	7.8
Community, social and personal services	5.4	6.8	7.1	5.7	6.8	13.1
Total GDP at factor cost	8.5	7.5	9.5	9.7	9.0	6.7

* Trade, hotels and restaurants, transport and communication (together) grew at 9 per cent in 2008-09.

Source: Central Statistical Organisation.

The above table points out that the growth in agriculture and allied activities decelerated from 4.9 per cent in 2007-08 to 1.6 per cent in 2008-09 due to the high base effect of 2007-08 and a fall in the production of non-food crops including oilseeds, cotton, sugarcane and jute. The manufacturing, electricity and construction sectors decelerated to 2.4, 3.4 and 7.2 per cent respectively during 2007-08 from 8.2, 5.3 and 10.1 per cent respectively in 2007-08. The slowdown in manufacturing could be attributed to the combined impact of a fall in exports followed by a decline in domestic demand. The rise in the cost of inputs during the beginning of the year and the cost of credit also reduced manufacturing margins and profitability and adversely affected the industry.

The construction industry went through a boom phase with growth as high as 16.2 per cent in 2005-06 and continued to grow, thereafter, the increase in the costs of construction due to a rise in the prices of inputs like steel and cement and interest costs had started to affect the industry. In certain segments of the industry, there was an excessive price build up in the form of a speculative bubble, related to limited supply of urban land for those segments. The rise in interest rates and the slowdown in housing loans also moderated demand. The double squeeze on the costs as well as the demand side and the fall in the liquidity in mid September 2008 precipitated a sharp downturn in this sector. In the second half of the year, demand had already moderated but costs remained high. The reason for higher growth in community, social and personal services during 2008-09 was attributed to an expansionary fiscal policy that was reflected as higher growth of Government Consumption expenditure.

Impact on Financial Sector

Following the collapse of Lehman Brothers in mid-September 2008, there was a full-blown meltdown of the global financial markets. It created a crisis of confidence that led to the seizure of inter-bank market and trickle down effect on trade financing in the emerging economies. Together with slackening global demand and declining commodity prices, it led to fall in exports thereby transmitting financial sector crisis to the real economy. It severely affected the countries with export led model of growth. The impact on Indian economy was less severe because of lower dependence of the economy on export markets and the fact that a sizeable contribution to GDP is from domestic sources.

The direct impact of the crisis on financial sector was

primarily through exposure to toxic financial assets and the linkages with the money and foreign exchange markets. Indian banks however had very limited exposure to the US mortgage market, directly or through derivatives, and to the failed and stressed international financial institutions. The depending of the global crisis and subsequent deleveraging and risk aversion however affected the Indian economy leading to slowing of growth momentum.

The effect of the financial crisis on emerging economies thereafter was mainly through reversal of portfolio flows due to unwinding of stock positions by FIIs to replenish cash balances abroad. Withdrawal of FII investment led to stock market crash in many emerging economies including India and decline in the value of local currency *vis-a-vis* US dollar as a result of supply-demand imbalances in domestic markets.

Impact on Balance of Payment

In India, the overall balance of payment situation remained resilient despite signs of strain in the capital account that manifested in the net reversal of FII flows of US 15.0 billion during fiscal 2008-09 and on current account through decline in exports. In 2008-09, the merchandise exports recorded a growth of 3.4 per cent reaching US 168.7 billion. While export growth was robust till August 2008, it became low in September and became negative from October 2008 to March 2009. The rupee depreciated by 21.2 per cent against US dollar during 2008-09. The US dollar however appreciated by 17 per cent against the broad index (FRB, New York) between March 2008 and March 2009 indicating that Indian rupee depreciated only 5 percentage points due to internal specific factors.

Impact on Money and Credit Markets

Money and credit markets have been affected indirectly through the dynamic linkages. The drying up of liquidity, fallout of repatriation of portfolio investments by FIIs affected credit markets in second half of 2008-09. This was compounded by the "risk aversion" of banks to extend credit in the face of a general downturn. The extent of external financial and monetary shock on the Indian monetary and financial system is best captured by the precipitous contraction in reserve money by more than 15 per cent between August 2008 and November 2008. Reserve money growth collapsed from 26.9 per cent in August 2008 to 10.3 per cent in November 2008 and further 6.4 per cent in March 2009. RBI adopted various monetary policy measures to prevent precipitous fall in narrow money M_1 and broad money M_3. Despite these, however, M_1 growth decelerated from 19.4 per cent in August 2008 to 10.3 per cent in November 2008 and further to 8.2 per cent in March 2009, while M_3 growth decelerated from 21 per cent in August 2008 to 18.7 per cent in March 2009. A series of unconventional measures actually helped to push up the rate of growth of bank credit from 25.4 per cent in August 2008 to 26.9 per cent in November 2008. However, this only partly offset the effects on short and long-term credit to Indian companies in the United States and EU markets because of freezing of financial markets. Subsequently, credit growth decelerated sharply to 17.1 per cent in March 2009.

SECTION III

POLICY MEASURES TO COUNTER ECONOMIC CRISIS

To counter the negative fallout of the global economic crisis on the Indian Economy, the Government responded by providing various measures. These measures have been discussed as follows:

- To facilitate the flow of funds from financial system to productive sectors, the Reserve Bank of India took a number of monetary easing and liquidity-enhancing measures including reduction in Cash Reserve Ratio, Statutory Liquidity Ratio and key policy rates. Between August 2008 and March 2009, RBI reduced Reverse-Repo and Repo Rates from 6 to 3.5 and 9 to 5 per cent respectively. CRR was reduced from 9 to 5 per cent. This helped in improving the liquidity in the system.
- To supplement monetary policy, Government adopted expansionary fiscal policy in the form of tax relief to boost demand and increased expenditure on public projects to generate employment and public

assets. In implementing the fiscal stimulus, the Government increased its spending on the plan by nearly 1 per cent of the GDP and 2.5 per cent of GDP on non-plan expenditure that included increased spending on fertilizers and food subsidy, agriculture debt waiver, defence, salaries and pensions. The Government renewed its efforts to increase infrastructure investments in telecommunications, power generation, airports, ports, roads and railways.

- Under institutional measures, the central Government adopted the policy of recapitalization of banks and consolidation of financial sector institutions. The Government merged 196 RRBs into 85 RRBs under the measure of consolidation and recapitalized public sector banks to maintain CRAR of 12 per cent.
- Domestic financial sector reforms and other measures include increasing access to finance, improving domestic resource mobilization, improving efficiency of banking sector, avoiding financial repression, improving supervision and regulation, strengthening property and contract rights, judiciary and rules of law.
- Measures to reform international financial markets include deepening of financial markets, moving towards a more inclusive system of global financial governance, satisfactory conclusion of Doha Round of WTO, etc. For this India is actively participating in G-20 meets.

SECTION IV

RECENT GROWTH DYNAMICS AND PROSPECTS OF INDIAN ECONOMY

Compared to other emerging economies, India has several strengths that can help an early mitigation of the adverse effects of the global financial crisis and the recession in major OECD economies. These strengths are:

- India has a relatively high share a services in GDP which tend to be less affected by cyclical downturns than manufacturing. This factor has operated in the second half of 2008-09 and is likely to continue in 2009-10.
- In last six years, the average annual growth of agriculture sector has been 4.4 per cent. During the past years this growth of agriculture and different rural development programmes including NREGS have kept the rural income and consumption strong and thereby domestic demand.
- India's domestic saving rate remains high and has resin sharply with higher growth during the last five years. The habit of savings and spending according to income levels have saved the economy from the crash.
- As a policy response to the growth slowdowns, the Government has designed the programme of infrastructure investment, which provides the basis for offsetting some decline in corporate investment in manufacturing by increased investment in infrastructure by government and by private sector through the PPP model.
- India continues to retain its position as a preferred destination for investments. In a recent UNCTAD study on assessing the impact of the current financial and economic crisis on global flows, it was found that India achieved a growth of 85.1 per cent in foreign direct investment flows in 2008, the highest increase across all countries. According to this study, FDI investments into India went up from US $ 25.1 billion on 2007 to US $ 46.5 billion in 2008 even as global flows declined from US $ 1.9 trillion to US $ 1.7 trillion during this period.
- The steep decline in commodity prices in the second half of 2008-09 along with the likely slack in global demand for at least the next 12 months would not only help in cutting down the import bill, but also have a favourable impact in effecting a reduction in

below the line deficit to less than the level in 2008-09. The reduction in oil and fertilizer subsidies would help bring the central fiscal deficit back towards the long-term trend.

- Over the past five years of growth, net exports were a depressant on domestic demand contributing (–) 17 per cent to the total increase in demand due to high oil prices. In the previous five years, net exports made a substantial positive contribution to domestic demand due to exceptionally low oil prices complemented by significant export growth. This is the substantial improvement over the negative contribution in the recent years.

The prospects of Indian economy are bright because the global recession has only slowed the economy and has not shrunk it. A large domestic market, resilient banking system and a policy of gradual liberalization of capital account have been key protectors of the economy. A number of forecasts and projections have been made on the prospects of the economy in 2009-10 ranging 4 to 7.5 per cent GDP growth. The growth of economy in first quarter of 2009-10 has been 6.1 per cent showing the bright prospects of future growth.

Challenges

There are certain risky factors that may hamper the growth of Indian economy. These are reduced availability of risk capital for the corporate sector due to equity disinvestment and repatriation, lower medium to long-term capital flows due to continuous deleveraging in the US economy, negative impact on Indian exports due to delayed revival of the OECD economies especially exports of gems, jewellery, leather products and garments could remain affected for some more time.

SECTION V

CONCLUSION

Thus it may be concluded that Indian economy is returning on its path of high growth rate of GDP (probably 8 to

8.5 per cent). There has been an increase in Foreign Direct Investment (FDI) during 2008-09 over the previous years. It also seems that Foreign Institutional Investors (FIIs) may return to Indian market. The credit market appears to be working normally and there is no dearth of liquidity in the economy. The index of industrial production is showing clear sign of revival. The stock market have already picked up. The implementation of the recommendations of Sixth Pay Commission and various programmes of social and rural development have boosted demand and helped in survival of the economy from global crisis. This indicates that India will soon be back on the new trend growth path provided the critical policy and institutional bottlenecks are removed. The policy measures to be adopted should address the short and long-term challenges and ensure the sustainability of growth and progress.

NOTES

1. **Subprime lending**—This is lending practice mainly in the form of mortgages for the purchase of residences. This lending practice is used to those borrowers who want to purchase residence but do not fulfil the usual criteria for borrowing at the lowest prevailing market interest rate.
2. **Foreclosure**—The process of seizing the home in case when a homeowner is delinquent in making payments to the bank is called foreclosure.
3. **Securitization**—It is a process through which lenders sell the right to receive payments on the mortgages they issue. Securitization is structured finance process in which assets, receivable or financial instruments are acquired pooled together as collateral for the third party investments.
4. **Speculative Borrowing**—Keynesian Economist Hyman Minsky described three types of speculative borrowings based on types of speculative borrowers. These borrowings can lead to a collapse of asset values by accumulation of debt. One is "hedge borrower", which borrows for making debt payments from cash flows from other investments. Second is "speculative borrower" which borrows with the belief that interest payment on loan will be made but principal amount will be rolled over into new investments and the third is "Ponzi borrower" who relies on the appreciation of the value of his asset (real asset) to refinance or pay off his debt but can not repay the initial loan.
5. **MBS**—Mortgage Backed Securities.
6. **Credit Default Swaps (CDS)**—These are insurance contracts typically used to protect bondholders or MBS investors from the risk of defaults.

References

Government of India, Economic Survey, 2008-09.

Lal, Subir, "IMF Predicts Slower World Growth Amid Serious Market Crisis," International Monetary Fund, April 9, 2008.

Singh, Chandra Kant, Economic Meltdown 2008: Global Perspective, R.K. Publications and Distributors, 2009, Delhi-110053.

The World Economy Bad or Worse, Economist.com 09/10/08. Retrieved 15/04/09.

Strategic Importance of Business Process Outsourcing in India's Service Sector

PRADEEP KUMAR SINGH, ANUP KUMAR AND U.S. RAI

INTRODUCTION

The emergence of India as one of the fastest growing economies in the world during the 1990s is attributable in significant part to the rapid growth of its services sector. During the 1990s, the Indian service sector grew at an average annual rate of 9 percent, contributing to nearly sixty percent of the overall growth rate of the economy. At the same time, India's exports of services displayed one of the fastest rates of growth in the world-over 17 percent per annum in the 1990s and grew two and a half times faster than the domestically focused part of the services sector.

Access to external markets and domestic reform have played an important role in creating a dynamic services sector in India. While factors such as the high income elasticity of demand for services, cost reducing and variety-enhancing technological advances, and changes in the method of organizing production favouring increased outsourcing have played a vital role, two other factors have played an equally critical role in sustaining this dynamism, namely access to a growing external market for services and the gradual, though partial, liberalization of the domestic economy. The analysis shows the strategic importance of Business Process Outsourcing in India service sector in different aspects as well as the problems and prospects in the context of economic crisis.

Over the past decade, Indian has made considerable advances in reducing the role of the state in the provision of key infrastructure services and opening service industries to domestic and foreign competition in telecommunications, banking, insurance, business and health services. Although the gains are hard to quantify, these reforms have undoubtedly produced economy-wide benefits both in terms of sectoral efficiency and growth performance.

SERVICES SECTOR'S GROWTH: A GLOBAL PERSPECTIVE

It has been theoretically argued and empirically estimated that as economic growth proceeds the service sector grows. In developed countries, the service sector is therefore the largest sector in terms of its contribution to total output. In 1990, the service sector contributed more than 60% of GDP in most developed countries. This share grew steadily and in 2003 the service sector contributed almost 70% of GDP in most of the developed countries. In contrast, this sector's contribution to GDP in developing countries of Asia ranged between 40% and 45% in 1990, with countries in South Asia such as Bangladesh, Pakistan and Sri Lanka averaging lower growth rates of around 47-48%. In the period 1990 to 2003, we find that the share of services in GDP remained more or less the same in many East and Southeast Asian countries while then has been a rise in its share in most South Asian countries. Like other developing countries of South Asia, India also witnessed a rise in the share of services in its GDP, but the rise is much more pronounced—it is almost 10%. Since 2003, the service sector has contributed more than 50% of India's GDP.

The only other country, which has witnessed such an increase, is Philippines when the share of services increased from

TABLE I

Contribution of Services to GDP in Select Developed and Developing Countries, 1990-2003

Country	*Services Contribution to GDP (%)*			
	1990	*1995*	*2000*	*2003*
ASEAN				
Cambodia	-	36.64	37.08	35.88
Indonesia	41.47	41.06	36.66	39.85
Lao PDR	24.26	25.08	24.57	25.50
Malaysia	42.59	45.65	40.47	41.80
Myanmar	32.20	30.10	33.07	-
Philippines	43.62	46.31	51.97	53.16
Singapore	-	66.20	62.83	64.96
Vietnam	38.59	44.06	38.73	38.22
SOUTH ASIA				
Afghanistan	-	-	19.77	-
Bangladesh	48.28	49.06	49.20	51.98
Bhutan	31.53	25.41	28.75	27.30
India	41.10	43.64	48.78	51.20
Maldives	-	-	-	-
Nepal	32.13	35.49	37.05	37.85
Pakistan	48.83	50.06	50.17	53.20
Sri Lanka	47.71	50.46	52.82	54.73
DEVELOPED WORLD				
United Kingdom	62.92	66.16	70.46	72.44
United States	70.09	72.10	73.95	-
Japan	58.15	63.90	66.38	-
Australia	67.20	68.46	70.70	-
Belgium	65.05	68.79	70.44	72.19
France	66.47	69.36	71.72	72.82
Germany	59.45	65.28	68.00	69.41
Italy	62.54	65.11	68.08	69.55
Luxembourg	66.31	73.20	79.64	78.89
Netherlands	64.79	67.61	70.34	-

Source: World Bank (2005), World Development Indicators.

around 43% to 53% in this period. The rising share of services-GDP is therefore not a unique phenomenon witnessed by India though the extent of this increase is much higher in India's case than other developing countries. Though the share of services in total GDP may not have raised much in many East and Southeast Asian countries, this does not suggest that the service sector has not grown over time in these countries. A fast growing manufacturing sector may lower the share of the services sector in GDP. Looking at the average annual growth rate in value added of the services sector in the period 1990 to 2003, we find that in many developing countries of ASEAN—such as Indonesia, Malaysia, Myanmar, Thailand and Vietnam-the growth in services value added has on an average been more than 7%. The corresponding growth in Bangladesh, Pakistan and Sri Lanka has been lower. In South Asia, only India and Maldives have experienced an average annual growth of more than 7%. Starting from a higher base, most of the developed countries have witnessed growth of less than 3% in their service sector.

Growth of the service sector in an economy is invariably accompanied by growth of employment in this sector. One reason for accompanied growth of employment is the slow rise in productivity growth in services as compared to the manufacturing sector. Different explanations have been put forwarded for slow growth of productivity in services as compared to goods, including the argument that when it comes to cost reduction for existing products or services, technological change is more frequent and more powerful in its effects in the commodity sector (Kuznets, 1957). It has also been argued that many services are subject to diminishing returns and because of their labour-intensive nature, the service-sector activities can not be made more efficient through capital accumulation, innovation, or economies of scale (Fuchs, 1980).

But lower productivity in services as compared to goods would imply that the shift of the economy towards a larger service sector might lead to a reduction in the economy's overall rate of productivity growth. The relationship between investment in new technology mainly information technology (IT), and productivity has been widely discussed but little understood. The huge increase in computerization overtime, especially in the 1970s and 1980s roughly coincides with the productivity slowdown that began in the early 1970s. it has also been widely reported that most of the productivity slowdown is concentrated in the service sector. This "productivity paradox" has led to big debate. Roach (1991) support the dismal performance of IT in the service sector. Roach argues that the long-learning period associated with new technology reduces the visible benefits from investments on new technology. Moreover, these investments show higher productivity only if they are widely used. Many a time the new technology is used along with the old technology leading to a slowdown in productivity. Slow productivity growth in the service sector has important implications for growth of employment in services as the share of this sector increases in total GDP. This implies that a higher share of services in GDP will invariably be accompanied by higher employment in the service sector. Examining the trends in service sector employment across different countries over time, we find that in developed countries, the service sector contributes around 70% of GDP and constitute 65-70% of total employment.

In sum, relative to other countries, we find that the contribution of services to GDP has been high in India though services have not been able to contribute as much to total employment as in other countries. Trade in services, however, is an important component of total trade in India.

Trends in Growth of India's Service Sector

Given the growing significance of services in India's GDP and trade but their low contribution to total employment, it becomes important to analyse the contribution of the service sector at the disaggregated level. At the aggregate level the service sector witnessed a phenomenal growth in the decade of 1990s. During the 1980s, this sector's output grew at the rate of 6.6% per annum, while during the 1990s the growth rate increased to 7.5% per annum. In the financial year from (1994-2004), the service sector in India has grown at an average rate of 7.9% per annum.

Share of Services in GDP

A striking feature of India's growth performance is that between 1950 and 1990, agriculture's share in GDP has declined by about 25 percentage points, while industry and services have gained equally. The share of industry has stabilized since 1990 and consequently the entire decline in agriculture has been picked up by the service sector.

Growth in India's service sector has also not been uniform across all services. A close scrutiny reveals that amongst services, business services have been one of the fastest growing

FIGURE 1

Average Sectoral Growth Rates (%) in India, 1994-2008

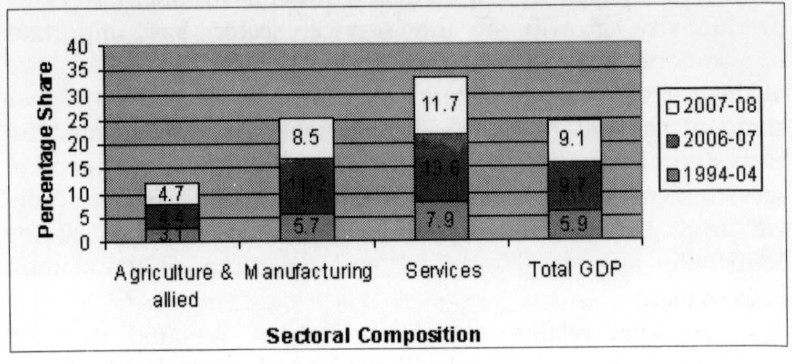

Source:: Economic Survey.

FIGURE 2

Average Sectoral Contribution (%) to India's GDP

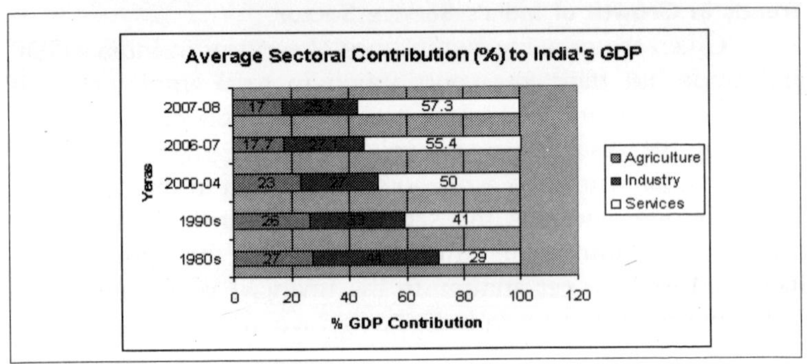

services in the 1980s, closely followed by banking and insurance. The prime drivers of growth in services apart from business services in the 1990s are communication services (with average growth of around 13.6%) and hotels and restaurants (with average growth of around 9%).

In services, the areas of policy focus, liberalization and high growth in India have been Software, ITES (including financial IT services) and BPO, besides emerging areas as healthcare (in particular diagnostics and surgeries), telecommunication and more recently in professional services,

TABLE 2

Index of Revealed Comparative Advantage

Year	*INDIA*			
	Transport	*Travel*	*Other Services*	*All Commercial Services*
1995	1.14	1.19	0.85	0.92
1996	1.17	1.22	0.80	0.90
1997	0.92	1.02	1.06	1.03
1998	0.68	0.81	1.26	1.26
1999	0.56	0.67	1.46	1.39
2000	0.45	0.57	1.56	1.54
2001	0.39	0.48	1.66	1.62
2002	0.49	0.42	1.64	1.56

Notes: (1) The Figures in the table are Balassa's Revealed Comparative Advantage (RCA) Index, computed as:

Rih= (Xih/Xit)/Xwh/Xwt), where

Rih= Balassa's Index of RCA

Xih= Country is export of product h

Xit= Total export of country I

Xwh= world export of product h

Xwt= total world exports A country is said to have revealed comparative advantage (disadvantage) in product h if Rih>1

(2) Other services being Communications, Construction, Insurance, Financial Services, computed and Information, Royalties and License fees, Other Business services, Personal, cultural and recreational Government.

Source: Based on data from Balance of Payments Statistics, 2004, IMF

distribution and government services. It should be noted here that unilateral services sector liberalization in India has been most focused is still restricted in many services which can lead to Intra-industry trade (IIT) with trading partners.

Growth of BPOs in Service Sector in India

Unlike its experience in trade in goods, India in a short span of time has emerged as one of the most dynamic suppliers of services in the world. Cross-border supply or Mode 1 of GATS involves the physical movement of a service across borders. One of the most prevalent forms of cross-border supply in services is global outsourcing (also termed as off-shoring) whereby some of the operations of a firm, such as business processes and back office non-core operations, are outsourced to service providers in other countries and delivered back to the outsourcing firm through internet, voice, and satellite-based communications. Trade in Mode 1 has emerged as the main driver for India's growth of trade in services. Both the domestic and international markets for Indian IT-ITES have been increasing steadily.

FIGURE 3

Growth of India'a Domestic Market and Exports of IT/ITE

(Billion $)

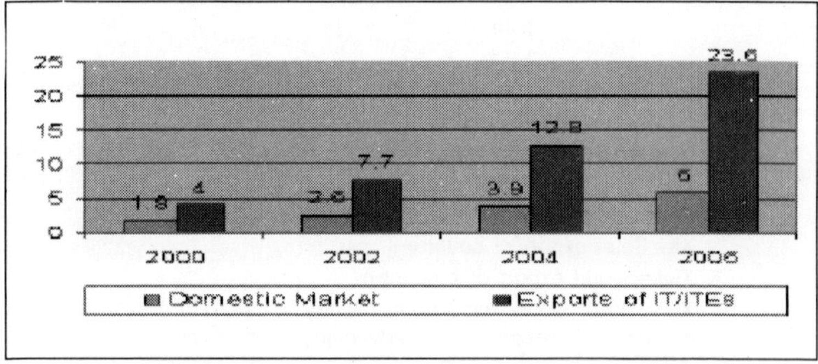

Exports have increased exponentially in the last six years (i.e. from $ 4 billion in 2000 to around $ 24 billion in 2006). The total market for Indian IT-ITES is estimated at around $ 30 billion in 2006. India's competitiveness in Mode 1 trade has been examined by many studies. The global services location index for 2005 shows that India remains the best offshore location by a wide margin although wage inflation and the emergence of lower-cost countries have decreased its overall lead. Close competitors in this field are China and Thailand. Improved infrastructure and relevant people skills have increased China's attractiveness as a low-cost option for servicing Asian markets.

India's competitive advantage in off-shoring arises due to its growing pool of highly skilled, low-cost workers in India around 3000 educational institutions train more then 200,000 software professionals and an equal number of non-engineering English-Speaking graduates every year. Estimates by firms, such as Gartner and Forrester, place the size of the global outsourcing (offshoring) market at about $ 185 billion today and project the size of this business to grow to over $ 500 billion, with the potential to create hundreds of thousands of jobs worldwide in services as wide ranging as customer relations, technical support, consulting, design, engineering, R&D, biotechnology, accounting, and human resource management.

However, in terms of destination of exports of IT-ITES, India's exports in Mode 1 are highly concentrated in a few countries. The US is the most important market for India, with exports constituting 71% of total software exports, followed by UK (14%). Indian software companies have recently begun diversifying to markets in Europe, Japan, Singapore, and Australia. India's trade with Brazil is also increasing steadily. The Indian IT-ITES sector is expected to exceed $ 36 billion in annual revenue in 2006, an increase of nearly 28% from the previous year, according to NASSCOM Strategic Review 2006. Exports are likely to account for nearly two-thirds of total revenues. The IT-ITES sector is expected to contribute 4.8% of GDP in 2006-07. Engineering, R&D and software products hold great opportunity for India as they are growing at 37%. India is increasingly becoming an offshore base for high-value, specialized services in areas such as research and development, bioinformatics, drug testing and pharmaceutical research, engineering design, and financial analysis. All leading listed IT service players in India have entered this segment with the bigger ones also serving some of the Fortune 500 companies. At all levels of the value chain, there is a huge cost advantage from outsourcing to India. For instance, costs of call centre operators, including salary and benefits, are around $ 3000 per year in India as compared to around $ 25,000 per year in the US. In the case of engineers and accountants, the cost in India is in the range of $ 6000 to $ 7000 per annum as compared to $ 55,000-60,000 per year in the US, amounting to a huge cost reduction for even the more skilled an high-value activities.

Importance and Justification of BPO Services in Indian Service Sector

The social impact of outsourcing is huge. Apart from providing age-gender-neutral employment to many thousands of people, it has substantial spillover effects. A wide range of ancillary services like housekeeping, security, catering, transport, real estate, etc. have received a boost. It has also triggered the creation of new training institutions and infrastructure, such as computer technical schools, diploma programmes and IT training and application courses in colleges and universities. It has encouraged spread of education, training, computer literacy and internet penetration. Although exports through cross-border supply in areas like BPO and ITES are largely unregulated and free, there is now an increasing unrest in developed countries with respect to Mode 1 trade. Consequently, while in 2003 only four bills restricting offshore sourcing-the practice of acquiring services from a non-US vendor-were introduced in the US, in 2004 the number went up to 40 federal bills and 200 state bills. This discourages offshoring of services by the US.

According to NASSCOM, India has become the most favoured destination for sourcing software and IT-Enabled Services with an export value of $ 12.8 billion in 2003-04. India in comparison with other locations ranks high in several critical parameters including level of government support, quality of the labour pool, English language skills, labour cost advantages, project management skills, and overall quality certifications. Every year, India produces 2.1 mn. graduates and 0.3 mn. post-graduates (including non-engineering colleges). The difference in wages between the US or the UK and India is more than 70-80% for many offshored processes. India will have to pursue its offensive interest in near-future in cross-border supply of services and negotiate with developed countries to bind in their existing liberal regimes with respect to offshore outsourcing of services. India also needs to promote its exports of services to other developing countries, mainly in East and Southeast Asia.

Problems and Prospects of BPO Industries in the Context of Global Economic Crisis

It is far too presumptuous to think that India is going to be hugely and adversely affected by the world recession mainly US economy slowdown. India's share of the global trade is too tiny for this. At the same time, however, one must always bear in mind the far reaching impact of globalization, which has, in turn, led to the interdependence of economies particularly where the

US is concerned. 25% of the India's IT exports, for example are to the US.

The United States is India's largest trade partner, source of foreign direct investment and external job opportunities for the Indian middle class. Any slowing of the US economy is likely to hurt India more today than at any time in the past. The fact is that the US is not only India's largest trade partner but that India has the highest trade surplus with the US and any slowdown in Indian exports to the US is likely to have a larger impact on the trade deficit than a slowdown in trade with European Union or developing Asia. The software segment is another main area of concern. The US has emerged as the biggest market for Indian software exports. A slowdown of the US economy will hurt the "new economy" in India since it is still largely export-dependent and has not yet found a domestic market large enough to offset any loss in the external market. But analysts and software CEOs argue that in a slowing economy, jobs are cut and companies invest in automation, so that the demand for software services and for IT products is likely to increase as the economy slow down.

Also, many US firms may offload work to lower-cost countries like India, especially in the area of data-processing and office management work, and that this is likely to increase the demand for new economy services in India rather than hurt them. On the negative side is the concern that firms tend to put on hold expansion plans and investment in new projects when there is a fear of a generalized slow down. This is likely to hurt demand for Indian IT services and products. The final outcome may be a combination of both factors. But one must realise that most of the companies who service the lower rung areas of maintenance, etc. will not really stand to loose. They may face a squeeze on their margins but the business will continue.

We can demonstrate the problems and prospects of BPO sector by using SWOT analysis as follows:

Strengths
- English speaking labour pool
- Strong IT background
- Superior Service Maturity
- Strong governmental support

Weakness
- Small players
- High attrition
- Infrastructure
- Bureaucracy

- Cost Competitiveness
- Indian domestic-market growth
- Geographic positioning

Opportunities	**Threats**
• Move up the value chain	• Emerging low cost nations
• Unexplored markets	• Rising costs
• Greater share of the market	• Backlash in US and Europe
	• Technology
	• Indian educational policy

SWOT ANALYSIS

Strategy and Predicted Policy Amendments for BPO Industries of India

The decline in growth of the global economy has been caused by a combination of global and country-specific factors. One universal cause has been the persistent rise in the energy prices during 1999-2000. Another key factor to the reduction in growth has been the sharp and sudden downturn in hi-tech investment in the second half of 2000. This weakened growth, notably in the US and Europe, while brutally reducing the export performance of many Asian countries. In the US, the output of hi-tech equipment accelerated at an annual growth rate to 70 percent in early 2000, before collapsing. The crisis worsened because not only was demand falling but the unit price equipment in the hi-tech sector also collapsed. US investment spending was sharply reduced, particularly on hi-tech equipment. The unexpected decline in the demand for hi-tech investment goods undermined stock prices, reversing the earlier surge in the value of new economy stocks.

A decrease in exports as a result of the US Economy slowdown will be certainly negative from the Indian standpoint but the decrease in oil prices (from a peak of $35 a barrel to $20-$22) will be positive for the Indian Rupee and the funds flow, given the US interest rate cuts, would be positive. However, the FDI track record will continue to be shoddy, so the effects would be neutral. The amazing growth of frontline IT companies at 55-

60% is a thing of the past. The global slowdown will definitely affect these companies. What inevitably needs to change is to shift our exports focus from being US-centric to newer markets.

FUTURE DIMENSIONS

The IT-Enabled Services industry in India began to evolve in the early 1990s when companies such as American Express, British Airways, General Electric (GE) and Swissair set-up their own offshore operations in India. MNCs like GE, HSBC, American Express, Dell computers, etc. have set-up base in India. Content development, which includes areas like engineering, design animation, network consultancy and management, and biotech research, is anther high revenue earner in the ITES industry. Some other emerging segments in the ITES industry are: HR, Payment services, administration, health-care, retail, telecom and hospitality. There is also increasing offshoring of upcoming service lines involving higher value-added activities such as engineering and design, knowledge processing and logistics.

According to UNCTAD, the preferred locations for call centres in the near future include India, the Philippines, China, South Africa, Mauritius, and the UAE. Of more than 300 Export-oriented IT projects in developing world, 37% went to India, 19% to China and 11% to Singapore during 2002-03. And the potential future locations for FDI projects related to IT services were India, the Russian Federation, Bulgaria, the Philippines, China, and Mexico in order of preference. India with its vast pool of cheap graduates and proficiency in English-speaking is well-positioned as an ITES destination.

In order to compete in the global marketplace, India needs to build a full spectrum BPO industry, in all its rich variety-not just dominance in the call centre business. We need our BPO workforce to see the industry as a place that can give them long-term and fulfilling career opportunities and not as a place where they come to get their accents neutralized and move on. We need customers to see us as a strategic, viable, and low risk alternative to 'doing it themselves' rather than as a tactical answer to next quarter's earnings problems.

References

Banga, R., 'Statistical overview of India's trade in services', "Trade in Services and India: Prospects and Strategies", Edited by Rupa Chanda, Co-published with CENTAD, Wiley-India, 2006.

Illiyan, A., 'Performance, Challenges and Opportunities of Indian software export', *Journal of Theoretical and Applied Information Technology*, © 2005-2008, JATIT.

IT Software and Services Industry in India—An Overview, "Electronics and Computer Software Export Promotion Council (ESC)", New Delhi.

Joshi, S., 'FDI in India's service sector: Determinants and implications', "Trade in Services and India: Prospects and Strategies", Edited by Rupa Chanda, Co-published with CENTAD, Wiley-India, 2006.

Kantak, A.N., 'Trends and Challenges in Business Process Outsourcing', Sri Sri Ravishankar Vidya Mandir, January 2007.

Nasscom, "Software Industry in India—A Strategic Review", National Association of Software and Services Companies, New Delhi, 2005-06.

Nasscom, "Software Industry in India—A Strategic Review", National Association of Software and Services Companies, New Delhi, 2006-07.

Nasscom, "Software Industry in India—A Strategic Review", National Association of Software and Services Companies, New Delhi, 2007-08.

Sustaining India's Services Revolution—Access to foreign markets, domestic reform and International negotiations, The World Bank, 2004.

Walters, R., Stapleton, T., and Andrews, R., "India's Services Sector—Unlocking Opportunity", Edited by Peter Judge, © Commonwealth of Australia, Australian Government, Department of Foreign Affairs and Trade, Economic Analytical Unit, 2007.

Impact of Global Recession on Indian Economy

A.K. KHAN

INFORMATION TECHNOLOGY

Until 2001, the Indian IT industry was climbing dizzying heights and reached unprecedented levels. It was the most envied industry With the fastest growth impetus, and the highest profit margins. This industry paid attractive salary, had challenging projects on hand and could earn millions of dollars to our country in the form of export revenue. All this came to an end with the onset of recession, which in turn created an adverse impact on Indian IT industry. This recession had a global impact and has affected many industries in the world, including India. However, the impact of recession has been very severe on the Indian IT industry when ccmpared to the impact of recession on other industries

Indian Tourism Industry

Tourism has become one of the largest and fastest growing industry, 'in the world.' It not only provides much needed foreign exchange but also provides maximum employment to our country. It is estimated that by 2010, it may contribute Rs. 1,30,000 crore in capital investment and will create 7 million jobs. Our country can provide various tourism such as nature, richness of architecture, culture, diversity, wildlife, festivities, shopping, ete. in one holiday, which show that our country has everything for everyone for all seasons. Out the present situation of our tourism industry is not up to the mark

Co-operative Sector

Although the genesis of cooperative movement is seen to give freedom of farmers and landless lobours from the clutches of moneylenders, subsequently, the cooperative organizations took a place as a tool of socio-economic development of mass movement and spread almost in every field of Indian economy. In the course of serving the poor and middle class people, the cooperative movement has made substantial contribution to the economic development of country and emerged as one of the inevitable part of Indian economy. During the period of last 105 years, the cooperative movement has passed through several revolutions and still they have evolved as the significant player of economic development. During the period of financial reforms followed by global economic recession the cooperative have positioned themselves steadily without trembling. The cooperatives being the organizations of poor with small means can not be termed as a vibrant one in regard to responding to the completion from private and foreign players. But the cooperative are sustaining with their core values and philosophy as enunciated in cooperative principles.

Indian Financial System

Recession has become synonymous with crisis financial turmoil, job cuts, pink slips, unemployment, uncertain future, etc. The current global financial crises are the cause of defaults on sub-prime mortgages in US. Sub-prime is a high risk debt offered to people with poor credit worthiness or unstable incomes. The US financial crises have affected many countries of the world and India is not an exception to it. Because of these financial crises, Indian economy is likely to lose 1% to 2% of GDP growth. Almost all sectors of the Indian economy are affected by this crisis.

Banking and Business Sector

The global recession which started in 2008 after the Subprime crisis and the unprecedented default or rescue of many financial institutions has strongly affected the credibility of the international banking system, damaging also the real economy. Due to this joint crisis, the credit crunch is severely affecting the economy in Western globalized countries. The truth is, we are going through the most severe global financial crisis since the days of Great Depression.

Retail Marketing Sector

The Indian Retail Industry is gradually inching its way towards becoming the next boom industry. The Retail industry in India has come forth as one of the most dynamic and fast paced industries with several players entering the market. But all of them have not tasted success because of the heavy initial investments that are required to break even with other companies and compete with them. The organized retail industry in India had not evolved till the early 1990s. Retail sector is one of the India's fastest growing sectors with a Five percent compounded annual growth rate. India is the country having most unorganized retail market. India's huge middle class and its untapped retail industry are key attractions for Global retail giants planning to enter into newer markets. Driven by changing life style, strong income growth and favorable demographic patterns Indian retail is expected to grow 25% annually. But due to the recession the rate of the development has become slow.

Rural Marketing

In recent years, rural markets have acquired significance, as the overall growth of the economy has resulted into substantial increase in the purchasing power of the rural communities. On account of green revolution, the rural areas are consuming a large quantity of industrial and urban manufactured products. In this context, a special marketing strategy, namely, rural marketing has emerged. A recession is a decline in a country's gross domestic product (GDP) growth for two or more consecutive quarters of a year. A recession is also preceded by several quarters of slowing down.

Insurance Industry

Since the initiation of economic liberalization deregulation and setting-up of IRDA, insurance industry in India has been changing fast. Before 1991, the life insurance market was virtually monopolised by LIC through. legislative measures. The other markets for insurance: like general insurance market, health insurance, market, etc. were also opened for other private players. Now, the entire insurance market is opened to the insurance marketers of the world. This has changed the competitive structure of insurance market significantly. It is evident from the fact that the strength of insurance agents registered 3.7 times growth between 1999 and 2008. Similarly, the branches of insurance and the number of insurance products have also multiplied significantly during this period. Unfortunately there has been an adverse impact of the global recession on the Insurance Industry

CONCLUSION

Global financial and economic breakdown have affected Indian economy also adversely. Enormous national problems like declining growth rate, increasing fiscal deficit and revenue deficit, widening current account deficit, increasing un-employment, negative mood of share markets, falling industrial growth and the overall negative mood of the economy. All components of Indian economy shows downturn trend during 2008 and 2009. Although in second quarter of 2009 Industry's growth increased by 6.8% in comparison to second quarter of 2008

REFERENCES

Brunnermeir, M.K. (2009): Deciphering the 2007-08 liquidity and credit crunch, *Journal of Economics Perspectives*, Vol. 23(1), Winter 2009, pp. 77-100.

Globalization: The Indian Scenario: S. Shiva Ramu, Wheeler Publishing, New Delhi.

Globalization and Development of Backward Areas: Edited by G. Satya Narayana, New Century Publication, New Delhi.

International Business: Environment and Management, V.K. Bhalla and S. Shiva Ramu, Anand Publication Pvt. Ltd., New Delhi.

National Commission for Enterprises in the unorganized sector (NCEUS) (Nov. 2008): The global economic crises and the informal economy in India, Govt. of India.

A Study Identifying Factors Considered for Evaluating the Global Economic Crisis

Kamesh Kumar and Shatyaki

GLOBAL ECONOMIC CRISIS AND INDIAN ECONOMY

A year ago, people were questioning if the subprime crisis that began in the summer of 2007 in the United States would spread to India. It was pointed out that India has not been a major investor in US subprime mortgages, and that the institutions of subprime lending, of piggy-back mortgages, of no-doc mortgages and of securitization of mortgages are not prominent in India.

Moreover, the Reserve Bank of India did not follow the policy of the Federal Reserve in the US of cutting interest rates to near zero levels at the height of a real estate boom. In the US, the Federal Reserve kept policy so loose that short-term real (that is, inflation-corrected) interest rates were in negative territory for roughly three years, from late 2002 to well into 2005, the very height of the real estate boom in the US. In India, the Reserve Bank did no such thing, and Indian real three-month rates generally stayed in the (positive) 1% to 4% range for almost all of the period since 2002.

So, it might well seem that the situation in India is completely different. There have been many optimists who have questioned whether India would have any serious fallout from the economic explosion in the US. Now, a year later, after a September 2008 which showed massive financial collapse in the US, we know India has been hit by the crisis. But it has not, so far, been a serious disruption. The seemingly inexorable rise in the Indian stock market has been clipped. The sensex rose about eight-fold from 2003 to the beginning of 2008, but now has had a correction, is down about 40% from its peak. It is only about 10% below what it was in the summer of 2007 though. The real estate markets in India have slowed and many home prices are falling sharply.

Even though the commonly-identified "causes" of the crisis in the US, the subprime mortgage revolution and the extremely loose monetary policy, were not in evidence in India, India is still seeing some of the same outcomes.

The most fundamental problem is found in the swings of overconfidence that was seen in many countries since the 1990s, overconfidence shared by millions, billions, of people. And this confidence has been very strong until recently.

In the US, consumer confidence rose to near-record levels at the time of the peak in the stock market around 2000. This high level of confidence, shared in many other countries as well, was related to the booming markets and booming economy of that time. The booming markets and economy were in turn substantially buoyed by the high confidence, in a feedback loop. With the global financial crisis spreading through Europe and Asia, it is time to objectively analyze where India stands.

The Governments of the US and European countries have already announced bail out packages to save their sinking economies. Taking a cue from them our own Reserve Bank of India has announced various measures, including drastic reduction in CRR, to inject liquidity in the market.

However, it is our share market that has taken the biggest hit. There is a marked difference between the Indian economy and those of the US and Europe. The present financial turmoil began with the sub-prime crisis in the US, wherein American financial institutions gave away trillions of dollars of bad home loans without considering the repaying capacity of the borrowers.

The inability of the American people to repay their loans led them to ask for extensions, and in many cases it led to the financial institutions acquiring their houses. As a result, the financial institutions were stuck with billions of dollars worth of securities but zero liquidity. This in turn forced investors to pull out and, subsequently, Wall Street came crashing down.

On the other hand, conditions in India are much different and much better. Loans that are given by Indian banks are absolutely solid. Though it's correct that sometimes Indian banks also indulge in unsafe lending, such loans normally don't exceed more than five to seven percent of the total loans given out by the banks. These Non-Performing Assets are also not completely bad debts. Indian banks may face criticism for their bureaucratic style of working with too much paper work, but they don't lend without solid collateral and good credit-worthiness.

Apart from this Indian banks have to mandatorily keep a major portion of their deposits with the Reserve Bank of India. These funds can then accordingly be released in case there is a liquidity crunch.

The impact of the global crisis has been transmitted to the Indian economy through three distinct channels, viz., the financial sector, exports, and exchange rates. On the financial front, the Indian banking sector was not overly exposed to the sub-prime crisis. While exports of both goods and services, still account for only about 22 percent of the Indian GDP, their multiplier effect for economic activity is quite large as the import content is not as high as for example in the case of Chinese exports. Therefore, an export slump will bring down GDP growth rate in this year. The third transmission channel is the exchange rate, as the Indian Rupee has come under pressure.

In terms of policy response, there is not much room for further fiscal policy action as the consolidated fiscal deficit of the central and state governments in 2008-09 is already about 11 percent of the GDP. Any further increase in fiscal deficit to GDP ratio could invite a sharp downgrading of India's credit rating and a loss of business confidence. It is more important to focus policy attention on removing some of the many remaining structural bottlenecks on raising the potential GDP growth rate. Essentially this will imply efforts at improving the investment climate both for domestic and foreign investors; removing the entry barriers for the entry of corporate investment in education and vocational training; improving the delivery of public goods and services; and expanding physical infrastructure capacities including a major effort at improving connectivity in the rural regions.

The Indian economy looked to be relatively insulated from the global financial crisis that started in August 007 when the 'sub-prime mortgage' crisis first surfaced in the US. In fact the RBI was raising interest rates until July 2000 with the view to cooling the growth rate and contain inflationary pressures. But as the financial meltdown, morphed in to a global economic downturn with the collapse of Lehman Brothers on 3 September 2000, the impact on the Indian economy was almost immediate. Credit flows suddenly dried-up and, overnight, money market interest rate spiked to above 0 percent and remained high for the next month. It is, perhaps, judicious to assume that the impacts of the global economic downturn, the first in the center of global capitalism since the Great Depression, on the Indian economy are still unfolding. The severity and suddenness of the crisis can be judged from the IMF's forecast for the global economy. For the first time in 60 years, the IMF is now forecasting a global recession with negative growth for world GDP in 2009-10. The IMF has revised its forecasts downwards thrice since July 2000, and it is not yet certain that this will be the last revision. The WTO has predicted that world trade, which has virtually collapsed in the second half of 00 is likely to decline by as much as nine percent in 2009-10. We have already seen exports from world's major exporters, like Germany, Japan and China, plummeting by more than 35 percent in the last quarter of 2000. The sharp decline in economic activity is despite the large stimulus, estimated at more than USD 3 trillion, those OECD economies have put in place. Yet the bad news does not stop. The worst downside scenario could be for the US economy being trapped in a Japan like "L" shaped recovery for the next few years. This will imply a further decline in world exports and softening of global commodity prices. In turn, it will result in sharp slowdown in world exports and result in widespread unemployment and social stress in major exporting economies. This could well generate irresistible protectionist sentiments and if governments do succumb to these, it will unleash the dreaded downward cycle which could see the global economy plunging over the precipice into a prolonged recession. It is, therefore, prudent not to underestimate the severity of the present crisis.

IMPACT OF GLOBAL CRISIS ON INDIAN ECONOMY

The impact of the global crisis has been transmitted to the Indian economy through three distinct channels, viz., the financial sector, exports and exchange rates. The financial sector including the banking sector, equity markets, external commercial borrowings and remittances has not remained unscathed though fortunately, the Indian banking sector was not overly exposed to the sub-prime crisis. Only one of the larger banks, ICICI, was partly affected but managed to thwart a crisis because of its strong balance sheet and timely action by the government, which virtually guaranteed its deposits. The equity markets have seen a near 60 percent decline in the index and a wiping off of about USD 1.3 trillion in market capitalization since January 2000 when the Sensex had peaked at about 1,000. This is primarily due to the withdrawal of about USD 1 billion from the market by foreign portfolio investors between September and December 2000. The foreign investors withdrew these funds in order to strengthen the balance sheet of their parent companies. Commercial credit, both for trade finance and medium-term advances from foreign banks has virtually dried-up. This has had to be replaced with credit lines from domestic banks but at higher interest costs and has caused the Rupee to depreciate raising the cost of existing foreign loans.

IMPACT ON INDIA AND POLICY RESPONSE

Impact on India's Poor Indians have reportedly fallen as oil producing economies in the Gulf and West Asia begin to suffer from decline in oil prices.

The second transmission of the global downturn to the Indian economy has been through the steep decline in demand for India's exports in its major markets. The first sector to be hit was the gems and jewellery which felt the impact in November itself and where more than 300,000 workers have lost their jobs. The negative impact has since covered other export-oriented sectors garments and textiles, leather, handicrafts, and auto components. The 1 percent decline in exports in February 2009 is the steepest fall in exports for the last two decades. It is unlikely that exports will recover within this year. While exports of both goods and services, still account for only about percent of the Indian GDP, their multiplier effect for economic activity is quite large as the import content is not as high as for example in the case of Chinese exports. Therefore, an export slump will bring down GDP growth rate in this year.

The third transmission channel is the exchange rate as the Rupee has come under pressure with the outflow of portfolio investments, higher foreign exchange demand by Indian entrepreneurs seeking to replace external commercial borrowing by domestic financing, and the consequent decline in foreign exchange reserves.

This is likely to continue because current account will remain in deficit and the capital account, which has been in deficit in the second and third quarters of 2000-09, will not generate the needed surplus to cover the current account deficit. This will imply further drawing down of foreign exchange reserves and continued downward pressure on the exchange rate. However, with foreign exchange reserves remaining at 110 percent of total external debt at the end of December 2000, investment sentiments should not be unduly affected in the near-term. The nearly 5 percent depreciation in the Rupee's exchange rate has partially nullified the benefits from the decline in global oil and gas prices and increased the cost of commercial borrowings.

The weaker Rupee should encourage our exporters and it is possible that with imports declining as sharply as exports, the country's trade deficit may actually improve in the short-run and the external sector balance may remain stable and not pose any major policy issue. Overall, it would be fair to say that the timing of the external shock from the global economic downturn has been rather unfortunate. Coming right on the heels of a policy induced contraction in economic activity, its initial impact, as reflected in the third quarter GDP growth falling to

5.3 percent and the steep decline in exports, has been perhaps exaggerated.

This negative impact has been, to an extent, ameliorated by the quick policy response both by the RBI and the Central government. The RBI has infused about USD 20 billion, as additional liquidity by cutting the CRR, lowering the SLR.

The RBI has also signaled its expansionary preference by cutting its repo rate, at which it lends funds to commercial banks from nine to five percent in less than six months. The reverse-repo rate has also been brought down to 3.5 percent to discourage banks from parking overnight funds with the RBI. Three fiscal stimuli have been announced between November 2000 to February 2009. These amounts to about 1.3 percent of the GDP. However, to these stimulus packages we should also add the fiscal outlay of measures announced in the 2000-09 Budget in February 2000. These included some measures that implied a hefty transfer of purchasing power to the farmers and to the rural sector in general. These included, farm loan waivers, funds allocated to the National Rural Employment Guarantee Scheme (NREGS), Bharat Nirman (targeted for improving rural infrastructure), Prime Minister's Rural Road Programme, and a large increase in subsidies on account of fertilizers and electricity supplied.

All this measures, taken more out of political considerations and not in response to the global crisis, have, nevertheless, helped to shore up rural demand for both consumer durables and non-durables.

We have modified the model to not only incorporate the impact of the external shock provided by the global economic downturn but also to take in to account the mitigating impact of the monetary and fiscal measures taken by the government. According to this model, Indian economy will grow by about 6.3 percent in 2000-09. The Economic Advisory Council to the Prime Minister has now also brought down its estimate of 2000-09 GDP growths to 6.5 to seven percent and not 7.1 percent as given by CSO in its advanced estimates and used for budget formation by the finance ministry. The GDP growth is likely to further decline to between 4 to 5.5 percent in 2009-10. Other agencies like the IMF, the World Bank and the ADB have also estimated Indian GDP growth in 2009-10 at similar levels in their latest forecasts released in March 2009. Thus, Indian economy will come down from the nine percent trend that it had achieved in the last four years. The growth targets for the 11th Five-Year Plan will also have to be surely lowered.

POLICY RESPONSE

There is not much room for further fiscal policy action as the consolidated fiscal deficit of the central and state governments in 2000-09 is already about 11 percent of the GDP. This is likely to rise further as further necessary public expenditures are announced in the next budget and economic activity slows down.

With inflation down at less than one percent and likely to remain below five percent in the coming months, there is room for bringing down the repo rate further. However, the more important issue is to try and induce commercial banks to bring down their lending rates as these currently remain at around 10 percent even for their prime borrowers. This is largely a result of the 'crowding out effect' of the large government borrowing programme. To address it, the government may have to consider monetizing its borrowing requirement so that liquidity is not squeezed out of the system. This poses the danger of stoking inflation in the medium-term but perhaps more importantly the breakdown of macro-prudential discipline that has been achieved after considerable effort. It would seem, therefore, that government's options for taking counter cyclical and reflationary measures in the short-term are rather limited.

According to us, it is more important to focus policy attention on removing some of the many remaining structural bottlenecks on raising the potential GDP growth rate. Essentially, this will imply efforts at improving the investment climate both for domestic and foreign investors; removing the entry barriers for the entry of corporate investment in education and vocational training; improving the delivery of public goods and services and expanding physical infrastructure capacities including a major effort at improving connectivity in the rural regions. These measures will constitute the package of second generation of structural reforms and will enable the Indian economy to climb out of the downward cyclical phase and then to extend the upward phase for a longer period than was achieved in the last cycle.

INDIA'S JOB GUARANTEE ACT EMERGING AS RAY OF HOPE IN GLOBAL MELTDOWN

A pioneering piece of legislation that recognizes work as a fundamental right and guarantees 100 days employment a year to those in rural areas who demand work is emerging as a ray of hope for India's poor, who have been left even more vulnerable by the aftershocks of the global financial crisis.

GLOBAL FINANCIAL CRISIS MAY BE OPPORTUNITY FOR INDIA

The Indian Minister of Commerce and Industry, Kamal Nath, says that current global financial woes may present an opportunity for India.

At the World Economic Forum's 24th India Economic Summit, held in partnership with the Confederation of Indian Industry (CII), Nath said that the real India included 300 million people living on less than one dollar a day. According to him, sustained growth depends on including people below poverty line also. He said that in order to do so, public and private sectors must partner to break through old educational models to train rural workers for the modern marketplace.

Manvi Sinha, resident editor at New Delhi Television (NDTV) said that the new educational models are about "skilling" to meet the new needs of the modern Indian economy. R Seshasayee, MD of Ashok Leyland said that a secondary education system that incorporated skill development was necessary. It is important to assess the real needs of industry as well as the desires of trainees before launching any skills development programme. Technology should be incorporated into skills training strategies.

Visty Banaji, Executive Director and President for group corporate affairs with Godrej Industries India, said that the slowdown in the economy has offered a substantial opportunity to get India's trade education house in order. Manvi Sinha, resident editor at New Delhi Television (NDTV), said that rural

India could be the agent of change itself because it is an engine of growth that is "chugging along". According to Nath, even though there are concerns related to the slowdown in the economy, India had the ability to overcome these concerns.

References

Business India Magazine.

Business Line Newspaper.

Economic Survey (Various Issues), Ministry of Finance, Economic Division, Govt. of India.

Inputs by Kamal Nath, Former Minister of Commerce in the World Economic Forum Report at 24th India Economic Summit.

Inputs by Rajiv Kumar, Director and Chief Executive, Indian Council for Research on International Economic Relations (ICRIER), New Delhi.

Ruddar Datt, "Poverty, Employment and Growth: Pre- and Post-Reform Experience", An article published in *IEJ*, Vol. 54, No. 4, Jan.-March 2007.

Sachs Jeffery D. and Warner Andrew (1995), "Economic Reforms and the Process of Global Integration", *Brooking Papers on Economic Activity*, Vol. 1, pp. 1-118.

The Times of India.

The Financial Express.

The Economic Times.

The Global report on financial crisis by Robert J. Shiller by internet.

World Development Report (2006), World Bank, Oxford University Press, New York.

www.businessline.in

12

Is India Really Immune to the Global Meltdown?

PURABI BORTHAKUR

The global meltdown, which was originated in U.S.A. has, now spread all over the world. The sub prime crisis that started in the later half of 2007 soon transformed into a global financial crisis in September 2008 after the collapse of Lehman Brothers. Lehman's collapse froze credit flows, stopped commodity market from operating normally and also even stopped equity market virtually in their tracks. This make economic environment uncertain and risky for which the year 2008 is one of the worst years in the world history. According to the estimates of International Monetary Fund (IMF), global Gross Domestic Product (GDP) is expected to decelerate from 5.0 per cent in 2007 to 4.1 per cent in 2008 and further to 3.9 percent in 2009. The economic growth in the most advanced economies such as U.S., Japan and Euro areas decelerated sharply mainly on account of the turbulence in the US sub-prime mortgage market and its spread to international financial market.

Now the effects of the global meltdown on Indian economy is a matter of great debate as whether the economy would be immune in this changing global scenario is an important question. While the advanced economics like USA, Japan and Euro areas is suffering worst, the Emerging Market Economies (EME's) suffered smaller fall. Fortunately the slowdown in Indian economy is not so high like advanced economies. In 2007-08 the real GDP of India was 9.0 percent, which was a satisfactory indicator for our country.

Though Indian economy continued to exhibit robust growth during 2007-08 (9.0%) yet this real GDP growth rate has moderated to 9.0 percent from 9.6 percent in 2006-07. The dream run of 9.0 percent of GDP growth was made possible due to the external capital support in terms of foreign direct investment and venture capital fund all through past ten years. The same is not available now. Therefore an attempt has been made to deal with some crucial indicator of our economy by highlighting the available factual information.

Objectives

The objective of this paper is:

1. to find out the extent of economic slowdown in India.
2. to provide the actual fact by the help of secondary data.
3. to compare the opinion of different market observer with the findings of this seminar paper.

Data and Methodology

The Study is basically based on secondary data published by RBI annual report 2007-08, *RBI Bulletin*, July 2009, different Magazine, Journal, etc. Besides some articles published in *The Economic Times, Assam Tribune,* Website, etc. are also been consulted at the time of preparation of this paper. To know the proper situation the economic indicators like real GDP, performance of agriculture, industry and service sector, balance of payment, FDI, external debt and foreign exchange reserves are taken into account. The collected data has been analysed with the help of simple statistical method.

ANALYSIS OF DIFFERENT MACROECONOMIC INDICATOR

1. Gross Domestic Product

According to Central Statistical Organisation's (CSO) revised estimates India's real GDP growth decelerated to 9.0percent in 2007-08 from 9.6 percent in 2006-07 and again decelerated to6.7 percent in 2008-09. Though agriculture and allied activities shows an upward trend in 2007-08 by 4.5 percent but it again falls to 1.6 percent in the year 2008-09. The slowdown of GDP is more clearly visible from the growth rate of successive quarter of 2007-08 and 2008-09 given in Table 2.

TABLE 1

Trends in Sectoral Growth in GDP at Factor Cost

(Growth rate in percent)

Item	*2005-06*	*2006-07*	*2007-08*	*2008-09*
1	*2*	*3*	*4*	*5*
Agriculture and allied activities	5.8	4.0	4.9	1.6
Industry	8.1	10.7	7.4	2.6
Service	11.2	11.3	10.8	9.4
Overall	**9.5**	**9.7**	**9.0**	**6.7**

Source: RBI Bulletin July 2009.

TABLE 2

Quarterly Growth of GDP at Factor Cost of 2007-08 and 2008-09

(in %)

Item	*2007-08*				*2008-09*			
1	*2*	*3*	*4*	*5*	6	7	*8*	*9*
	Q1	Q2	Q3	Q4	Q1	Q2	Q3	Q4
GDP at factor cost	9.2	9.0	9.3	8.6	7.8	7.7	5.8	5.8

Source: Economic Survey Report, 2008-09, published in *Protiyogita Darpan*, August 2009.

2. Agriculture

In India although the share of agriculture in GDP has declined below one fifth (shown in Table 3), yet it employs 52 percent of the workforce. The overall food grain production increased to 230.7 million tonnes in 2007-08. According to CSO's revised estimate real GDP growth of agriculture and allied activities recovered to 4.5 percent during 2006 –07 from 3.8 percent during 2006-07. But the rate again decelerated to 1.6 percent (Table 1) in the year 2008-09. This fact shows the deepening impact of global crisis and a slowdown in Indian economy.

TABLE 3

Share of Agricultural to GDP at Factor Cost

(Amount in Rs. crores)

Item	*2005-06*	*2006-07*	*2007-08*	*2008-09*
1	*2*	*3*	*4*	*5*
Agriculture and allied activities	511114 (19.5)	531315 (18.5)	557122 (17.8)	566045 (17.0)
Industry	506519 (19.4)	569775 (19.5)	602032 (19.2)	617882 (18.5)
Service	1598468 (61.1)	1779028 (62.0)	1970563 (63.0)	2155448 (64.5)
GDP at factor cost	2616101 (100.0)	2871120 (100.0)	3129717 (100.0)	33393375 (100.0)

Note: Figure in parentheses is in percent.
Source: *RBI Bulletin*, July 2009.

3. Industry

The industrial upturn which started in April 2002 and peaked by the end of 2006-07 moderated during 2007-08. In terms of Index of Industrial Production (IIP) industrial growth decelerated from 11.5 percent in 2006-07 to 8.5 percent in 2007-08 and again to 3.9 percent in 2008-09. But recently IIP index clocked 7.8 percent in June 2009. This indicates that Indian economy is in recovery stage.

4. Service Sector

According to the revised estimates released by CSO, real GDP of the service sector moderated from 11.2 percent during 2006-07 to 10.7 percent during 2007-08 due to deceleration in financing, insurance, real estate and business services and construction. According to revised estimates of GDP for 2008-09 released on May 09 by CSO the growth rate in the service sector further decreased to 9.7 percent. This indicates that there is a downfall of service sector due to the contraction of world economic activity.

5. Balance of Payment

India's balance of payment (BoP) position continued to remain comfortable during 2007-08. Although merchandise export growth remain robust the trade deficit widen during the

TABLE 4

India's Balance of Payment Position during 2007-09

(USD million)

Serial No.	*Item*	*2006-07*	*2007-08*	*2008-09*
1	*2*	*3*	*4*	*5*
1.	Export	128,888	166,163	175184
2.	Growth rate in percent		28.9	5.4
3.	Import	190,670	257,789	294,587
4.	Growth rate in percent		35.2	14.2
5.	Trade balance (4-2)	-61,782	-91,626	-119403
6.	Invisible (net)	52,217	74,592	89,586
7.	Current account balance (6+7)	-9,565	-17,034	-29,817
8.	Capital account balance (including error and omission)	46,171	109,198	9.737
9.	Change in reserve (-indicates increase, +indicates decrease)	-36,606	-92,164	20,080

Source: *RBI Bulletin*, July 2009.

TABLE 5

Composition of India's External Debt (both long-term and short-term)

(in USD billion)

Item	*Short term*	*Long term*	*Total*	*Percent of GDP*
1	*2*	*3*	*4*	*5*
2005 end March	17.72 (13.3)	115.25 (86.7)	132.97 (100.0)	18.5
2006 end March	19.54 (14.1)	118.59 (85.9)	138.13 (100.0)	17.2
2007 end March	28.13 (16.4)	143.20 (83.6)	171.33 (100.0)	18.1
2008 end March	47.00 (20.9)	177.77 (79.1)	224.77 (100.0)	19.0
2009 end March	49.37 (21.5)	180.52 (78.5)	229.89 (100.0)	22.0

Note: Figure in parentheses indicates percentage to 'total'.
Source: Website:http:/India budget.nic.in and by the author.

year. Though there is a substantial surplus in invisible account yet current account deficit was continued to fall during the year. During the year 2008-09 the current account deficit was USD 29.8 billion as against USD 17.0 billion for the corresponding period of 2007-08. With net capital inflows far exceeding the current account deficit, the overall balance of payment recorded a significant surplus which was reflected in an accretion of USD 252 billion to the foreign exchange reserve at the end March 2009.

6. External Debt

India's external debt was USD 229.89 billion in end March 2009 which was USD 224.77 billion in end-March 2008. The ratio of external debt to GDP increased to 22.0 percent at end March 2009 from 18.1 at end march 2007. It can be concluded that

India's debt position is bearable till now. Because the ratio to GDP was 30.8 percent at the end March 1995. The debt service ratio has declined steadily over the years and stood at 4.6 percent at end March 2009. As seen from table5, the share of short-term debt in total debt increased to 21.5 percent at 2009 from 13.3 percent in 2005. Further India's foreign exchange reserves provided a cover of 109.6 per cent to the external debt stock at the end March 2009.

7. Gross Domestic Saving

Gross domestic saving as a percentage of GDP at current prices was 31.7 at 2004-05 which increases to 37.7 in the year 2007-08. From the composition of gross domestic saving it can be concluded that though household sector takes a dominant role yet the contribution from this sector is continuously decreasing. On the other hand both private corporate sector and public sector shows an upward trend in the structure of gross domestic saving.The following two table shows the fact clearly.

TABLE 6

India's Gross Domestic Saving at Current Prices

(amount in Rs. crores)

Item	*2004-05*	*2005-06*	*2006-07*	*2007-08*
1	*2*	*3*	*4*	*5*
Household sector	716874 (22.8)	864653 (24.1)	994895 (24.1)	1150134 (24.3)
Private corporate sector	212048 (6.7)	276550 (7.7)	342284 (8.3)	416936 (8.8)
Public sector	68951 (2.2)	86823 (2.4)	137926 (3.3)	212543 (4.5)
Gross domestic saving	997873 (31.7)	1228026 (34.2)	1475105 (35.7)	1779613 (37.7)

Source: *RBI Bulletin*, July 2009.

8. Gross Domestic Capital Formation

Capital formation is considered as an important determinant of economic development Gross domestic capital formation which was 32.1 percent of GDP in 2004-05 increased to 39.1 percent in 2007-08.

FIGURE I

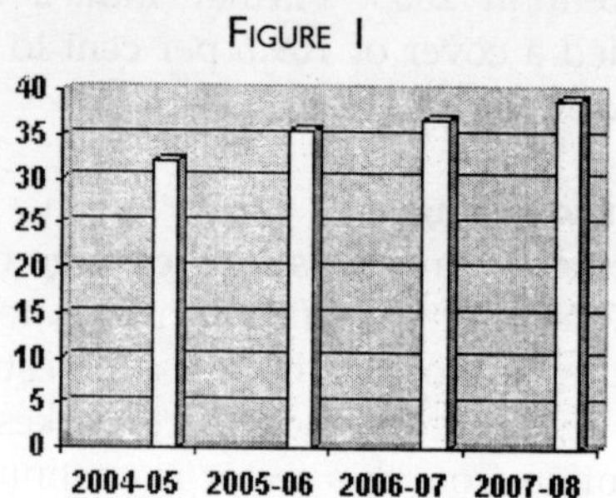

In the above figure base line indicates year and the vertical column indicates the rate of Gross capital formation to GDP. The figure indicates that it is continuously increasing.

It depicts the increasing trend of Indian economy.

9. Foreign Direct Investment (FDI) Inflow

Foreign investment in India during 2007-08 were driven by foreign direct investment and portfolio investment inflows. Gross inward FDI at USD 32.4 billion during 2007-08, which was USD 22.1 billion in 2006-07. India, is the second most favoured destination after China. FDI inflow to India was USD 35 billion in 2008-09 which shows the reflection of confidence of foreign investor in the growth prospect of Indian economy.

10. India's Outward FDI

The global economic crisis has made Indian firms wary of further expansion abroad. Consequently actual foreign direct investment outflows, which rose to a historic level of nearly USD 18 billion in 2007, fell by 6 percent in 2008 to under 17.0 billion. The contraction in India outward FDI is continuing in the year 2008-09. India's FDI outflow during the year 2008-09 declined to USD 15,947 million from USD 18,749 million in the year 2007-08. In that year manufacturing sector was the single largest component of India's FDI outflow.

11. Foreign Exchange Reserve

India's foreign exchange reserve increased to USD 309.7 billion at end March 2008 as compared with USD 199.2 billion at end March 2007. India became the third larger holder of foreign exchange reserve among the EME's during 2007-08. The foreign exchange reserve stood at USD 252 billion at end March 2009.

CONCLUSION

From the analysis of the above indicator it is clear that global meltdown has affected Indian economy to some extent. Despite the slowdown in growth, investment remained relatively buoyant, growing at a rate higher than that of GDP.

During the period of 2007-08 gross domestic saving as a percentage of GDP at current prices stood at 37.7 percent. The growth performance of Indian economy is also noteworthy in the global context as the growth of Indian economy is faster than world economy. To provide adequate liquidity, Reserve Bank of India (RBI) took steps by decreasing CRR, Repo, Reverse Repo rate and statutory Liquidity Ratio (SLR).

Considering these facts it can be concluded that India will overtake the global crisis in the near future. In support of this conclusion following predictions are included:

1. *Prediction of OECD*: Organisation for Economic Co-operation and Development(OECD) in it's semi-annual economic outlook has projected India's growth at 5.9 percent for 2009-10 and 7.2 percent 2010-11 in the wake of recovery signs in the global economy.
2. *Prediction given by CMIE*: According to the projection of Centre for Monitoring Indian Economy (CMIE) despites falling exports the Indian economy would grow by 6.6 percent in 2009-10 on the back of strong domestic demand and market recovery. CMIE also predicts that the economy is likely to bounce back to 9 percent growth path by 2010-11.
3. According to U.K. Sharma, Chairperson and managing Director of UTIAMC the measures taken by the government of India were bound to result in positive development.

The IIP number clearly indicates that the worst is behind us. The economy and markets are on a recovery path. Development of past 3-4 weeks gives us comfort that market can self correct.

4. Consumer confidence in India is on an upward trend. A.C. Nielson conducted a survey on global confidence during the second quarter of 2009 which reveals that India registered a 13 point rise in the confidence survey which reflects early revival of the economy.

In the same tune it can be concluded that though India's some economic indicators have worsening yet India continues a robust growth and strong foreign exchange reserve. After all no country including India remained immune to the global economic shock.

References

Business World, July 2009.

Economic Survey Report, 2008-09 from web

Protiyogita Darpan, August 2009.

RBI Bulletin, July 2009.

Reserve Bank of India (RBI), Annual Report, 2007-08.

The Assam Tribune, August 13, 2009.

The Assam Tribune, August 19, 2009.

The Economic Times, June 7, 2009.

The Economic Times, August 7, 2009.

Website: http:/ India budget.nic.in

13

Global Economic Crisis and its Impact on India

S. Natchathira Jothi

Globalisation has ensured that the Indian economy and financial markets cannot stay insulated from the present financial crisis in the developed economies. Present economic crisis is not really a general economic crisis; it is specifically a crisis of global capitalism. Capitalism does not say that profits must be made only by ethical means. The essence of capitalism is pursuit of profit. From its birth, capitalism has been an expanding, globalizing mode of production. As Prof. Marx puts it, 'Capital is nothing but self-expansion of value'. Five major investment banks on New York city's main financial location, the Wall Street, which were considered the icons of the new kind of banking called investment banking, have all disappeared or been transformed: Bear Stearns (taken over at throw-away prices by J.P. Morgan, with US government guarantees); Lehman Brothers (allowed to go bankrupt); Merril Lynch (taken over by Bank of America); Morgan Stanley and Goldman Sachs, both or which have converted themselves from being investment banks to ordinary banks. They have all become part of the history now. So the investment banking model is dead. It is merely banking, insurance and stock markets which are in crisis. There is a crisis in the real economy, in the sense that the industrial output in the advanced capitalist countries is falling and unemployment is rising.

CAUSES OF THE CURRENT CRISIS

The process of global integration plays a vital role. It is not merely one of liquidity. It is the crisis of solvency. In other word, many financial firms are bankrupt. Businessmen are seeing a huge recession. Markets are dull. And demand is not picking up. So nobody wants to invest, nobody wants to lend. The loan agreement between the borrower and the bank is not the end of the matter. The bank converts a set of such loans it has created into a saleable financial asset through a process known as securitization. It creates, from out of the loans it has extended and which are assets owed to the bank by the borrowers, instruments—financial paper-which can be bought and sold in financial markets. Persons trading in these instruments do so because they expect to make profits by buying them at a lower price and selling at a higher price. Banks were lending massively without due diligence to assess whether the borrower can repay or not. That is what is called sub-prime lending.

The key and basic point is the inability of capitalism to sustain demand at a high enough level to maintain full employment and to avoid cyclical fluctuations in both output and employment. Huge increase in borrowing was encouraged by rapid financial innovation which supposedly reduced and transferred the risks by borrowers, such as sup-prime home loan borrowers. An important reason why this massive expansion of complex financial products, built on a foundation of shaky housing loans, could go on for many years is because of a growing culture of weak regulation of financial institutions and markets that prevailed in the US, UK and some other countries for the past two decades. Finally, the enormous increase in imprudent borrowing and excessive lending was fuelled by old fashioned greed, which fuelled the huge asset price bubbles in housing, stock markets and commodity prices.

IMPACT OF THE CRISIS ON THE INDIAN ECONOMY

The U.S financial crisis has had its reverberations on both developed and developing world. The impact of global financial crisis is stronger and longer than expected. There is evidence of economic activity slowing down. At the same time, headline inflation, as mea—sured by the wholesale price index, has fallen sharply and the decline has been sustained, pointing to a faster than expected reduction in inflation. India has been spared the panic that followed the collapse of banking institutions, such as Fortis in Europe and Merrill Lynch, Lehman Brothers and Washington Mutual in the US. Indian banks have taken less risk than their peers abroad.

The most immediate effect of that crisis on India has been on outflow of foreign institutional investment from the equity market. India's GDP growth estimates for the current fiscal (2008-09) has been down graded from 9 percent to 7.4 percent and for the financial year (2008-09) from 8.5 percent to 7 percent. The element of GDP growth driven by off-shore flows (along with skills and technology) will be diluted; correction in the asset prices which were hitherto pushed by foreign investors and demand for domestic liquidity putting pressure on interest rates. While the global financial system takes time to "nurse its wounds" leading to low demand for investments in emerging markets, the impact will be on the cost and related risk premium. The impact will be felt both in the trade and capital account. Indian companies which had access to cheap foreign currency funds for financing their import and export will be the worst hit. Also, foreign funds (through debt and equity) will be available at huge premium and would be limited to blue-chip companies. Reduced capacity expansion leading to supply side pressure; increased interest expenses to affect corporate profitability and increased demand for domestic liquidity putting pressure on the interest rates. Consumer demand in developed economies is certain to be hurt by the present crisis, leading to lower demand for Indian goods and services, thus affecting the Indian exports. Export-oriented units will be the worst hit impacting employment; reduced exports will further widen the trade gap to put pressure on rupee exchange rate and intervention leading to sucking out liquidity and pressure on interest rates.

The impact on the financial markets will be the following: Equity market will continue to remain in bearish mood with reduced off-shore flows, limited domestic appetite due to liquidity pressure and pressure on corporate earnings; while the inflation would stay under control, increased demand for domestic liquidity will push interest rates higher and we are likely to witness gradual rupee depreciation and depleted currency reserves.

The reserve bank of India lowered the interest rates at which it lends to banks; it lowered the Statutory Liquidity Ratio (SLR) and the Cash Reserve Ratio (CRR). SLR is 25 percent or less. But banks are keeping a much higher percentage of the deposits with the RBI. Overall, while RBI would inject liquidity through CRR/SLR cuts, maintaining growth beyond 7% will be a struggle. The banking sector will have the least impact as high interest rates, increased demand for rupee loans and reduced statutory reserves will lead to improved NIM while, on the other hand, other income from cross-border business flows and distribution of investment products will take a hit. Banks with capabilities to generate low cost CASA and zero cost float funds will gain the most as revenues from financial intermediation will drive the banks' profitability. Given the dependence on foreign funds and off-shore consumer demand for the India growth story, India cannot wish away from the negative impact of the present global financial crisis but should quickly focus on alternative remedial measures to limit damage and look inwards to sustain growth.

Foreign institutional investors (FIIs) operating in India are taking money out of India. In 2007, these FIIs brought in 20 billion dollars plus while in the first ten months of 2008 they have taken out 19 billion dollars. When the FIIs take money out of India, stock markets tend to crash. When foreign capital goes out in large amounts, there is a big demand for dollars. This means the demand for dollars against the rupee goes up. As a result, the rupee value goes down against the dollar. Our imports became much more expensive. This in turn leads to a generalized pressure on prices. There is a tendency to inflation. Cost of food and other basic commodities rise whenever the rupee declines in value against the dollar. So, stock market declines and currency value goes down.

Our economy is much more vulnerable to global commodity prices that it was 20 years age. It is much more vulnerable to financial flows. So, both in terms of commodities and in terms of capital, the Indian economy is much more vulnerable to changes in the international economy. The reduction in government expenditure in order to minimize deficits, without increasing resource mobilization through taxation of the rich leads over time to serve supply constraints as well. Declines in rural development expenditure have hurt agriculture and rural development badly over the years since 1991. They have caused considerable rural distress by lowering the purchasing power of the rural population. Twenty years of liberalization, privatization and globalization (LPG) policies have greatly weakened agriculture. Our food grains output had been stagnant from 1999-2007. The rate of growth of food grains output over last 10 years is less than one percent per year.

SUGGESTIONS TO MINIMIZE THE NEGATIVE IMPACT OF THE CRISIS

Financial sector regulations should be strengthened. A focus on the real sector of the economy instead of the obsession with the financial markets is needed. Expenditure that will directly benefit the peasantry rural and urban labour and small and medium industries and enterprises including those which are export oriented and those in retail trade should be focused. The state must spend money to actively promote foodgrains output. Reasonable input prices, remunerative procurement prices and importantly extension of procurement to all major crops are essential to enable rapid recovery of the rural and agrarian economy.

The important policy measure has to be the provision of some degree of protection against imports for domestic agricultural output. We must demand that the government of India abandon the system of targeted public distribution of food grains (TPDS) and revert to the earlier system of universal PDS. We must bring down the prices of diesel and petrol, given the considerable decline in the global prices of petroleum, not just marginally as the government has done, but substantially. The government of India must consult state governments; consult organizations of working people, kisan sabhas, agricultural workers' unions, trade unions. A complete reversal of neoliberal policies; putting in place careful regulatory oversight of the financial sector; massive fiscal stimulus through expenditures directed at improving the purchasing power of ordinary people and the economic viability of peasant agriculture, small and medium industry and small retail trade; and measures to control prices by importing essential commodities from time to time is needed. Protection must be provided to domestic agriculture and a massive effort to increase the output of food grains. The IMF's chief economist Olivier Blanchard has warned that the global crisis is set to worsen and that the situation will not improve until 2010; he also has said that the IMF does not have the funds to solve every economic problem. Massive withdrawals of investment from emerging countries could represent hundreds of billion of dollars, which is so significant that the IMF alone can not counter them. The IMF had spent a fifth of its $250 billion fund in the first two weeks of November alone. The only solution he has suggested is that the central banks should lower interest rates to as close to zero as possible.

Nationalization of the entire banking system along with the major companies is needed to solve this problem. Other speculative instruments like options, derivative and future prices must be disallowed as well as by the National Exchange, who would advice the banks to invest directly to the companies as they do in both Germany and Japan today.

The unprecedented global economic crisis has definitely taken a toll of India's economic performance. Most likely it has also reduced our potential for economic development in the next 3 or 4 years. However, despite the severity of the global crisis, Indian economy has demonstrated considerable resilience, in part to the strength of our agricultural sector. With sound and determined economic policies growth momentum of 7-7.5 percent in a year or two should be recovered. The challenge for our policies and programmes is to convert this potential into performance.

References

Global Economic and Financial Crisis: Essays from Economic and Political Weekly, By Orient Longman Publishers (Author).

Global Economy, Robin Hehnel.

Global Financial Meltdown: How We can avoid the Next Economic Crisis. By Read, Colin (Author).

http://en.oboulo.com/global-crisis-and-its-impact-on-the-indian-economy-65052.html

http://www.thehindu.com/2008/10/18/stories/2008101851380900.htm

Mercy corps-coping with Economic Crisis.

www.amazon.co.uk/...Global-Economic-Crisis.../0745329438-Cached-Similar.

Impact of the Global Financial Crisis on the Indian Economy

PUSPA TARAFDAR

Global financial markets are showing strains on a scale and scope not witnessed in the past three quarter of a century. What started with elevated losses on US sub prime mortgages has spread beyond the borders of the United States and the confines of the mortgage market. Risk spreads have ballooned, liquidity in some market segments have dried up and large financial institutions have admitted significant losses. This process caused a huge financial meltdown and a sharp economic slowdown in practically all industrialized countries. Many have termed it the "worst financial crisis of the last century."

It is well known that financial crisis can inflict severe havoc on economies. Somehow, financial crisis are identified with the Great Depression that followed the stock market crash of 1929. It is generally known that financial crisis are crippling in their impact.

A recent study on the impact of financial crisis by Reinhart and Rogoff (2008) seems to bear out this gloomy view. In the view of authors "Broadly speaking, financial crises are protracted affairs." Reinhart and Rogoff (2008) claim that using a variety of indicators—asset price inflation, size of current account deficit and slowing down of economic growth the present U.S financial crisis qualifies as "severe".

The "financial crisis" is a very broad term that covers a whole range of events, including crashes in the housing market, stock market, foreign exchange market, current account of nations and of course, problems afflicting the banking sector. There is evidence that really severe financial crisis are those in which banking sector is affected.

Until October 2008, the impact of the financial crisis on the world economy was expected to be modest. It was Lehman collapse that changed the situation dramatically. The impact of the financial crisis may not have been as severe but for the decision to let Lehman fail. This accords with the widespread belief that the decision to allow Lehman to go into bankruptcy was a policy blunder. The Lehman collapse had important implications for the impact of the financial crisis on the Global Economy. The decision to let Lehman fail appears to have been a blunder of colossal proportions.

The broader point is that we cannot afford to take a mechanistic view of financial crisis and their economic impact going by averages estimated from the past. The quality of policy response can make vast difference in the impact on the economy.

These events have challenged policy-makers, and the responses have varied across regions. The Bank of England participated in the bailout and ultimately, the nationalization of a depository, Northern Rock. The U.S Federal Reserve has introduced a variety of new facilities and extended its support beyond the depository sector. These events have also challenged economists to explain why the crisis developed, how it is unfolding and what can be done.

Several articles search for the roots of the crisis in public policy, either monetary or regulatory. Cecchetti has a series of questions about the extraordinary monetary policy actions taken to alleviate the crisis. He argues that crisis are endemic to modern economics and should not necessarily be blamed on monetary policy. A well functioning financial system needs both deposit insurance and a central bank with regulatory authority. Other economists blame the crisis on in low US interest rate. Common with IMF and other analysis the de Larose Report contributed the causes of the crisis to macroeconomic issues, fundamental failures in assessment of risks, the role of credit rating agencies, corporate governance failures, and failures of regulatory, supervisory and crisis management.

Reinhart reviews five major financial crisis in industrial economics and concludes that the current economic problems have a great deal of precedent. These events have also challenged economists to explain why the crisis developed, how it is unfolding and what can be done, to avoid the reoccurrence of the crisis.

The present paper makes an attempt of examine extent of the spread of the crisis on Indian Economy and the policy response adopted so far to mitigate the impact of the crisis on the economy.

By and large there was general consensus that current regulations and supervisory practices failed to mitigate the recent cycle in leverage, credit expansion and housing prices, little was done to tighten regulation in the upswing.

Many other economists have come out with plans for financial reform and regulations (for example, www.Voxeu, org). A recent review of these mainstream reform reports notes that "the various reports agree broadly on the 'principles' that regulation should follow, and in particular they should be based on rules rather than discretion and should address well-identified externalities.

In fact, for dealing with systematic risk, many of the proposals call for more complicated value at risk modeling, but not for firmer oversight and regulation; they do not agree on what type of regulations so-called "large and complex financial institutions" should be subjected to. Though there is agreement on the need to reduce the pro-cyclicity of the financial system, there is no agreement on how to do it. There are some sets of proposals that are taking quite seriously the fundamental changes that need to be made in the regulatory system. They include the proposals being developed by the presidential commission on reforming the financial system at the United Nations, headed by Joseph stiglitz. All of them call for significant strengthening of the rule-based regulation that will significantly curtail the destructive tendencies of the financial markets.

James Crotty's writing elaborates, there were a number of

fatal flaws in the lightly regulated financial system that led to these crisis which can be combined into four key problems—

1. Asymetric and perverse incentives that lead financial actors to take an excessive risk.
2. A regulatory framework that was lax at best, and virtually non-existent in the case of the "shadow banking system".
3. Financial innovations and structures that were murky and opaque.
4. A system that was at root procyclical in "its underlying dynamics."

The New Financial Architecture (NFA) has widespread perverse incentives that create excessive risk, exacerbate booms and generate crisis. The NFA is based on light regulation of common banks, even lighter regulation of investment banks and little if any regulation of banking system. Credit rating agencies that play a crucial role in the NFA were also infected by perverse incentives. The supporters of NFA would argue that the reform would inhibit useful innovation, but it is now clear that the social cost of financial crisis that cause real sector problems far exceed their possible social benefits.

A number of previous suggestions might help restrict excessive growth of financial assets in the boom. But they may not, by themselves, eliminate the excessive growth of financial assets. To assure control of the rate of expansion of financial assets, regulators should impose counter cyclical capital-asset ratios. We can put an end to this analysis by stating that none of these proposals or any other serious regulations will be implemented unless there is a dramatic change in the political economy of regulation. Also there must be a broad political mandate in support of serious financial regulatory reforms.

DECOUPLING THEORY

As soon as the financial crisis spread in the U.S economy, the economic leaders in several emerging market economies and India assured that their financial systems with recent impressive growth were safely insulated from the western economies. The basis of their optimism was based on the popular decoupling theory which was strongly endorsed by the economists in May 2008. The decoupling theory mainly asserted that growth in Asian Economies were decoupled from growth trends in west and that the growth process in Asia (ASEAN-3, CHINA AND INDIA) would not only be continuous but also may help western economies to pull them out of the recession. The strength of the Asian Economies lies in their recent adoption of market oriented policies, their regional integration via trade and investment relationships and global inflows of capital. However, recent data from sources such as IMF and other international organizations, as well as national sources, is at variance with the decoupling thesis. The IMF'S World Economic outlook (WEO—January 2009) concedes that "financial market conditions have remained extremely difficult for a longer period than envisaged in November 2008 despite wide ranging policy measures to provide additional capital and reduce credit risks". Growth estimates for 2008 and projections for 2009 and 2010 have been scaled down considerably in advanced economics and Asian economies. As far as the Asian EMEs are concerned the growth of ASEAN-5 stands at 2.7% in 2009 and 4.1% in 2010, of China at 6.7% in 2009 and 8% in 2010 and of Indian at 5.1% in 2009 and 6.5% in 2010. This is far from the levels that the decoupling theory would lead us to expect, and instead speak of a substantial deceleration in 2009 followed by a recovery in 2010.

It seems that the channels of contagion have been substantially under estimated It is well known form the literature that there are four potential channels of contagion, namely, (i) trade channel (comprising both merchandise and invisibles); (ii) foreign capital flows; (iii) contamination of financial assets; and (iv) interdependence of asset markets especially equity, bonds and housing markets.

TRADE CHANNEL

As demand contracts in the crisis affected economies, exports from other countries are adversely affected. A substantial proportion of exports of key merchandise items is to the Western Economies (and Japan) both of which are in the grip of a recession-*cum*-depression situation. Exports to these countries constituted nearly 22% of our total exports in 2007-08. The prospects for Indian Export in 2009 is rather gloomy because of unabated fall in incomes in the economies of the U.S., E.U and Japan.

According to the central statistical organization (CSO) data, 2007-08.export growth plummeting to 7.5% from 18.9% registered in the earlier year. However, for estimation of the demand generation impact of exports (by the foreign trade multiplier analysis what is relevant is the command of export earnings over domestic consumption and investment. It is easy to observe how important export slowdown was in causing decline in GDP growth in general and industrial growth in particular during 2007-08. Exports of goods and services less export related imports (E.L.E.M) were a little over 20% of GDP in 2006-07, but their share in total autonomous expenditure was nearly 30%. This together with the fact that between 2006-07 and 2007-08, there was a 15.8 percentage fall in ELEM attests to the enormous significance of exports engineering the GDP deceleration.

There can be little doubt that the global crisis has seriously aggravated the decelerating phase of the Indian Economy. It is useful to take note of some of the stricking features of the Indian macro economy during this period. First, the slowdown in GDP and industrial growth became much pronounced from the fourth quarter of 2007-08 and the first quarter of 2008-09, that is more than three to six months after the eruption of the sub-prime crisis.

Growth Rate of India's GDP and its Components (2000-01 to 2008-09)

		2000-01	*2001-02*	*2002-03*	*2003-04*	*2004-05*	*2005-06*	*2006-07*	*2007-08 (QE)*
1.	GDP at Market prices	4.0	5.2	3.8	8.4	8.3	9.2	9.7	9.2
2.	Agriculture, forestry, fishing	-02	6.3	-7.2	10.0	0.0	5.9	3.8	5.1
3.	Industry	6.4	2.4	6.8	6.0	8.5	8.0	10.6	7.5
4.	Services	5.7	6.9	7.5	8.8	9.9	11.0	11.2	11.1
5.	Gross Investment	-3.5	-2.9	17.0	19.9	19.5	19.4	10.9	16.9
6.	Export of good and services	18.2	5.7	21.8	5.8	28.1	14.8	18.9	7.5
	2007-08 (QE)								

Source: Central Statistical Organization, GOI, National Accounts Statistics, 2008, RBI's website as represented in *EPW*, March 28, 2009, pp. 95-96. QE – Quick Estimate.

The proximate source of this was the sharper slowdown is in both private consumption and aggregate investment from early January 2008. Second, over March-August 2008, export as well as import growth was significantly higher than in the pre-crisis period—something which cannot but be viewed as counter intuitive in the context of global economic woes. It is only from September, 2008 that the crisis seems to have finally taken its toll of the country's trade flows. Finally, with a much sharper deceleration of investment and private consumption and a steep downturn of export growth from the third quarter of 2008-09 the economy seems to have entered a new phase and been sucked into the maelstrom of the global crisis.

FINANCIAL CONTAGION

After one year of the outbreak of the crisis the financial sectors of developed countries were affected, causing mounting losses, a string of bankruptcies, and a severe jam in the flow of credit in the inter bank money market. Indian banks have not been seriously rocked by the global financial turmoil due to small exposure of Indian banks to US asset backed securities. However, the crisis has cast its long shadow on Indian Financial Markets and hence on the real sector of the economy.

With increasing relaxation of capital account transactions and close integration of the domestic economy with international financial markets, the first significant impact of the global crisis was on the country's capital flows, especially commercial borrowings (ECBS) and foreign institutional investment (F11). Almost immediately after the crisis surfaced (net) ECBS and F11 registered a steep fall between October and November 2007, from $ 3.6 billion and $ 5.7 billion to $ 2.2 billion and minus $ 1.6 billion, respectively. The reversal of capital flows has led to a steady fall in the value of the rupee despite substantial running down of foreign currency assets by the Reserve Bank of India (RBI); between October 2007 and November 2008, both the nominal effective exchange rate (NEER) and the real effective exchange rate (REER) went down significantly, the former by 11.6% and the latter by 12.8%.

To the extent domestic producers relied upon ECBS for funding their projects partly or wholly, drying up of this source of finance might have played a role in the significant dip in investment growth since the outbreak of the crisis F11 outflows might also have had a negative impact on domestic investment. The sharp fall in F11s followed by their withdrawal contributed to the bursting of the Indian stock market bubble. However, a substantial $3.2 billion F11 outflow in January 2008 triggered a relentless bear run, making the BSE plunge by 52% (to 9,350) between December 2007 and January, 2009.

Finally, despite the resilience of Indian Banks, the global financial meltdown has had some adverse consequences for credit financed economic activities. Widespread banking troubles created serious credit crunch for traders. The problem of accessing credit was not confined to traders alone. Though Indian Banks remained relatively unscathed, they became extremely choosy in extending loans, especially to buyers of real estates and consumers durables—the two categories of economic agents who have so far played an important role in sustaining domestic demand.

GLOBAL INFLATION

For a little over a year after the outbreak of the financial crisis, the world economy experienced, between September 2007 and October 2008, a pronounced stagflationary phase, with growth slowdown on the one hand and rising inflation on the other (Rakshit, 2009). For Organization for Economic Co-operation and Development (OECD) countries, the y-o-y consumer price index (CPI) inflation, starting from a low 1.9% in August 2007 exhibited an uninterrupted increase to peak at 4.9% in July 2008. The global inflation was driven mostly by commodity prices, especially prices of energy and agricultural goods. So far as the Indian Economy is concerned, since prices of practically all petroleum products are administered and trade in agricultural goods is far from free, transmission of global inflation to domestic prices occurred with a time lag, from November, 2007. However, with wholesale price index (WPI) inflation rising from 3.1% in October 2007 to 12.8% in August 2008, the price pressure in India was significantly greater than that in advance countries. Though the world wide commodity price-led inflation did not owe its origin to the Global Financial

Crisis, it reinforced the decelerating tendencies in the Indian Economy. The sharp rise in the prices of food and fuel led to a fall in the demand for industrial products and services and strengthened the recessionary forces already at work in the domestic economy.

Finally, the drying up of external sources of borrowing, the sharply rising costs of production of investment goods, the bursting of the stock market bubble, and the domestic credit crunch especially in respect of loans for housing and consumer durables—all these acted as major impediments to domestic demand. However, no less important was the role of government policies or their absence.

As discussed in earlier global financial crisis can affect the economies in three related ways : reduction in Indian companies' access to overseas finance, lowering domestic liquidity and causing stock prices to fall. Adverse global conditions have limited Indian firm's access to global fiancé in various forms. There is a much broader impact on the Indian economy arising from foreign inflows in forms such as foreign direct investment (FDI) and foreign institutional investment (F11). These inflows had contributed to accretion of foreign exchange reserves. Any accretion of reserves enhances domestic liquidity, any decline in reserves constitute a reduction in liquidity.

It is fair to say that when liquidity becomes scarce, the impact on investment and economic growth is greater than is suggested by the current account deficit gap of 1.5% of GDP. Most projections place economic growth for 2008-09 at around 7% and even lower for 2009-10.

Turning new to the policy response both fiscal and monetary policy have responded to the crisis although there is much debate about the adequacy of efforts on the two fronts, especially the monetary front.

The focus of fiscal policy has changed from fiscal stabilization to providing a growth stimulus. It is held that debt financed government expenditure would stimulate aggregate demand, capacity utilization, and profits due to expansionary fiscal measures is likely to raise not only the current gross domestic product but also the long-term growth potential of the economy.

A quick way to estimate the fiscal stimulus would be to

take the difference in the fiscal deficit for the Financial Year 2007-08 and that for Financial Year 2008-09, including off budget items. The figures are 3.1% and 7.8%. The difference of 4.7% may be said to constitute the additional fiscal stimulus in Financial Year 2008-09. With the consolidated deficit of the centre and states in region of 10-11% for 2008-09, any further stimulus was limited.

The stimulus packages being worked out in India might not be confused with the packages in the US and Britain. In true Keynesian sense, the US stimulus packages are geared to boosting aggregate effective demand. The objective conditions prevailing in countries like India is however altogether different. It may be argued that the true rational of the stimulus package ought to be to address long-term, rather than short-term issues in countries that are still remarkably low in terms of their average level of living. As per the world development Report India is at $950 per capita income figure whereas China is at $2,360 and the US is at $46,040.

For a country that has over a quarter of population below the poverty line as per official Planning Commission figures, the obvious moral imperative is one of placing exchange entitlement or simply purchasing power in the hands of the poor and the destitute.

An obvious way of thinking of stimulus strategies in our context would be to pump money into rural infrastructure to revitalize the vast agricultural sector that now contributes a bare 18% of gross domestic production (GDP) whereas about 60% of the population of the country is still dependent on it.

Removal of infrastructural bottlenecks has been accorded top priority by all Indian economists. The bottlenecks are no doubt supply side factor, however, as the Indian experience suggests, they also tend to depress private investment and reduce aggregate demand. Such linkage suggests that demand management policies in India would have to be different from those followed in the United states or the U.K and require dovetailing into long-term programmers of economic transformation and growth.

The tax cuts in fiscal stimulus are largely expected to benefit higher income households, who may not spend the entire additional income put in their hands by tax cuts. Again much of the infrastructure activity today (such as integrated township, highways and ports) is highly capital intensive, with negligible multiplier spending or employment effect.

On the monetary policy front there has been a flurry of activity—the repo rate was reduced in a succession of steps from 9% in September 2008 to 5% in March 2009, the CRR was also reduced from 9% to 5% over the same period, whereas the statutory liquidity ratio (SLR) was brought down by 1% to 24%. These measures have released more than 4,00,000 crores of liquidity into the system.

The package of policy measures is not really having the intended impact of reviving the real sector. In spite of the more than Rs. 40,00,000 crores of liquidity released into the financial markets, the credit off take has been remarkably poor.

While tendency for bank credit to the commercial sector to fall and for bank's holding of government bonds to rise during downward phase of the trade cycle was also present earlier, such pro-cyclicity has been greatly accentuated with the adoption of Base 1. All economies face this problem, but it is much more serious in countries like India. Hence arises the need for moving toward a system that contributes toward sound risk management, but does not make bank credit a major source of volatility or inefficiency of the macro economy.

Deposit Insurance, A well-designed rule-based deposit insurance scheme-one that insulates a commercial bank's retail customers from financial crisis should be first step in protecting the banking system from future financial crisis.

CONCLUSION

The past quarter century of deregulation combined with rapid pace of financial innovation helped create the conditions that led to the devastating financial crisis. The severity of the global financial crisis and the, depth of the global economic recession that has accompanied it demonstrates the, utter bankruptcy of the deregulated, global neo liberal economic regime established three decades ago. From the last quarter of 2008 both the financial stress and contractionary forces have become significantly stronger in the developed as well as developing countries including India.

When the recent crisis eventually came, the leading policy-makers have tended to ask for a return to a Keynesian like state that creates a fiscal stimulus, without the other necessary changes in supporting the non-capitalist structure. This may, in itself, increase the instability/volatility in the overall system. Given the long lags in fiscal policy or monetary policy easing, fiscal stimulus runs the danger of creating a future high inflation phase. Therefore the short run policies and actions taken need to be consistent with the long-run objective of a viable financial system.

With increasing relaxation of capital account transactions and close integration of domestic economy with international financial markets the first significant impact of the global crisis was on the country's capital flows (in either direction) which have had potentially destabilizing consequences. Under such circumstances, it is necessary to impose key capital controls for a specified period of time. There is no doubt that policy of the Reserve Bank of India not having gone in for full capital account convertibility has been proven to be a right decision. There is the need for changes in both regulatory norms and bank's own operation and management in some crucial areas.

The stimulus packages in U.S, U.K, Germany and Singapore incorporate special measures to help the vulnerable sections of society. In India very little have been done to relieve the distress caused by the crisis to the vulnerable sections of society.

References

Crotty James and Gerald Epstein (2009): Regulating US Financial System to avoid another meltdown, pp. 89-92, *EPW*, March 28, Vol. 44, No. 13.

Crotty James (2009): Profound structural flaws in US Financial system that helped cause the financial crisis. *EPW*, March 28, Vol. 44, No. 13, pp. 123, 134, 135.

Felton, A. and C. Reinhart (ed.): The First Global Financial Crisis of the 21st Century. (www.Voxeu.org)

Mohan, T.T. Ram (2009): The Impact of the crisis on the Indian Economy, *EPW*, March 28, Vol. 44, No. 13, pp. 110-14.

Nachane, Dilip M. (2009): The fate of India unincorporated, *EPW*, March 28, Vol. 44, No. 13, 115-17, 119-21.

Nayak, Pulin B. (2009): Anatomy of the Financial Crisis between Keynes and Shumpeter, *EPW*, March 28, Vol. 44, No. 13, pp. 162-63.

Rakshit Mihir (2009): India midst the global crisis, *EPW*, March 28, Vol 44, No. 13, pp. 95-96, 100-04.

Rakshit Mihir (2009): Money and Finance in India, Vol. II, Oxford University Press, New Delhi, pp. 270-78, 280-82.

Reserve Bank of India (2005): Handbook of Statistics on the Indian Economy, 2004-05, Mumbai.

Sheng, Andrew (2009): The first Network crisis of the 21st century: A regulatory Post Mortem, *EPW*, March 28, Vol. 44, No. 13, pp. 73-74.

Vakulabharanam Vamsi (2009): The recent crisis in global Capitalism: Towards a Marxian understanding, *EPW*, March 28, Vol. 44, No. 13, pp. 149-50.

Global Meltdown and Indian Economy

Anil Kumar Thakur, Manindra Kumar Singh and P.S.K. Sudheer

The on-going process of globalization has brought stupendous growth of inter national finance. The major part of this inflow of foreign investment is in the form of port folio investment popularly called foreign Institution Investment (FII). It is the consideration of the relative rate of return on capital determined by the market forces which dictate their cross country movement as well as nature of investment to be undertaken. Any fluctuation within the macro fundamentals of the economy or other disturbance in the global world can withdraw the investment leading to perpetuation of crisis. East Asian crisis was the first signal. However, that did not affect the Indian economy much because of the poor financial integration at that time. Now with the increasing integration of Indian Economy with global financial system, our economy is also fully exposed to global financial crisis.

The present global melt-down is a result of the risks of globalization. It all began with the one and all American dream, that every American should have a home. Regardless of who you are and what you do, if you are an American, you should have something called a home. Real Estate business was in boom, and financial agents thought that there was not a better time to give away loans. The household sector was given a boast with increased monetary supply by commercial financial companies. People were given loans regardless of their credit rating. It was never expected that their boom in the real estate business would come to such an abrupt end, and prices would reach all time low. The U.S. Economy, being a capitalist driven economy, did not brother to indulge it self in the policies pursued by the prominent financial giants. Gradually these financial giants in this business started feeling the heat as sub-prime clients who defaulted in their repayment of loans. The properties which was mortgaged by the clients were not even covering the principal amount of the loan, leave alone the principal and interest commitments. The credit offered to the people in indiscriminate fashion, achieving short-term goals and ignoring warnings from the leading economists about long-term sustainability of the policy, back fired completely and companies like Lehman Brothers, Merill Lynch and Freddie Mac's bad assets reached magnimous proportions. An acute credit shortage was experienced in the economy, and simultaneous negative effect-started occurring. The credit lynch meant that borrowing interest rates shot up in the market, companies slowed down their investment policies, production declined, lay offs increased, consumption decreased and the whole economy followed the downward spiral.

What stands out glaringly in the crisis episode was the regulatory failure. The regulatory failure was two fold. First, some parts of the financial system were either loosely regulated or were not regulated at all, a factor which led to regulatory arbitrage with funds making more towards the unregulated segments. The second failure lies in the imperfect under standing of the implication of various derivation products. In one sense, derivative products are a natural corollary of financial development. They meet a felt need. However, if the derivative products become too complex to discern the risk lies they become a major source of centers. Rating agencies in the present episode were irresponsible in creating a booming market in suspect derivative products. Quite clearly there was a mismatch between financial innovation and the ability of the regulators to monitor them. It is ironic that such a regularatory, failure should have occurred of a time when in tense discussions were deing held at Basle and else where to put in place a sound regulatory frame work (Rangrajan, 2009).

The crisis surfaced around August 2007 with the bursting of the bubble in the sub-prime mortgages in the US as reflected in the credit markets. Eventually, the sub-prime crisis had affected financial institutions in the US, Europe and else where including the shadow banking system comprising inter alias investment banks, hedge, funds, private equity and structured investment vehicles, and in the process, had caused within six months a huge financial meltdown, a string bankruptcies and a sharp global imbalance and slowdown in practically all industrialized countries. The collapse of the Lehman Brother in Mid-September 2008 further aggravated the situation leading to the crisis of confidence in the financial markets. The Reserve Bank of India Governor, D. Subharao (2009) has rightly pointed out that from three channels : the trade channel affecting the capital and current account of balance of payments, the financial channel and the confidence channel, it arose. The resulting uncertainty cascaded into a full-blown financial crisis of global dimensions.

IMPACT ON TRADE

Government of India's Economic Survey Categorically stated that "the sub-mortgage loan crisis is the major financial crisis of new millennium whose origin is in US housing market. Subsequently this spread to Europe and some other parts of the world. The sub-prime crisis has also impacted the emerging economies. India has remained insulated from this crisis. The banks and institutions in India do not have marked exposure to the sub-prime and related assets in natured market. Further, India's gradual approach to the financial sector reforms process has played positive role in keeping India immune from such international shocks. But the presumptions is wrong. Recent growth in India is dependent upon greater global integration, related to financial deregulation that spurred consumptions as well as credit boom and combined with fiscal concessions to spur consumption among the richer population of the country.

This led to rapid increase in aggregate GDP growth at the cost of greater employment generation and agrarian improvement. The proliferation of financial activities thus became combined with rising asset values to enable credit-finance consumption surge among rich and middle classes in our country. These developments in the financial sector resulted in drastic reductions of activity in the real sector and those were transmitted quickly to the real sector with adverse effects.

The credit-financed consumption spark, which in turn generated higher rates of investment, did not match with the growth of the domestic market. This mismatch was reflected in the Indian economy. Besides the deepening of the global crisis and subsequent deliver again and risk aversion however affected the India economy leading to slowing of growth momentum. It has fallen rom 9.7% in 2009-07 and 9% in 2007-08 to 6.7 in 2008-09 and exacted to 6% in 2009-10. Indian economy was seriously affected by the trade channel through drastic reduction in earning from exports of goods followed by a fall in global demand. There was significant decline in merchandise exports, reflecting fall in exports of all commodity groups. The biggest falls were recorded in the export of rice, raw cotton, readymade garments, sugar and morasses iron one, iron and steel, gems and jewelry. More generally, small and medium industries were adversely affected whenever there was such type of stress in the financial and real sectors. There has also been spillover effects on invisibles through lower remittances from non-residents and earnings from tourism. Thus the fall out of the crisis has also permeated on to the service sector. Despite that, imports continued to grow. So, the trade deficits as well as the current account deficit has increased. What made things worse was that capital was also leaving India, causing the capital account to turn negative during the third quarter of 2008-09; which altogether indicating a net out flow of US$ 3.7 billion as against the inflow of US$ 31.0 billion in 93 of 2007-08 attributable to not outflow under portfolio investment, banking capital and short-term credit. Net external commercial borrowings remained lower at US$ 3.9 billion in Q3 of 2008-09 (US$ 6.2 billion in Q3 of 2007-08) as the liquidity conditions tightened in the international financial market and external commercial borrowing became more difficult and expansion in the net portfolio flows to India turned negative as foreign institutional investors rushed to sell equity stakes in bid to replenish overseas cash balances. This had knock-on-effect on the stock market and the exchange rates through creating the supply-demand imbalances in the foreign exchange market.

The policy-makers' stress on acquiring excessive capital flows before the on set of the global financial crisis, led to increase in foreign exchange reserves as well as contributed to monetary expansion which fuelled liquidity growth. WPI inflation reached a trough of 3.1% in October, 2007, month before global commodity price inflation zoomed to double digits from low single digits. The rising oil and commodity prices contributed to significant rise in prices with annual WPI peaking at 12.9% in August 2008. So, it is obvious that such global crisis will adversely affect upon works of India through falling employment, lower wages and more adverse working conditions and indirectly through reduced access to public goods and services. The global crisis also meant that the economy has had been experiencing extreme volatility in terms of fluctuation in inflation level.

IMPACT ON INDIAN CULTIVATORS

Indian agriculture has been adversely affected by the global meltdown crisis. In liberalized world, the Indian farmers have to work in highly uncertain and volatile international environment. Volatile crop prices often leads the farmers to respond to the wrong signal and they finding no other alternatives have to adjust themselves by margin their crop pattern. This requires for them new varieties of seeds and other inputs supplied by MNCs. Small and marginal farmers find themselves in real difficulty if crops fail or output prices remain low. They have also to face continuous rising prices of inputs. Financial liberalizations measures caused significant slowdown in the growth of bank credit, particularly from commercial banks to rural areas and a relative fall in proportion to bank credit flowing to the priority sectors specially agriculture. Bank credit to agriculture fell from 22.3% in 2007-08 to 17.3% in 2008-09. Thus the impact of slowdown in rural banking fell disproportionately on poor and small borrowers. There is ample evidence here in India that the deep crisis of the cultivable community which has been associated with to a proliferation of farmers suicide and other evidences of distress such as migration and even hunger deaths in different parts of rural India, has been related to the decline of institutional credits (Ghosh, 2009). The global meltdown in commodity prices particularly in energy, metals and agricultural inter mediates across the world, most of which are tradable, was led to corresponding decline in domestic prices (Economic Survey, 2008-09). The fall in international prices of several commodities (both agricultural and non-agricultural) has impinged on small producers and farmers' income via import competition as well as low prices in sectors such as cotton and oilseeds production. Farmers now face lows prices of their output even as food prices have continued to increase.

IMPACT ON EMPLOYMENT

Major markets have been seriously affected by the global financial crisis with a dearth of employment opportunities. According to some sample surveys namely conducted by Ministry of Labour and employment, there was decrease in employment about half a million workers during 2008-09. The most affected sectors were gems and jewelry, transport and auto mobiles, construction, and automobiles. The employment decline is more rapid in case of export units. There has also been substantial declines in money wages for daily contracts and piece rate work for the usual workers and migrant workers, the latter coming from the far-off backward and most distressed regions of the country. What emerges, in fact, in that the employment squeeze in the organized sector in the recent years has a tremendous impact on the unorganized sectors via backward linkages with the farmer. Even the National commission for Enterprises in the unorganized sector is of the view that the recent global crisis has impacted serious repercussions on the Indian economy and especially the poor who are the unorganized workers working in sectors like construction, handlooms, textiles, apparel, leather products, gems and jewelry, metal product, carpets, oil mills, marine products and handicrafts. The situation urgently calls for a revival from the part of the government in the form of major fiscal stimulus comprising of (i) Programmes to boast pro-poor public investment in physical and social infrastructure, (ii) expansion in scope and coverage of social security schemes, for the unorganized workers so that they are immediately assured of a minimum level of social protection, (iii) Schemes/ Programmes which protect and promote incomes of the poor.

A weakening of demand in the US affected our IT and Business Process outsourcing sector and the loss of opportunities for young persons seeking employment at lucrative salaries abroad. India's famous. IT sector, which earned about $ 50 billion as annual revenue was feared to fall by 50% of its total revenue. This would reduce the cushion to set-off the deficit in balance of trade and thus enlarge our balance of payments deficit. It has now been estimated that sluggish demand for exports would result in a loss of 10 million jobs in the export sector alone (Datt, 2009). Therefore, an export slump would bring down GDP growth rate in 2009-10.

Rupee has come under pressure with outflow of port folio investments, higher foreign exchange demand by Indian entrepreneurs seeking to replace external commercial borrowing by domestic financing, and the consequent decline in foreign exchange reserves from US$ 299.2 billion in March 2008 to US$ 241.4 billion in March 2009. This is likely to continue because current account will remain in deficit and the capital account which has been in deficit in the second and third quarters of 2008-09 will not generate the needed surplus to cover the current account deficit. This will imply further drawing down of foreign exchange reserves and continued down ward pressure on the exchange rate (Kumar, 2009).

India has the option of turning the crisis into opportunity. The most binding constraints to growth and inclusion need to he addressed, which in involve : improving infrastructure, developing the small and medium enterprises, building skills and targeting social spending at the poor. Systematic improvements in the design and governance of public programmes are crucial to get results from public spending. Improving the effectiveness of programme that account for 9-10% of GDP will, therefore, be an important part of the challenges. The most important challenge faced by Government during this time is to ensure a balance during this time is to ensure a balance between inflation and growth and also to stimulate ensured growth of demand and equality in income distribution.

Indian economy has certain inherent strengths which would help in meeting the challenges a head. We are still a large untapped market especially in rural areas which can sustain internal demand. A vast poal of Science and technology graduates and millions of people who are familiar with English language and adopt better to the global situation are its strong limbs. India being a largest democracy of the world, existence of free media keeps the government in check and provides some insurance against excesses. Most importantly, India with half of its population being below 25 will remain the youngest country in the world. Given the appropriate skill, they will outwit challenges in any field (Reddy, 2009). While there are indication that the economy may have weathered the worst of the downturn, impart, due to the resilience of the economy and also various monetary and fiscal measures initiated during 2008-09, never, themes, the situation warrants close march on various economic indicators, including the impact of the economic stimulus and developments taking place in the international economy. Taking policy measures that squarely address the short and long-term challenges would help achieve tangible progress and ensure that the outlook for the economy remains firmly positive.

To sum up the discussion; the East Asian Crisis of 1997 is the fore runner of he financial crisis that has emerged basically in US economy, particularly in the form of sub-prime crisis during the middle of 2007. It has adversely affected both the developed and emerging economies including Indian economy. The recovery phase has started in the US economy but at a very slow pace. So, the global economy is still not free from the danger of meltdown to continue some more years. The need of today is not just the pumping of liquidity into the Indian economy but also in addition the injection of demand. This can occur only through direct fiscal action by government. In India, larger government expenditure has to be oriented towards a substantial increase in agricultural especially food grains output. The new paradigm must entail infrastructure and food grain-led growth strategy on the agriculture and rural sector, which ears simultaneously remove both recession and food crisis is India. Development should be done with a human face with the realization that people are both the means and end of development. India is one of the emerging market economies and cannot remain immune from such types of crisis and so is suffering the after-effects of this financial tusunami unleashed in the U.S. while there are indication that the economy may have weathered the worst of the downturn; the situation warrants close watch on various economic indicators, including the impact of economic stimulus and developments taking place in the international economy. In the backdrop of current crisis, it is important that the regulatory system should be efficient as the growing integration of Indian financial sector with the global system besides many advantages, also increases the vulnerability of the financial sector. The fundamental problem is essentially internal and has to be sorted out domestically. The problem relating to Indian economy is principally a supply side problem unlike the case of advanced countries. So, only Keynesian pump priming will hardly help in long-run. It is imperative to break the supply side bottlenecks to come out of the Crisis.

References

Acharya, Shankar, 2009: India and the Global Crisis, Academic Foundation Ltd. World Bank, 2009: World Development Report, 2009 Washington D.C.

Agenor, P.R. (2002): Does Globalisation Hurt the poor ? World Bank, Washingtan D.C.

Ghosh, Jyati (2009): The Global Financial Crisis and the working class in India, Prabhat Kar Memorial Lecture delivered at Jadavpur University, on the 13th June, 2009.

Government of India (2008-09): Economic Survey, Ministry of Finance.

Karmakar, Asim K. (2008): "India's External Delit An Evaluation of its Status during the reform Period", *Rebindra Bharti Journal of Economis*, Vol. II, March, 2009.

Kumar, Rajiv (2009): Global Financial and Economic Crisis : Impact on India and Policy Response, Indian Council for Research on International Economic Relations (ICRIER), New Delhi.

Nachare, D.M. (2009): India and the Global Crisis, Academic Foundation Ltd.

Ram Mohan, T.T.: "The impact of the crisis on the Indian Economy" in Global Economic and Financial Crisis, Essay from *Economic and Political Weekly*, orient Blckswan Pvt. Ltd.

Rangrajan, C. (2009): The International Financial Crisis and its impact on India, Bureau of Parlimentary Studies and Training, Loksabha Parliament House, New Delhi.

Reddy, V.V. (2009): India and the Global Financial Crisis, Orient Blockswan, New Delhi.

Subha Rao, D. (2009): "Impact of the Global Financial Crisis on India : Collateral Damage and Response", Speech delivered in Tokya, 18 February, 2009.

16

Global Economic Crisis and its Impact on the Indian Economy

V.B. CHAURASIA

This paper makes an attempt to analyse the present global economic crisis. It discuss the severity and impact of crisis on world economy, especially on Indian economy; reasons, policy measures and their future implications on economies with concluding remarks. The global financial system has suffered its greatest crisis for last two years since 'Great Depression of 1930'. The main reason of present crisis is a collapse of confidence in some leading banks in capitalised countries. The core of the crisis has been an interplay between macroeconomic imbalances and financial market developments. Global imbalances occurred with accumulation of large current account surpluses in many Asian and oil-exporting countries and correspondingly growth in fiscal deficit and current account deficit in the US and other parts of the Euro area. The Asian exports became highly competitive due to these weakened currencies and resulting in significant current account surpluses that increase saving-investment gap in the emerging economies. These countries accumulated significant foreign exchange reserves which were invested predominantly in US government securities. This led to a marked increase in global liquidity and a consequent reduction in real risk-free interest rates. Moreover, strong growth and unprecedented stability in prices witnessed by the global economy that was significantly contributed inter alia by productivity gains with integration of China, India and other emerging economies into the world economy allowed for easy monetary policy.

The US banks offered exotic mortgages to subprime borrowings in the expectation that booming real estate market will continue and the security cover will be more than adequate and therefore these banks indulged in securitisation. The Collateralised Debt Obligations (CDO) and Credit Derivative Swaps (CDS) are resulting in terms of ballooning subprime loans and a fall in risk premia. The continuation of this scenario depended on rising housing prices and low interest rates. The subprime crises had created credit crunch that drying up of liquidity in the short-term and affected across the regions and countries from US to Europe, to Australia and to Asia. Financial markets are expected to remain strained during 2009. It has caused asset values to fall sharply across advanced and emerging economies, decreasing household wealth and thereby putting downward pressure on consumer demand. The associated high level of uncertainty has prompted household and businesses to postpone expenditures, reducing demand for consumer and capital goods. At the same time, widespread disruptions in credit are constraining household spending and curtailing production and trade. The IMF has revised its forecast for global growth to 3.4 percent for 2008, 0.5 percent for 2009 and 3 percent for 2010. These growth rates of US for the same period 1.1 percent, –1.6 percent and 1.6 percent; for Euro area 1.0 percent, –2.0 percent and 0.2 percent respectively. The EMEs and developing economies are expected to grow 6.3 percent, 3.3 percent and 5 percent respectively for the corresponding period. The pickup is likely to be unusually gradual in the coming quarters.

The Indian economy is also affected fro the global crises. As the RBI Governor, D. Subbarao has pointed out that India has been affected in three ways. First is the exit of foreign equity that resulted in capital flow reversal and put pressure on the exchange. Secondly, through drying up of overseas bank credits for both Indian corporates and Indian banks, which shifted credit demand from external sources to the domestic ones. Lastly, exports were hit because of the declaration of global economy.

These effects can be analysed in the following manner. The economy and the stock market is closely related and reflects the buoyancy of the economy. In the US a recession is yet to be declared by the Bureau of Economic Analysis but, investors are worried a lot. They spend less as they fear stock values will fall and thus stock market fall on negative sentiments. The BSE Sensex crashed by nearly 13% in just two trading sessions in January 2009. The BSE Sensex slipped by over 55 percent between December 31, 2007 and December 30, 2008. This fall could be attributed to large disinvestments by FIIs of US $ 12.3 billion during this period. If the risk aversion of the foreign investors persists, capital flow in the form of FII disinvestment may continue, exerting further downward pressure on exchange rate through the capital account of the balance of payments. Depreciation in rupee further adversely affected balance of trade and creating downward pressure from current account as well.

There is much broader impact on Indian economy arising from foreign inflows like FDI and FII. These inflows had contributed to accretion of foreign exchange reserves and any decline in reserves constitutes a reduction in liquidity. The gap between domestic investment and savings, i.e. current account deficit is around 1.5 percent of GDP. In 2007-08, the capital inflows amounted to 9 percent of GDP which is excess of current account deficit. It is clear that around half of the portion financed by corporate savings and the major portion of balance came from external sources. Therefore, when liquidity becomes scarce, the impact on investment and economic growth is greater than is suggested by the current account deficit of 1.5 percent of GDP. The current account deficit is expected to widen during 2008-09. IMF estimates is to be 2.8 percent of GDP in 2008. Growing liquidity crunch in international financial markets and consequent reverse flow of capital impacted the portfolio investment and funding of investments in the other sectors of the economy. The decline in asset prices evident in stock market, housing and real estate sector coupled with slow down in fresh investments due to inadequate availability of external funding impaired domestic demand in the system.

The primary source of contagion has been the trade channel in India. Therefore the real sector has been affected more than the financial sector. It is true that the exposure of domestic private sector banks, as well as some nationalised banks and foreign subsidiaries, to toxic assets and CDOs in the US and EU has come to light but the volume of total exposure is limited. Indian banks loses due to their direct and indirect exposure to subprime crisis are estimated at US $ 2 billion. The impact of subprime crisis on the Indian corporate sector has been adverse and it would depend on three factors—First, share of external commercial borrowing (ECBs) on variable rate of interest; Second, currency composition and third, the share of hedged debt portion of the total ECBs. So, there has been a huge substitution of foreign credit with the domestic credit. The impact of subprime crisis on the corporate sector would be moderated to that extent if this substitution is facilitated through appropriate monetary measures. Beside, the government sector is also affected indirectly through the spill over impact of subprime credit market developments on domestic interest rates and there could be an increase in the cost of government borrowings.

Indian exports are closely linked with US, EU, Japan, China and other countries. As these economies contracts and world economy experiences slowdown, it signals an adverse impact on Indian exports. The Commerce Ministry expects that total exports to be between $ 170 billion and $ 175 billion in 2008-09. The worst affected sectors are gems and jewellery, textiles, especially handloom sector, leather and leather products, cotton and manmade yarn, tea, edible oil, marine products, handicrafts and carpet. All these industries are highly labour intensive so that the impact on labour employment is to be quite substantial. In case of external sector, signs of slowdown preceded overall trends in manufacturing and services sector. Growth in exports during April-January of current year declined sharply to 13.2 percent against a rise of 24.2 percent in the previous year. Since October 2008, there has been a net fall in exports in each month compared to the corresponding period of preceding years. Exports remain weak and a renewed downturn in the West—the primary market for Asian goods or a turnaround in the rise in Asian stocks, could pose major risks.

However, the trade impact are not only confined to merchandised items but have spilt over into the exports of invisibles. Private transfers and remittances from non-resident Indians are likely to decline. It is about 3.48 percent of the GDP and represent a significant item of the balance of payment. In addition, miscellaneous services which includes software services, communication, financial and business services, accounting for about 3.32 percent of the GDP. This is facing the prospect of huge decline in exports as demand for these services is primarily from the US. Apart from demand side, Indian external trade could be adversely affected by violability in the exchange rate. Therefore, exchange rate volatility has significant in the short-term in respect to employment, output and distributional consequences.

Considering all these effects, the estimated growth of Indian economy for 2009 is 5.1 percent and 6.5 percent in 2010 which is below than previous two years growth rates of 9.3 percent and 7.3 percent in 2007 and 2008 respectively.[5] Prime Minister's Economic Advisory Council (PMEAC, August 2009) estimated that the Indian economy is expected to grow between 6 to 6.5 percent in 2009 due to rise in factory output by 7.8 percent in June 2009. However, the weak monsoon could have some adverse impact on the overall GDP. Ignorance of agriculture sector shows that the per capita cereal output in the world economy has declined in absolute terms over the last more than two decades and this fact has been at the root of the growing world hunger. So it is need of the hour to look this sector seriously.

Slackness in real economic activity and lower commodity prices have dampend inflation pressures. In context of the advanced economies, inflation is expected to decline from 3.5 percent in 2008 to 0.25 percent in 2009 and 0.75 percent in 2010. Moreover, some advanced economies are expected to experience a very low or negative consumer price increases. As far as, emerging or developing economies are concerned, inflation is also expected to 5.75 percent in 2009 and 5 percent in 2010. Headline inflation in Indian economy turned negative since July 2009 but prices of food items are increasing sharply has serious concern for policy initiative.

The social costs of recession can be seen in the form of

massive unemployment. The International Labour Organization presents a dire picture of Global Employment Report for January 2009. This report gives three alternative scenario (optimistic, moderate and worst) of world unemployment, it projects an increase in world employment ranging from 18 million under optimistic scenario to 51 million in case of worst scenario over the years end 2007 to end 2009. The corresponding figures for South Asia range from 4 million to 17 million. On the basis of these data, one can estimate job losses in India to be between 1.3 million and 6 million over this period. The Labour Bureau was also conducted a official survey of the unemployment impact of the global crisis with a focus of eight sectors those are highly affected from global crisis. The survey estimated a total job loss of 50,000 over the quarter September-December 2008. Extrapolating this trend is conjunction with the official growth projections in the EAC (2009), the estimated job losses roughly would be 1.5 million over the entire recessionary phase, i.e. 2008 to Dec. 2009. The unemployment situation in unorganised sector or informal sector is relatively higher than organised sector as previous is dependent on later. As per definition of National Commission for Employment in the Unorganised Sector (NCEUS), the informal sector accounts for about 50 percent of the GDP and employs 86%, i.e. 393 million out of a total workforce of 457 million. Small producers and traders dependent on export markets have already been badly affected in industries such as textiles, apparel, handlooms, gems and jewellery, leather products, oil meals, carpets, handicrafts and marine products. These industries are highly labour intensive and about 1.5 million jobs have already lost in these industries.

The present global recession created huge unemployment in several countries and they, especially US and Europe; have adopted many measures to protect employment for domestic workforce. Since October 2007, about 66 new trade restrictions measures have been introduced in the form of tariff and non-tariff barriers. In addition, several bailout packages targeted at export-oriented units are tantamount to export subsidies and hence trade distorting.

Though, the Indian Economy is not affected directly from global economic crisis but it affected indirectly through trade and investment channel and that can be seen in downward trend in growth rate, investment, output and employment level. Therefore, appropriate measures, i.e. mix of monetary and fiscal, have been taken by the government to achieve the goal of revival without stagflation. The principal monetary measures since October 2008 are—reduction in the repo rate from 9 percent to 5 percent and reverse repo rate from 6 percent to 3.5 percent; CRR also reduced from 9 percent to 5 percent and SLR brought down from 25 percent to 24 percent. The RBI estimates that these measures have released about Rs. 4,00,000 crore of liquidity in the system. Fiscal stimulus (in three stages) mainly comprised 4 percent and another 2 percent cut in excise duty, Rs. 20,000 crore towards bank capitalization over the next two years, 2 percent reduction in service tax, greater borrowing access to state government and the India Infrastructure Financing Co. Ltd. The total burden of fiscal stimulus on the government exchequer at Rs. 81,000 crore which is about 1.82 percent of GDP at current prices. Apart from these, Sixth Pay Commission payouts, farm loans waivers and election expenditure are also in the nature of fiscal stimulus.

However, these measures have serious danger on economic front. First, the size of India's consolidated fiscal deficit (Central and State government together) is now to be estimated between 11 percent to 12 percent of the GDP for 2008-09 at current prices. Second, the long-term interest rates will be increased which put pressure on government borrowings. Third, general tax cut will not increased effective demand as it benefits to higher income households who may not spend the entire additional income. Fourth, infrastructure spending could turnout to be procyclical due to long gestation period and has less effect on employment. The risk of deficient monsoon can put pressure on prices of food items as it reduces farm yield and hurt industrial output growth through lower rural demand for consumer goods.

Therefore, an appropriate policy measure does help to reduce severity and period of economic downturn. Financial sector policies should focus on the recognization of credible and coordinated loan loss and providing support to the financial institutions. Indian banking system remains sound, healthy and well capitalized that provide more room for credit disbursement. Banks, non-governmental organisation and micro-finance institution should focus to provide required capital as they are able to create employment at large scale. Low inflation would support consumption demand and reduced input cost for corporate sector.

Fiscal stimulus packages should rely primarily on temporary measures and be formulated within medium-term fiscal frameworks that ensure the envisaged build-up in fiscal deficits can be reversed as economies recover and that fiscal sustainability can be attained in the face of demographic pressure. Decline in energy prices will provide a further space for more infrastructure funding. Lastly, extensive social safety net and rural infrastructure development expenditure would protect extreme decline in domestic demand. India's industrial output growth in June 2009 (7.8 percent) is second highest in the world behind China (10.8 percent in July, 2009). The manufacturing sector grew by 7.3 percent and consumer durables sector grew by 15.5 percent in the same period triggering hopes of a strong economic rebound in the coming months.

Notes

1. These (CDO) are rated by credit rating agencies based on the past repayment history and the value of the underlying house property that are mortgaged to the lender.
2. CDS are tradable derivatives which offered protection against credit risk for a commission.
3. The quarterly estimates and projections of World Economic Outlook (WEO), Jan. 2009 account for 90 percent of the world purchasing power parity weights.
4. The quarterly estimates and projections of WEO, Jan. 28, 2009 account for approximately 76 percent of the emerging and developing economies.
5. IMF World Economic Outlook Projections, Jan. 28, 2009.

References

Economic Advisory Council to the Prime Minister (2009). *Review of the Economy*, 2008-09, January.

Gopinath, T. (2008): "Does Subprime Mortgage Crises in the US Impact India? : An Exploration", *The Indian Economic Journal*, Vol. 56, No. 3, Oct.-Dec., 2008.

IMF World Economic Outlook (2009), 28 Jan.

International Labour Organization (2009): "Global Employment Trends", January.

National Commission for Enterprises in the unorganized sector (2007). "Financing of Enterprises in the Unorganized Sector and Creation of a National Fund for the Unorganized Sector", Government of India, November.

Ram Mohan, T.T. (2009): "The Impact of the Crisis on the Indian Economy", *Economic and Political Weekly*, Vol. XLIV, No. 13, 28 March.

Rao, Govinda, M. (2009): "The 3rd Stimulus Package and Fiscal Conundrum", *Business Standard*, 3 March.

Rao, Govinda M. (2009): "The Fiscal Situation and a Reform Agenda for the New Government", *EPW*, Vol. XLIV, No. 25, 20 June.

Subbarao, D. (2009): "Impact of the Global Financial Crisis on India : Collateral Damage and Response", Lecture in Tokyo, 18 February.

The Economist (2008): "The Decoupling Debate", 6 March.

Financial Meltdown and its Impact on the Indian Economy

K. Hari Haran

The paper brings out various aspects of 'Financial Meltdown and Its Impact on Indian Economy'. Indian Economy is passing through a severe global economic crisis since the Great Depression of the 1930s. Across the countries, fiscal stimulus packages and monetary easing of unprecedented magnitude and scope have been very slow in arresting the decline and the year 2009 is not expected to see a reversal of the trend. According to the World Bank forecast, the global economy as a whole is expected to grow by just 0.9 per cent in 2009, in contrast to 2.5 per cent in 2008 and 3.7 per cent in 2007.

It is quite interesting to note that observations of Sri S. Venkitaramanan, a former Governor of Reserve Bank of India, on the global financial crisis and its impact on India. Banks and Financial Institutions in India have not experienced the kinds of losses and write-downs which similar institutions in Western World have faced. Pointing out the panic situation following the collapse of Fortis in Europe, Merrill Lynch, Lehman brothers and Washington Mutual in USA, India has fortunately been spared from such reactions. The wise and judicious policies followed by our Central Bank and Government of India, were responsible for this saving grace. The policy of Indian Banks to the effect that "The lesser risks you take, the more you will be safe" may also be held responsible for this achievement. He also quotes the path-breaking study of Sri Narasimhan, an experienced central banker, which was authorized by former Finance Minister Dr Manmohan Singh. The "classic reports" have given the policy framework for the Government of India and Reserve Bank of India to formulate the structure of India's Banks and Financial Institutions. He adds: "Sri Narasimhan model was based on adequate capitalization, good provisioning norms and well structured supervision. Both the Government of India and the Reserve Bank of India accepting his recommendations have duly implemented them. Due credit should be given to these two for having avoided the temptation of total capital convertibility. While judging the related freedom of Indian Banking system from the recent recessional trend in the US, an important fact to be borne in mind that Indian Banking system is basically owned by the public sector.

In addition, the depositors reposed greater confidence in State-owned banks than those of private. Another report he refers is the one produced by Dr. Raghu Ram G. Rajan, former counsellor of I.M.F. and presently a Professor at Chicago University. This report includes a number of very useful suggestions which deserve to be examined and implemented to the extent possible to keep the Indian Financial System—modern and efficient. He urges that the RBI could follow the example of the U.S. Federal Reserve in the matter of distribution of profits. Further, he points out that the behaviour of the RBI is in sharp contrast to that of the U.S. Federal Reserve.

Another example offered by Federal Reserve related to inflation. The U.S. Federal Reserve measures inflation on the basis of consumer price index and not on the basis of wholesale price of sale price index as is prevalent in India. If we follow the consumer price index in measuring inflation, India can afford to have an interest rate of roughly 5% lower than the one in force at present. This can make a significant difference to the fiscal fortunes and the growth of Indian Economy.

There is no precise road map to deal with the global financial crisis that is adversely impacting the Indian economy.

Unlike in the rich countries where the crisis travelled from the financial sector to the real sector, in India, it travelled the other way about. In September last, nobody knew the evolution of the crisis in the subsequent three months. Now nobody knows what will happen in the next three months. It was not possible for any Central Bank much less the RBI, to have a road map for everything as we did not have a contingency plan.

An official survey was recently undertaken by the Labour Bureau which focussed on 8 major sectors which included mining, textile, automobile, conduction, transport and the IT/BPO industries to assess the loss of the job as a result of the economic slowdown in India. The total estimated employment in all the sectors covered by the survey went down from 16.2 million during September 2008 to 15.7 million during December 2008, implying a job loss of about a million. After September 2008, the Survey points out that employment in all industries declined at an average rate of 1.01% per month. The Survey adds that it is not surprising that in Asia that was experiencing robust growth till recently has been affected quite adversely by the global financial and economic crisis. As the financial crisis unfolded, foreign financial investors in need of capital to cover losses and meet margin calls at home-unwound the position in Asia, resulting in collapse in stock markets in many Asian economies. Apart from China, Vietnam and India which had seen their stock market outperforming their global "Competitors"—also recorded the steepest falls. The global economic recession slowed export growth in these increasingly export-driven economies. All this generated an Asian version of the global financial and economic crisis, which is what the collapse in aggregate growth, figure reflects.

The Unorganised Workers' Federation has commissioned a study on the impact of global economic crisis on construction workers in the unorganised sector. Being part of the initiative on the National Campaign Committee on unorganised sector workers, the results of this study would be available by September. More than 2.5 lakh construction workers are affected by the slowdown. Health education of children and housing for any of these construction labourers from other Sates are poor. The suffering of the labourers in the construction industry has increased due to the prevalence of child labour, absence of voting rights and denial of benefits of the welfare schemes of the Government of India. This segment will see signs of recovery from the economic recession in the second half of this year and a distinct improvement in growth will be witnessed in 2010/ 2011. It was false to contend that the country escaped from a serious impact of the crisis due to economic reforms. The financial reforms were intended at improving efficiency and the global crisis would have a ripple effect on the structure of capital. The need for cutting excise duty and enhanced public spending, especially in infrastructure development, was strongly felt. The crisis had its roots in the sub-prime lending crisis which was a result of housing loans obtained beyond of their repaying capacity by the borrowers.

The Interim Budget 2008-09, presented in Parliament asserted that India has arrived on the international economic scene. Notwithstanding the global financial crisis and recession, India had posted a 45% growth in foreign direct investment (FDI) receiving $23.3 billion between April and December 2008 India's FDI was a record of $ 32.4 billion. The 7.1% rate of GDP growth in current year made India the second fastest growing economy of the world. The fallout of global slowdown on Indian economy has resulted in according approval to 37 infrastructure projects for Rs. 70,000 crores from 2008 to 2009 by Government of India.

In his recent article on the above topic, Mr. Ranabir Ray Choudhry, has declared the Indian economy was strong enough to weather the storm currently raging in the world economy and emerge from it unscathed. Quoting the inference of the former Finance Minister Mr. P. Chidambaram, that India should not be unduly worried by the talk of a strong recession grappling the developed economy, he points out that the export sector has been doing well, despite a rapidly appreciating rupee making Indian product costlier in the world market. The Finance Minister has reiterated that the Indian economy growing at 7% plus is a job creating economy. As it is, the growth has been reduced which in fact, is the biggest admission on the part of the authorities that the Indian economy is not an island into itself Placing ourselves in the midst of an economic crisis, the worst since the great depression would be in the fitness of things that people are made aware of the need to bring out the best in the rational economy to tide over the difficult times ahead. It is not possible for the Central Bank to lay a road map of precise stops to deal with the global financial crisis which is adversely impacting the Indian economy. He attributes this to the absence of a precise road map. We are responding to the crisis as it impacts on us.

According to a study seven million people are directly employed by the Trans National Corporation in the entire third world, i.e. the figure is smaller than the annual fresh entrants into the Indian Labour market. On the other hand, in comparison to the few jobs that they have been creating, the Multi National Corporations have been destroying many more jobs. Faced with competition from these highly capital intensive mega-corporations, Indian private sector big business houses have begun restructuring the operations and are shedding lakhs of workers every year. The public sector undertakings have virtually stopped all fresh recruitment, and in addition have also begun retrenching workers in a big way under voluntary retirement schemes. Globalization and the entry of MNC's into Indian economy are also leading to the mutual decimation of India's small scale industrial sector. As a result, small scale industry's have been downing shutters in tens and thousands. From the above, it is obvious that the total number of jobs being destroyed by the MNC's is far more than the miniscule number of jobs they have been creating. Consequently, the unemployment situation which was already bad when the economic reforms began in 1991, has become "alarming"—a word used by the Prime Minister himself while speaking on the unemployment problem in the Rajya Sabha in March 2000. The workers in the organized sector and the small scale industries constitute less than 20% of the country's total work force which was estimated at 314 Million as per the 1991 census. The rest of the overwhelming bulk of India's work force comprises agricultural workers, small plantation owners like rubber growers, fishfolks, dairy workers and the like and those working in the traditional manufacture like handlooms. Globalisation is threatening to destroy the very livelihood of these hundreds of millions of working people. The Exim policy is going to affect the sustenance of millions in the unorganized sector like fisheries, dairy sector, handlooms, agriculture, etc. in a major way. They will now have to compete with these highly subsidised imports from the developed countries. Thus, it is globalization-and its related conditions-an imposed by World Bank and International Monitory Fund on Indian agricultural sector as part of economic reforms- on a banla-upt Indian economy by India's creditors are responsible for pushing the economies of millions of India, small and marginal farmers into a precarious state, driving many of them to commit suicide.

In this connection Edward Goldsmith, the Founding Editor of the Ecologist and a cult figure of the environmental movement has remarked that globalization will destroy millions of jobs in the organized sector small scale industries and also devastate the livelihood of hundreds of millions working in India's unorganized sector.

In his article for the Global view point, Barrack Obama President of US reminds us that we are living through a time on global economic challenges that cannot be met by half measures or the isolated efforts of any nation. He says for the first time in a generation, the global economy is contracting and trade is shrinking. Trillions of dollars have been lost, banks have stopped lending and tens of millions will lose their jobs across the globe. The prosperity of every nation has been endangered, along with the stability of the Governments and the survival of people in the most vulnerable parts of the World. The current economy crisis is unfolding before us faster than even the most pessimistic predict of experts. As many as 27 million people could become unemployed while 140 million others in the region's developing economies could be forced to face extreme poverty. In Asia, working women will be affected more severely and differently than the males. Mr. Amelita King Defardin, Senior Technical Adviser in the Policy Integration and Statistics Department of the International Labour Office, who made these observation has also suggested suitable remedies to win over the crisis of meltdown. It is therefore critical that when Governments, employers and worker's organisation sit down to discuss policies to fight the social and economic effects of the crisis, they do so from the perspective of women as well as men. When it comes to the social aspect of policy responses, basic health care, maternity and education of women must be included. According to another report since the melt down began in September, the

U.S. economy has seen on an average, a loss of around one thousand jobs a day.

In India too, job losses are now finding some mention of migrant labourers who left their villages seeking work when they were left with no other option. In this context a comment of such workers is worth considering: "There is nothing to send back to the village and nothing to go back to the village for". In contrast to this, the Kleptocreates the top bosses of US Financial firms flourish by divine right. The very gangs which created the melt down are rewarded with huge amount of tax payers' money, so that they can go back to doing something they were doing before.

The World Bank projected world output to grow by a mere 0.9% in 2009—(compared with 2.5% in 2008 and a high of 4% in 2006) and world trade to contract by a significant 2% (compared to positive rates of growth of 6.2% in 2008 and high of 9.8% in 2006). The recently released preliminary edition of the OECD'S Economic Outlook for 2008 shows that GDP in most OECD countries declined in the third quarter and is likely to fall also in the fourth.

According to the OECD, for most countries: a recovery to at least the trend growth rate is not expected before second half of 2010 implying that the down turn is likely to be the most severe since the early 1980 leading to a sharp rise un employment. Another estimate from the Bank of Korea predicts that by Korean economy, the fourth largest in Asia, would shrink by 1.6% in the fourth quarter of 2008, and grow only at 2% in 2009, and 3.7% for full 2008. The recent crisis had a number of consequences in the developed countries. It made households, more cautious in their spending and borrowing behaviour, resulting in a collapse of consumption spending. The crisis also resulted in a collapse in the value of assets held by Banks and Financial Institutions pushing them into insolvency. While there is a wide agreement that what is needed is a globally co-ordinated and huge fiscal stimulus, the actual effort on the ground remains fragmented and meagre. Because of this, the results are disappointing threatening to make this crisis the most protracted in a wrong time. The year 2008 is likely to be remembered as a year in which a crisis of immense proportions unfolded.

The financial meltdown could result in reversal of globalization as the affected Governments increasingly occupy spaces they have once vacated for the free markets to drive enterprise and growth. The spirit of competition and challenge that were so important to spur growth would suffer when Government started attaching strings to stimulus packages to salvage the economy and try to gain dominate status in private enterprises. The roots of the recession did not lie in the market policy but were caused by unchecked capitalist greed where money chased money in a bloated speculative bubble.

The right formula should involve strong but unobtrusive regulatory systems within a free market, as international trade had accounted for 50% of global growth in the past two decades. However, the bright spot amidst all the gloom and doom was the opportunity for India to convert the crisis into an opportunity. India's inherent advantages to make the most of this crisis lay in the concept of trusteeship spearheaded by Mahatma Gandhi that sets the benchmark for good governance, its demographic dividend of having a large proportion of youth when western societies were aging and its fairly high level domestic consumption of goods and services. However, for this to happen India needed a combination of strong and stable political leadership and measures to trigger inflow of overseas capital by convincing foreign investors and Banks of the strengths of its regulatory mechanisms.

To sum up, it is pertinent to reiterate the erudite views expressed by Hon'ble Mr. M. Veerappa Moily, former Chairman, Administrative Reforms Commission, Government of India, New Delhi, In his Convocation Address at Kuvempu University, Shivamogga, Karnataka State: "The recent crisis in the global financial system has had a cataclysmic impact on the global financial centres, with major banks failing in the U.S. as well as in Europe, drying up of inter bank credit and the loss of perhaps trillions of dollars in capital value on the world's stock markets." These events, triggered by the sub prime lending crisis in the U.S., have now started to affect the real economy with rising cost of borrowings, spiralling unemployment figures in the major world economies, rising levels of home loan foreclosures and bankruptcies and a general crisis of confidence in the economies around the world.

India's economy is estimated to grow at 7% which is down from 9.3%. The principle reasons for this relatively modest decline expected in economic growth in India are the following:

1. A large and diversified consumption base-India is perhaps the only major economy driven primarily by domestic demand.
2. India's trade of GDP ratio is much smaller than that of China.
3. India's financial markets remains relatively sequestered from the global financial markets. India has healthy extra balance, a low ratio of short-term external debt to GDP, substantial foreign exchange reserve and the country has still not gone in for complete capital account convertibility.

The global financial crisis will also affect the poor in India. Since 1980, India's 6.2% average annual growth rate has brought an estimated 30 million, out of its 1.1 billion people, out of extreme poverty. But an estimated 250 million Indians remained under the extreme poverty line in 2005. According to the latest world bank poverty estimate (PDF) an 827 million Indians earned less than $2 a day, the median poverty line for all developing countries.

Now, India is happily endowed with the luminous leadership of Dr. Manmohan Singh, our esteemed Prime Minister and the eminent economist who will provide the blue print to face the crisis. Old adage says that 'success is when preparation meets opportunity'. We should prepare ourselves to enter the threshold of success. 'Whatever the mind can conceive and believe, the mind achieve'. Every failure carries with it a seed of an equivalent advantage. Perpetual enthusiasm is our multiplier.

Therefore, while the global recession has chilling prospects for many countries; we in India should be able to ride out the storm on the strength of our aspiring and upwardly mobile poor and our legions of youngsters who can unleash a demographic dividend for our nation. Let us rebuild our traditional economy and keep our heads high.

References

A time for global action, Barack Obama.

Asian Face of the global reception, CP. Chandrasekar and Jayati Ghosh, *Business Line*, 16.12.2008.

Behind the Triple Global Crisis, Utsa Patnaik, *The Hindu*, 4.11.2008.

"Back to Basis": Boosting Public Expenditure Enhanced Demand for Goods and Services Can Combat Economic Slowdown, A. Rangachari, *The Hindu*, 19.01.2009.

Depression economic returns, Paul Krugman.

Don't Blame Keynes, Gorge Monbit.

Economy headed for more pain in 2009, S.D. Naik.

Economy will see recovery this year, S. Rangachari.

Fiscal Spurs may be in order, S. Venkitaramanan, Former Reserve Bank of India's Governor, *Business Line*, 03.11.2009.

Global Recession: How Deep and for How Long?, C.P. Chandrasekar and Jayati Ghosh, *Business Line*, 16.12.2008.

"Global financial crisis": Reflection on its impact of India, S. Venkitaramanan, Former Reserve Bank of India's Governor.

"Globalisation and the Poor", Jay R. Mandle.

"Globalisation: Challenge and Opportunity", Joseph S. Nye, Martin Wolf, M.A. Thomas.

"Globalisation: Governance and Identity, Guy Lachapelle.

Is India an Island economy?, Ranbir Roy Choudhury.

New innovation Strategies to meet economic slowdown, Priscilla Jebaraj.

'... we all fall down', S.S. Tarapore, *Business Line*, 21.11.2008.

Reflections on the global economic crisis, Markandey Kaju.

Repeat of Great Depression Unlikely, Aravind Subramaniam.

Revenge of the glut, Paul Krugman.

"Selling Globalisation", Machael Vesetif.

"Stimulating Developments", S. Venkitaramanan, Former Reserve Bank of India's Governor.

2008: A forgettable year, S. Venkitaramanan, Former Reserve Bank of India's Governor.

The Hindu, Survey of Indian Industry, 2009.

The Industrial Recession: New or Ongoing?, C.P. Chandrasekar and Jayati Ghosh, *Business Line*, 18.11.2008.

The Meltdown: whose crisis is it, anyway?, P. Sainath.

The Tragedy of economy, T.C.A.. Srinivasa Ragavan, *Business Line*, 21.01.2009.

International Economic Crisis and the Indian Economy

MD. REYAZUDDIN AND YOGENDRA KUMAR SINGH

INTRODUCTION

Recent data on trade patterns in Latin America are partially consistent with the need for concern about Dutch disease in the region. The terms of trade have notably risen in Colombia, Chile and Uruguay, for example, indicating that the prices of their main exports are increasing faster than those of their imports. Specialisation has also increased, with most Latin American countries showing a higher degree of export concentration in commodities than at the beginning of this century. The trend towards greater specialization in commodities is most marked in Venezuela, Ecuador, Bolivia and Chile; the exceptions are Costa Rica and Argentina.

More reassuring is the fact that real exchange rates have not appreciated as much as could be feared. Macroeconomic stability has also been maintained, with inflation contained. Fiscal reform is in part to be credited for these successes, especially recently established oil and stabilisation funds. New transparency rules, such as freedom-of-information laws, should further stimulate responsible and accountable policies.

The result was an informal and illegal market in which the desired economic rights could be traded. Also, the lure of higher profits led producers and sellers (i) to have little concern for quality such that many deliberately produced and sold inferior quality products, and (ii) to resort to the creation of artificial shortages by not releasing to the market all of the products that were available for selling. Bardhan (1997) defines corruption as the use of public office for private gain, in which an official entrusted with the responsibility for certain public duties engages in malfeasance for personal enrichment that is not easy to monitor. He says that corruption has multiple effects on economic development. For example, it diminishes the efficiency of economic transactions, because corrupt officials will delay or otherwise obstruct those transactions until they receive their expected favours. Also, the payment of a bribe to receive an investment license tends to reduce the incentive to invest. Honest investors will see the futility of competing with dishonest investors who are guaranteed, through their bribes, to receive the privilege of investment rights. To fully understand the widespread nature of the corruption that existed in India at this time, it is necessary to consider the roles played by the many participants. For example, business people bribed government officials not only for the right to enter a particular line of business, but also to prevent others from entering that same line of business. Government officials made payoffs to politicians to receive the premium government positions that would allow them to easily contact businesses to seek illegal income and wealth. Indeed, as Wade (1985) indicates, those officials could earn far more through bribes and other corrupt behaviour than they could earn in salary. Consumers bribed government officials, politicians, and business people to receive a particular amount of a scarce goods or a higher quality version of the goods. Even individual and organizations outside India took part in the corruption. Some bribed both officials and politicians, particularly those connected with the revenue and police departments, to smuggle scarce goods into India at a high profit.

The complex system of government controls, including price ceilings, along with the resultant corruption, meant that decision making was arbitrary and the transactions non-transparent. The result was an increase in transaction costs. For example, businesses had to spend more to "stay connected' with appropriate government officials and politicians. And consumers, in addition to waiting in line to purchase needed products and services, also made illegal payments for what they should have received at a reasonable price in the first place. It has already been explained how India's government grew in size as it played an increasing role in controlling the economy. It grew even further in trying to be appropriately vigilant in dealing with the increased corruption among government officials, businesses, and other participants.

Price controls were only one example of the regulated economic environment. Another example of a harmful policy was the control of ownership of private capital (both income and wealth) by Indian nationals in India and also by foreign nationals doing business in India. Such policies, coupled with high individual and corporate income tax rates and high customs and excise duties, led to outcomes similar to those resulting from price ceilings namely, increased corruption and higher transaction costs.

TRADE FOR ECONOMIC DEVELOPMENT

The rise of India in the global economy has had important effects on Latin America and been the subject of passionate public debate. Both these Asian giants have outperformed Latin America since the mid-1990s in terms of growth, exports, FDI attraction, and innovation, giving rise to considerable pretension in the region. While there are many examples of business co-operation between Latin America and the Asian giants, and trade agreements are being signed between their governments, public opinion has at times seen Asia's increased presence as a threat to national industries. A closer look at the real impact in Latin America of the world's rapidly growing trade with China and India nevertheless offers a much more encouraging assessment.

The United States, the European Union and Japan are where most third-market competition takes place between Latin America and the Asian giants. That competition is fiercest in the United States, which alone received 57 per cent of Latin American exports in 2006. China and India have been increasing their market shares in the United States — and, in the case of China, have already overtaken Mexico's share, for example. Closer inspection shows, however, that only a few countries in Latin America face much trade competition with China and India, and that the latter do not constitute a significant threat to Latin America as a whole. Figures and provide indicators of export competition between China and India and selected countries. The competition is measured by comparing the trade structure of each country with that of China. A high score indicates similarity in export structures, which suggests more third market competition.

The data show that the export structures of most Latin American countries are very different from Chinese and Indian export structures, implying that they have little to fear from China's and India's export dynamism. Other emerging economies such as Thailand, Hungary and Malaysia are facing substantially tougher competition from Chinese exports. Mexico and Central America are the exceptions to this general pattern in Latin America of non-competition with China. Latin America's competition with India is similarly low, with El Salvador, Brazil and Argentina apparently facing the most exposure to competition, and emerging economies in other regions — notably Pakistan, Romania, Turkey and Bulgaria — facing much tougher competition with India. Not surprisingly, Latin American countries that export mainly commodities face the least trade competition with China and India, as the latter are net importers of these products. Paraguay, Venezuela, Bolivia and Chile thus suffer the least from Chinese and Indian trade competition.

Equally significant is the fact that rapid growth in China and India is opening important export opportunities for Latin American countries. Thus, while Mexico's export structure suggests it is the most vulnerable amongst Latin America's large countries to Asian competition in third markets, especially in manufactures, Mexico is also one of the Latin American countries, together with Colombia and Venezuela that stands to gain the most from increased commodities exports to China and India. Indeed, of the biggest Latin American and Caribbean exporters, are specialised in commodities, and both China and India are prime importers of these products. Their heightened demand for oil and minerals has already substantially increased Latin America's export earnings, which have benefited both directly, from the increased volume of the region's commodities exports to China and India, and indirectly, from the increase in world prices for the region's commodities exports to Asia and elsewhere induced by strong Asian demand. Few countries in Latin America, in contrast to Southeast Asian developing countries for example, appear likely to benefit from potential intra-industry trade growth with China and India, however. Mexico and Brazil may be partial exceptions in this regard, as they may have some potential to benefit from intra-industry trade in manufactures with the Asian giants.

While China's and India's growth dynamism thus offers major benefits for Latin American exporters of primary goods, including oil, minerals and agricultural products, the principal risk is that as commodity exports become more valuable and commodity exporters see their incomes rise, they will rely on commodity exports to the detriment of other sectors. As is well-documented in the literature on the so called Dutch disease, surges in commodity export income, while increasing both growth and government revenues, can have substantial adverse effects if they are not managed responsibly. Surging commodity exports can easily drive up a country's exchange rate, which induces a long-term decline in non-commodity exports, notably manufactures, to the detriment of economic development.

ENHANCING COMPETITIVENESS

The current commodities boom also intensifies the need for both governments and firms in Latin America to redirect windfall revenues towards strategic growth-enhancing activities in order to maintain growth beyond the natural-resource bonanza. These activities include building up capabilities in innovation, education and physical infrastructure. They are needed to strengthen the competitive position of the economy's non-commodity exporters, including those involved in intra-industry trade, and to offset the negative impact of any exchange-rate appreciation. Diversifying the economy and taking advantage of no commodity export opportunities also require a sound business environment, and it is important that

Latin American countries be attractive destinations for FDI and for cooperation on innovation. Yet spending on innovation remains insufficient, and what is spent goes largely to basic research with little private-sector participation. Education, too, remains a major challenge, even for the region's best performers.

Moreover, for those parts of Latin America's economy that do compete against Chinese and Indian exports, including much of Mexico's and Costa Rica's manufacturing export industries, as well as labour intensive sectors in other parts of Latin America and the Caribbean, proximity to the United States offers a major potential competitive advantage in goods where fast delivery or short turn-around times are crucial.

These goods include clothing whose fashions change frequently and rapidly, for example, and intermediate automotive and electronic products in lean production systems that rely on just-in-time delivery of manufactured inputs. To take competitive advantage of proximity to the United States nevertheless requires well-performing infrastructure, in transportation as well as in telecommunications. Yet current infrastructure investment levels in Latin America remain substantially below those of Asian countries, and many countries need to rethink their infrastructure-investment strategies.

Infrastructure thus constitutes a potentially critical part of Latin America's response to increased competition from Asia. Mexico needs to exploit its geographical position fully by improving infrastructure and Latin America as a whole needs to invest more and better in infrastructure. Such investment is also likely to help reduce inequality and poverty. It requires a well-organised public sector capable of managing infrastructure projects while maintaining fiscal discipline and engaging the private sector.

Today all over the world inflation has become a buzz word among the academicians, politicians and the public in general. Several people offer several reasons for the prevalence of inflation in various countries. The Deputy Chairman, Planning Commission, Prof. Montek Singh Ahulwalia is of the opinion that inflation is prevailing all over the world due to globalize contact of India with other countries is prone to inflation in India. Even a country like China inflation is prevailing. The President of USA is of the opinion that in India the inflation is taking place be-cause of increase in income of par-ticularly of the middle income people the consumption of food is increasing. Mr. Sharad Pawar the Agricultural Min-ister of Union Government is of the view that, if you stop export of food grains from India to other countries, that inflation can be controlled.

Mr. Chidambaram, the Union Finance Minister has announced several fiscal measures to control inflation such as increase in export duty, decrease in import duty particularly on agricultural commodities. Many academicians feel that due to increase in oil prices at an exorbitant rate, the food grains prices are increasing. Due to steep increase in shipping charges for the import of food grains, the prices are increasing. Mr. Kamalnath, Union Commerce Minister, is of the view that we can jump for the immediate imports of food grains, thereby inflation could be controlled. Leftists are of the opinion that there are several black marketers in the country who are hoarding plenty of quantity of food grain and creating artificial scarcity in the market. They requested the government to dishoard those stocks and release to the market so that prices will be controlled and such people to be punished severely for such unlawful activities.

THEORETICAL FOUNDATION FOR THE ECONOMIC CRISIS

The Classical Economists held the view that if demand is greater than supply this will lead to inflation. But this is not true. Since 1970 in India we are not only self sufficient in food grains but also exporting. For example, the food grains, production in the year 2007-08 is estimated at 219.3 million tonnes. The production of cereals is expected at 205 million tonnes in 2007-08. The production of pulses is expected to remain almost at the 2006-07 level. The production of the oil seeds estimated to reach to 27.2 million tonnes. The production of cash crops particularly cotton is likely to remain buoyant.

Our total exports have increased from 18,477 million US$ in 1990-91 to 1,28,083 million US$ in 2006-07. Thus, both, our production and exports are on the rise. Exports as a percentage of GDP in 1990-91 were 5.8 per cent has increased to 14 per cent by 2006-07. All this indicates that the inflation in India is not because of supply shortage.

Neo-Classical Economists such as Fisher contend that

increase in money supply leads to increase in prices given velocity of Money circulation and total transactions are kept constant. But this theory is developed only with reference to full employed countries. Moreover there are several empirical studies which showed that increase or decrease in money supply does not lead to changes in the prices, as money is only a measuring rod of goods and services. There are instan-ces in Indian Economy where prices have decreased even though money supply increased (This was prevalent during the Janata Government rule in India).

Thus neither the increase in money supply nor the shortage of food grains supply is the cause for the present inflation in India. Indeed for the last so many years we are maintaining the buffer stocks of food grains part of which was eaten by rats. The procurement of rice in the year 2006-07 is of the order of 250.8 lakh tonnes where as the procurement of wheat in the year 2007-08 has reached to 111.3 lakh tonnes. As on January 2008, we had 19.2 lakh tonnes of rice and wheat as buffer stocks, when this is the situation of production and existence of buffer stocks, there is no reason for the prevalence of inflation.

REASONS FOR THE ECONOMIC CRISIS

(I) Increase in Petroleum/Diesel and other Petroleum product prices.

(II) Increase in Indirect taxes including surcharge on several commodities which adds up to prices.

(III) Increase in oil prices have caused increase in transport prices, for example, it is estimated that, the freight charges by ships has increased 300 per cent for the last one year. This also adds up to prices.

(IV) Development of Black market. The subsidized goods such as kerosene, gas, rice, wheat have been diverted to black market with a view to create artificial scarcity in the market and earn exorbitant profits.

(V) The Development of middlemen also contributed for vice of inflation. In every organization/sector the mid-dlemen/broker is prevailing who charges for his services more than the legal price. For example, in

Chittoor district of Andhra Pradesh tomatoes are sold at 13 paisa per kg (which is lower than the input cost).

(VI) The government food price policy.

There are two objectives of the food policy of the government viz.

(a) Government declares MSP (minimum support price) for major food crops such as paddy, wheat, maize, sugar cane, etc. This is aimed at protecting the farmer from the clutches of the money lenders/rural traders/the contractors/village land lords, etc. Whatever the farmer produces is to be purchased by FCI for the last several years but of late the government is only declaring MSP and not purchasing all that is offered for sale by the farmer. Since the FCI has not been able to store the excess output because of the lack of storage facilities the farmer is left to market forces generally at the time of harvest the excess supply of the product takes place. However, the farmer cannot afford to wait for some time because he has to clear the debts/ loans he has taken for various pur-poses. Thus he is subject to loss and it is the traders/middle men/contractors/ landlords who purchase excess product gains because he can afford to wait for some months and when stocks are cleared in the open market and the prices start rising they will sell their product in the organized markets. Therefore inflation is taking place. The prices commission who generally take into consideration cost of agricultural in-puts in fixing MSP (Narasimhulu, 2008).

(b) The second aim of the food policy of the government of India is to protect the consumers by selling the food grains (collected by FCI) through PDS (public distribution system) at subsidized prices. This is aimed at protecting the consumer. But due to the implementation of the new economic policy the public distribution system is not effective.

Differential prices are charged by PDS, one for BPL (below poverty line) and another for APL (above poverty line). The WTO is not in favour agricultural subsidies in general and food subsidies in particular.

CONCLUSION

For India, the possibility of deflation is remote. First, the current declining inflation is just a one-time number and far from any trend. Second, the number is not final and could be revised upwards. Third, private consumption still forms around 60 per cent of GDP and is expected to be steady, preventing prices from falling due to lack of demand. Fourth, the consumer price inflation is still rising. Fifth, the policy-makers have been proactive trying to contain the fallouts from global crisis on the overall demand (A. Agrawal, 2008). However, no worst-case scenario can be ruled out for the current times. We are witnessing scenarios few could have predicted. Pre-crisis global economies were enjoying what was termed as Great Moderation—a phase of high growth and low inflation, both with low volatility. And now, the advanced economies are facing prospects of recession plus deflation. The meltdown in prices of oil and com-modities has also happened after reaching record highs. Hence, the Indian policy-makers need to maintain vigilance and be proactive.

References

A. Bonne (1998), Studies in Economic Development, p. 7.

A. Madison (1970), Economic Progress and Policy in Developing Countries.

Ahulwalia, M.S. (2002), Economic Reforms in India since 1991: Has Gradualism Worked, *Journal of Economic Perspectives*, Vol. 16(7).

Bhalla, G.S. (2000), "Political economy of Indian development in the 20th century: India's road to freedom and growth," Presidential Address at the 83rd Annual Conference of the Indian Economic Association, University of Jammu, Jammu and Kashmir, 30 December.

Burdekin, R.C.K. and P.L. Siklos (2004), Deflation: Current and Historical Perspectives, Cambridge University Press, Cambridge.

C.P. Kindleberger (2005), Economic Development, (Second Edition), p. 3.

Di Lodovico, Amadeo M., William W. Lewis, Vincent Palmade and Shirish Sankhe (2001), "India from emerging".

Gupta, S.P. (1999), "Development experience of the nineties and search for a new paradigm," A.K. Dasgupta Memorial Lecture at the 82nd Annual Conference of the Indian Economic Association, Guru Nanak Dev University, Amritsar, December 29.

Joshi, Vijay, (2001), "Capital controls and the national advantage: India in the 1990s and beyond," Oxford Development Studies, Vol. 29, 3, pp. 305-20.

Karunaratne, Neil Dias (2001), "Revisiting capital account convertibility in the aftermath of the Currency Crisis," Intereconomics, Vol. 36, 5 September/ October, pp. 264-71.

Krueger, Anne O. (1993), Political Economy of Policy Reform in Developing Countries (Cambridge, MIT Press).

Narisimhulu, M. and Padmaja (2008), Inflation in India: Why, What, How and Then, *Southern Economist*, Bangalore, September 1.

P.A. Baran (1957), The Political Economy of Economic Growth, U. Hicks, Learning About Economic Development, Oxford Economic Papers, February, 1957.

Pant, M. (2008), World Recession: The Way forward, *The Economic Times*, Kolkata, November 14.

Poole, W. (1999), Is Inflation Too Low? Federal Reserve Bank of St. Louis Review, Vol. 81(4).

Shastri, S. (2008), Inflation and Economic Growth in India: Empirical Investigation, *Southern Economist*, Bangalore, May 1.

Simha, S.L.N. (2008), Inflation: some observation, *Southern Economist*, Bangalore, June 1.

Singh, Ranbir (2007), Changing Social Scene in India, *Kurukshetra*, August.to Surging," *The McKinsey Quarterly*.

Tuteja, Usha (2008), Protect poor from food Inflation, *The Economic Times*, Kolkata, December 21.

_______(2008), Economic Survey, 2007-08, Government of India, New Delhi.

________(1985), Inflation and Economic Growth, *Bank of England, Quarterly Bulletin*, Vol. 35.

Housing Bubble and Credit Derivatives as Factors Behind the Financial Crisis

VINOD KUMAR SINGH AND NIRAJ KUMAR VERMA

VULNERABILITY OF FINANCE

There are sets of inter-related facts which seem to capture the nature of this financial vulnerability. First there emerged a set of financial institutions and companies that were in the lending business almost like usual commercial banks, but had no "lender of the last resort". They resembled instead a shadow banking system which lacked the explicit backing of a monetary authority on the one hand and escaped largely its regulation on the other. In true spirit of free market enterprise, finance could go on innovating new credit instruments with little regulation.

Second without a lender of the last resort at the top, innovative shadow banking resulted in what may be aptly be described as a circular rather a vertical network of credit interdependence. These shadow bankers, especially large investment banks, through mutual underwriting insured each others' debt with derivatives as the most prominent debt instrument and then went into "securitization" of these debts by mixing them in different ways.

Finally, by treating each others debt as asset in the capital base for lending could be expended enormously. "Low margin, high volume" by pushing loans to more risky borrowers became the name of the game. This was symbolized as sub-prime lending. The capital base itself became increasingly vulnerable due to the magnifying effect of each defaulted loans, as each loan is linked or correlated with the assets base of several other shadow bankers.

COLLATERALISED DEBT OBLIGATIONS

In fact, three things became clear in mid 2007. First, low income or sub-prime US households that had borrowed heavily from banks and finance companies to buy homes were defaulting heavily on their debt obligations. Next, the size of this sub-prime housing loan market was huge at about $1.4 trillion. Three, Wall Street's financial engineers had packaged these loans to really complicated financial instruments called CDOs (Collateralized debt obligations) American and European banks had invested heavily in these products.

CDO price started plummeting as defaults on US home loans rose. Falling prices dented banker's investment portfolios and these looses destroyed banks capital. Default mortgage loans are the primary reason for the financial crisis sweeping the world. (Rao, 2008)

The ongoing financial turmoil, described as 'the crisis of the Century' by Alan Greenspan, Former Federal Reserve Governor, had its reverberations on both developed and developing world. Credit markets appear to be drying up in the developed world.

The sub-prime mortgage crisis triggered by a dramatic rise in mortgage delinquencies and foreclosures in the United States had a major effort on financial markets and banks. According to Ban Ki-Moon, Secretary General of the United Nations, what was a purely financial crisis has become an economic crisis, spreading across the globe.

As the financial meltdown translates into a declined in wealth (the stock markets and real estate markets) and income (reduction in jobs), the world economy is poises for contraction. Pant of Centre for International Trade and Development School of International Studies, JNU, saw the stark similarities with the Great Depression of the 1930.

The usual argument for the onset of recession was that the US was living beyond its means as reflected in its huge and glowing trade deficits. The US economy like India in Asia is a net importer of commodities but a net exporter of services.

The world economy today boasts of several global co-ordinating mechanisms unlike in the 30s. There is a remarkable degree of co-ordination today between Central Banks of various countries. Similarly, the WTO is a useful mechanism to combat trade protectionism. We know that tariff wars led to a major contraction in world trade in the 30s. Given the globalized nature of today's world, only multilateralism can reverse pessimistic expectations.

A recession is always demand led. The US has remained dominate, accounting for about 30% of world demand in 2007. It then stands to reason that the easiest recovery from recession will come about through demand recovery in the US.

Bursting of the housing bubble was viewed merely as a correction, the defaults in the US sub-prime mortgages as misfortune, and the failure of important financial institutions as collateral damage. In April 2008, IMF estimated more than $ 1 trillion financial loss and predicted a sharp slowdown in the global economy.

TRIGGERS OF THE US FINANCIAL CRISIS

Copious analysis, investigations, research, and introspection of the current mayhem will go on for years. The following seven triggers seem to emerge as the pillars that shoulder responsibility for the crisis:

A. Reckless Sub-prime Lending

Most of this decade saw reckless lending in the US credit market through mortgage loans, car loans, credit cards, etc. to borrowers with impaired or limited credit histories. These sub-prime loans encompassed loans with no down payments, no verification of income, jobs and assets (referred to as NINJA loans), initial payment only of interest negative amortization, teaser interest rates, etc. According to news letter, Inside Mortgage Finance, US lenders added a total of $ 2.5 trillion in sub-prime mortgages between 2002 and 2007.

B. Origination and Distribution Model

The origination, securitization and servicing model (also known as the O&D model) proliferated in the US on the back of a booming mortgage credit market. The O&D model worked something like this; Typically a huge investment bank (HIB) – such as the big five investment banks, Bears Sterns, Lehman Brothers, Merrill Lynch, Morgan Stanley, or Goldman Sachs- would encourage mortgage banks countrywide to make home loans, often providing the capital, and then the HIB would purchase these loans and package them into large securities called residential mortgage backed securities (RMBS). They would package loans from different mortgage banks and different regions.

Since it was hard to sell some of the lower levels of these securities, the HIB would take a lot of the lower level tranches and put them into another security called a collateralized debt obligation(CDO). That the outstanding CDOs are estimated at $ 3.9 trillion against the estimated size of risk of the sub-prime market of $ 1 to 1.3 trillion is a revealing index of the multiplier effect of securitization structures and CDOs.

C. Proliferating Derivatives

To be sure, the credit boom was accompanied by proliferation of complex, illiquid, and inherently high leverage, over the counter (OTC) credit derivatives. The OTC market was bereft of any central counter party risk management mechanism such as a clearing corporation that acted as a CCP. The rate of growth of CDS has been breathtaking. According to the International Swap Dealers Association (ISDA) the notional amount outstanding of CDS grew to a staggering $ 62.2 trillion at 2007 year end, up from a modest $ 0.92 trillion at 2001 year end, depicting a compound annual growth rate of an astounding 102%, and making credit default swap (CDS) the fastest growing financial instrument of all times. Despite its growth to a staggering $ 62.2 trillion at 2007 year end, the market for CDS was entirely unregulated.

It appears that the US Fed could not let Bear Stearns enter bankruptcy because – and only because—the trillions of dollars of credit default swaps on its books would be wiped out.

D. Excessive Leverage

Leverage is a double edged sword. It is the life blood of business and economic growth when used wisely and moderately. Indeed, economic activity would come to a grinding halt if no credit or leverage were available from the banking or shadow financial system. Concomitantly, without lending the banking system would have no avenue to deploy their deposits, except in treasury securities. The role of leverage and credit is central to growth. Yet, excessive leverage leaves little margin of error if things go wrong, and can have a damaging impact. In any economy financial firms tend to use more leverage than the real economy firms. It is this inherent leverage nature of banks and financial firms that forms the basis of regulatory capital requirements and other regulations to which these firms need to be subjected to in the larger public interest.

Not surprisingly, as the downturn in the US housing market proceeded, these investment banks were caught in a vicious circle of credit derivative losses.

With extreme leverage providing little margin for error, what initially started as a liquidity problem quickly precipitated into a solvency problem. The annals of model finance will take note of year 2008, *inter alia,* as the year in which an era of powerful, iconic, high octane, non- bank Wall Street investments banks came to an end.

E. Housing Market Downturn

The years that preceded the recent turbulence saw an exceptionally strong performance of the world economy. Following the global slowdown of 2001, the world economy had recovered rather rapidly, posting record growth ratios in 2004, 2005 and 2006. This strength went hand in hand with unusually strong performance in financial markets and the financial system more generally, underpinned by the strength of asset prices. Pretty much globally, residential property prices had been rising rapidly.

Against the backdrop of historically low interest rates

and booming asset prices, credit aggregates alongside monetary aggregates had been expanding rapidly. Despite the rapid increase in credit, however, the balance sheets and repayment capacity of corporations and, to a lesser degree, households did not appear to be under any strain. But debt to income ratios in the households sectors exhibited a marked upward trend, on the back of a major rise in mortgage debt.

After a prolonged rise in housing prices 2000 to 2005 on the back of an eco system of easy availability of credit at low interest rates, the US entered a phase of a housing price correction in 2006, perhaps the worst in US history with no sign of it bottoming out any time soon. Indeed, the prolonged the housing price correction on the back of an extremely leveraged system turbo changed with complex CDO and CDS, ensured that what began initially as a sub-prime crisis morphed into a general credit deterioration touching prime mortgages.

CONCLUSION

Banking policy needs to moderate the recurring cycle of financial crisis, cycles that are not needed to particular instruments, institutions or individuals. The externalities from an individual bank failure both to other banks and thence to the wider economy are just so much greater. A raging financial crisis is threatening to shake capitalism to its roots.

The Federal Reserve, under Greenspan's undisputed leadership, was guided by a market fundamentalist approach. The Efficient Market Hypothesis of Eugene Fama along with the influence of ideas of complete rationality as the dominant feature of economic system had come to become conventional wisdom. Greenspan had a different philosophy—it was not the business of Federal Reserve to control speculation in asset prices. Let us recall the scene in the early 1990s. For many, the sustained buoyancy of Wall Street was the expression of a new renaissance of American Capitalism; technology stocks were dominating the market at inexplicable levels, for above their fair values.

Asset bubbles may have respondent to monetary policy adjustments if liquidity had been squeezed early enough.

The bubble ultimately burst. The midnight international following the Long-term Capital Management debacle sent out a different kind of signal. The market developed the belief that if there is any crisis a Wall Street, Greenspan would be savior.

Banks had been extensively using techniques such as securitization and creation of derivative instrument to pass on risks that they would have otherwise held in their books. This approach, dubbed as the "originate and distribute" model, was widely held as one that had transformed the banking industry into a less risking and more profitable business. As it turned out, these claims proved to be empty boasts.

Bruised by stock market losses, Americans started buying houses in a big way. The easy credit policy created an age of leverage. High and unsustainable leverage was accompanied by high investment in the housing. As at the time of equity bubble, the mistake was not only to set interest rates too low, but also to stand back even as wildly imprudent policy were being openly pursued by mortgage lenders. This financial crisis is defined by bursting of two bubbles—in housing and in the credit markets—bubbles that were deeply interconnected.

If the originators of loans were generating risky assets and investors were packaging these into securitized products and then selling these products to investors all across the globe, were not the regulators getting concerned about systemic risks.

If the widespread use of these instruments had the potential of exponentially increasing the risks in the financial systems all over the globe, should not the authorities have stepped in to limit and supervise the use of such financial instruments ? Extensive use of such instruments needed to be strictly supervised. The Federal Reserve kept its hand off and believed that the market would correct distortions, if any. It turned out to be a " story of great tragedy".

References

Bhaduri, Amit (2009): 'Understanding the Financial Crisis', *Economic and Political Weekly*, March 28-April 3, 2009, Volume XLIV, No. 13, pp. 123-25.

Chithelen, Ignatius (2008): 'Global Financial Crisis—A Long Way From Recovery', *Economic and Political Weekly*, Sept. 6 to 12, 2008, Volume XLIII, No. 36, p. 16.

Dua, Ajay (2008): 'The Impact of Slowdown on India', *The Economic Times*, 12 Nov. 2008.

Greenspan, Alan (2008): 'The World Must Repel Calls to Contain Competitive Markets', *The Financial Times*, 5 August 2008.

Ki-Moon, Ban (2008): 'Connecting the Solutions', *The Economic Times*, 18 Nov. 2008.

Kumar, Arun (2009): 'Tackling the Current Global Economic and Financial Crisis: Beyond Demand Management', *Economic and Political Weekly*, March 28-April 3 2009, Volume XLIV, No. 13, pp. 151-57.

Kumar, N. Kiran (2009): 'Economic Recession in US and its Impact on India', *Southern Economist*, Volume 48, No. 4, June 15, 2009, p. 31.

Madhavi, N.R. (2009): 'Current Financial Crisis and RBI's Prescriptions', *Southern Economist*, Volume 47, No. 18, Jan. 15, 2009, p. 45.

Madhavi, N.R. and Gadade, S.T. (2009): 'The Impact of Financial Crisis on India', *Southern Economist*, Volume 48, No. 1, May 1, 2009, p. 27.

Mohan, T.T. Ram (2008): 'From the Subprime to the Ridiculous', *The Economic and Political Weekly*, Volume XLIII, No. 45, Nov. 8-14, 2008.

Nayar, Pulin B. (2009): 'Anatomy of the Financial Crisis: Between Keynes and Schumpeter', *Economic and Political Weekly*, March 28-April 3, 2009, Volume XLIV, No. 13, pp. 158-63.

Pant, Manoj (2008): 'World Recession: The Way Forward ?', *Economic Times*, 14 Nov. 2008.

Rao, D. Subba (2008): 'R.B.I. Governor, *The Times of India*, Oct. 12, 2008.

Reuters (2009): 'Japan Plans Fresh Bailout Package', *The Economic Times*, 28 Jan. 2009.

Selvaraj, Anitha (2009): 'Current Financial Crisis: Its Impact on the Indian Economy', *Southern Economist*, Volume 28, No. 2, May 15, 2009, p. 5.

Strauss, Kahn, Dominique (2008): 'Systemic Solutions for Systemic Crisis', *The Economic Times*, 30 Sept. 2008.

Vaidyanathan, A. (2009): 'Reviving the Economic: Problems and Prospects', *The Economic and Political Weekly*, Volume XLIV, No. 6, Feb. 7-13, 2009.

The Global Economic Crisis and the Indian Economy

T.G. GITE

INTRODUCTION

Long-term Structural Factors Behind the Crisis

The immediate cause or trigger of the crisis was the bursting of the United States housing bubble which peaked in approximately 2005-06. High default rates on "subprime" and adjustable rate mortgages (ARM), began to increase quickly thereafter. An increase in loan incentives such as easy initial terms and a long-term trend of rising housing prices had encouraged borrowers to assume difficult mortgages in the belief they would be able to quickly refinance at more favorable terms. However, once interest rates began to rise and housing prices started to drop moderately in 2006-07 in many parts of the U.S., refinancing became more difficult. Defaults and foreclosure activity increased dramatically as easy initial terms expired, home prices failed to go up as anticipated, and ARM interest rates reset higher.

The financial crisis of 2007-09 has been called the most serious financial crisis since the Great Depression by leading economists, with its global effects characterized by the failure of key businesses, declines in consumer wealth estimated in the trillions of U.S. dollars, substantial financial commitments incurred by governments, and a significant decline in economic activity. Many causes have been proposed, with varying weight assigned by experts. Both market-based and regulatory solutions have been implemented or are under consideration, while significant risks remain for the world economy.

Home Price Bubble

The immediate cause or trigger of the crisis was the bursting of the United States housing bubble which peaked in approximately 2005-06. High default rates on "sub-prime" and adjustable rate mortgages (ARM) began to increase quickly thereafter. An increase in loan incentives such as easy initial terms and a long-term trend of rising housing prices had encouraged borrowers to assume difficult mortgages in the belief they would be able to quickly refinance at more favourable terms. However, once interest rates began to rise and housing prices started to drop moderately in 2006-07 in many parts of the U.S., refinancing became more difficult. Defaults and foreclosure activity increased dramatically as easy initial terms expired, home prices failed to go up as anticipated, and ARM interest rates reset higher. Falling prices also resulted in homes worth less than the mortgage loan, providing a financial incentive to enter foreclosure. The ongoing foreclosure epidemic that began in late 2006 in the U.S. continues to be a key factor in the global economic crisis, because it drains wealth from consumers and erodes the financial strength of banking institutions.

While the housing and credit bubbles built, a series of factors caused the financial system to become increasingly delicate. Policy-makers did not recognize the increasingly important role played by financial institutions such as investment banks and hedge funds, also known as the shadow banking system.

Causes of the Crisis

The crisis can be attributed to a number of factors pervasive in both housing and credit markets, factors which emerged over a number of years. Causes proposed include the inability of homeowners to make their mortgage payments, due primarily to adjustable rate mortgages resetting, borrowers overextending, predatory lending, and speculation and over building during the boom period, risky mortgage products, high personal and corporate debt levels, financial products that distributed and perhaps concealed the risk of mortgage default, monetary policy, international trade imbalances, and government regulation. Two important catalysts of the sub-prime crisis were the influx of moneys from the private sector and banks entering into the mortgage bond market and the predatory lending practices of mortgage brokers, specifically the adjustable rate mortgage, 2.28 loan. Ultimately, though, specific to the bailout of Wall Street and the financial industry moral hazard lay at the core of many of the causes.

SUB-PRIME LENDING

U.S. Sub-Prime Lending Expanded Dramatically, 2004-06

In addition to easy credit conditions, there is evidence that both government and competitive pressures contributed to an increase in the amount of subprime lending during the years preceding the crisis. Major U.S. investment banks and government sponsored enterprises like Fannie Mae played an important role in the expansion of higher-risk lending.

The term subprime refers to the credit quality of particular borrowers, who have weakened credit histories and a greater risk of loan default than prime borrowers. The value of U.S. subprime mortgages was estimated at $1.3 trillion as of March 2007, with over 7.5 million first-lien subprime mortgages outstanding.

Mortgaged-base Securities

In the years leading up to the start of the crisis in 2007, significant amounts of foreign money flowed into the U.S. from fast-growing economies in Asia and oil-producing countries. This inflow of funds combined with low U.S. interest rates from 2002-04 contributed to easy credit conditions, which fueled both housing and credit bubbles. Loans of various types (e.g., mortgage, credit card, and auto) were easy to obtain and consumers assumed an unprecedented debt load. As part of the housing and credit booms, the amount of financial agreements called mortgage-backed securities (MBS), which derive their value from mortgage payments and housing prices, greatly increased. Such financial innovation enabled institutions and investors around the world to invest in the U.S. housing market. As housing prices declined, major global financial institutions that had borrowed and invested heavily in subprime MBS reported significant losses. Falling prices also resulted in homes worth less than the mortgage loan, providing a financial incentive to enter foreclosure. The ongoing foreclosure epidemic that began in late 2006 in the U.S. continues to drain wealth from consumers and erodes the financial strength of banking institutions. Defaults and losses on other loan types also increased significantly as the crisis expanded from the housing market to other parts of the economy.

A Global Savings Glut is Good for Growth—but risks are mounting

The more a country saves, the more it has available to invest. And the more it invests—in computers, factories, or infrastructure—the more productive its economy becomes and the faster it can grow. The global savings glut also forces investors to operate without many of the signposts they used to depend on.

Generally, the flow of surplus global savings to the United States has caused Americans to spend more and save less. In recent speeches, Bernanke—a member of the Federal Reserve Board and nominated as head of the White House Council of Economic Advisers—has shown how. In the 1990s, some of the savings surplus went into the hot U.S. stock market, boosting prices further. Feeling wealthier—because their stock portfolios had fattened—Americans decided they could save less and shop more.

Something similar has happened in recent years, except through the housing market. Foreign funds poured into U.S. bonds and mortgages, keeping interest rates down. Low interest rates on mortgages increase housing demand and prices, making Americans (again) feel wealthier. People borrow against the inflated values of their homes. That reduces U.S. saving and increases consumption.

TRIGGERING OF THE CRISIS

Increased Debt Burden or Over-leveraging

U.S. households and financial institutions became increasingly indebted or overleveraged during the years preceding the crisis. This increased their vulnerability to the collapse of the housing bubble and worsened the ensuing economic downturn.

Nobel laureate Paul Krugman described the run on the shadow banking system as the "core of what happened" to cause the crisis. "As the shadow banking system expanded to rival or even surpass conventional banking in importance, politicians and government officials should have realized that they were re-creating the kind of financial vulnerability that made the Great Depression possible—and they should have responded by extending regulations and the financial safety net to cover these new institutions. Influential figures should have proclaimed a simple rule: anything that does what a bank does, anything that has to be rescued in crises the way banks are, should be regulated like a bank." He referred to this lack of controls as "malign neglect."

A commodity price bubble was created following the collapse in the housing bubble. The failure of gatekeepers, including auditors, boards of directors, Wall Street analysts, and career politicians.

Decoupling Theory

In economics, decoupling is often used in the context of economic production and environmental quality. In this context, it refers to the ability of an economy to grow without corresponding increases in environmental pressure. In many economies increasing production (GDP) would involve increased pressure on the environment. An economy that is able to sustain GDP growth, without also experiencing a worsening of environmental conditions, is said to be decoupled. Exactly how, if, or to what extent this can be achieved is a subject of much debate.

Similarly, decoupling can refer to "breaking" the link between a dependent variable and its cause for a specific industry or activity. For instance, decoupling green house gas emissions from increasing electrical power generation.

Channels of Contagion

The study of financial contagion is growing in importance with the expanding global scope of financial markets. Financial contagion is defined as a shock to one country's asset market that causes changes in asset prices in another country's financial market. He channel that seems to best explain financial contagion is the cross-market rebalancing channel. Shocks occurring in one market are transmitted to other markets thought the cross-market rebalancing channel when investors react to a shock by readjusting their portfolios in other markets. Financial contagion is defined generally as "a price movement in one market resulting from a shock in another market." Contagion can be defined more restrictively as "a shock in one country that generates price movements in other countries that are excessive relative to 'full information fundamentals." A great cause of instability in emerging markets is financial contagion, as witnessed by the recent financial crises in emerging markets. Reducing financial contagion would increase the stability of emerging markets, and thus lend itself to fostering stability in developing countries

Employment Dimension

This meltdown is rapidly turning into a jobs and social crisis. Labour market conditions are weakening throughout the world, as companies are cutting production, closing factories and dismissing workers. Our latest projections (to be released officially tomorrow) indicate that the unemployment rate in the OECD area could approach 10% by 2010 compared with 5.6% in 2007. This implies that the crisis could swell the rank of the unemployed in the OECD by about 25 million people, by far the largest and most rapid increase in OECD unemployment in the post-war period.

And the job crisis is spreading rapidly around the world. The International Labour Organization estimates that world-wide unemployment could increase by 40 million people by the end of this year.

The most disadvantaged labour-market groups—youth, low-skilled, immigrants and temporary workers—are already bearing the brunt of the rapidly rising unemployment. They are the first to lose their job and tend to have only limited access to social safety nets. And since they also face serious difficulty in finding a new job, they run the risk of becoming long-term unemployed or discouraged.

INDIAN POLICY RESPONSE

Impact on Indian Economy

Both the Government of India and the Reserve Bank of India responded to the challenge in close coordination and consultation. The main plank of the government response was fiscal stimulus while the reserve Bank's action comprised monetary accommodation and counter cyclical regulatory measures.

Monetary Policy Response

The Reserve Bank's policy response was aimed at containing the contagion from the outside—to keep the domestic money and credit markets functioning normally and see that the liquidity stress did not trigger solvency cascades. In particular, RBI targeted three objectives: first, to maintain a comfortable rupee liquidity position; second, to augment foreign exchange liquidity; and third to maintain a policy framework that would keep credit delivery on track so as to arrest the moderation in growth. RBI reduced the interest rates aggressively and rapidly, reduced the quantum of bank reserves impounded by the it and expanded and liberalized the refinance facilities for export credit. Relaxed external commercial borrowings (ECB) regime for corporate and allowed non-banking financial companies and housing finance companies access to foreign borrowing.

The unconventional measures taken by the RBI include: a rupee-dollar swap facility of Indian banks to give them comfort in managing their short-term foreign funding requirements, exclusive refinance window as also a special purpose vehicle for supporting non banking financial companies, and expanding the lendable resources available to apex finance institutions for refinancing credit extended to small industries, housing and exports.

Taken together, the measures put in place since mid-September 2008 have ensured that the Indian financial markets continue to function in an orderly manner. Taking the signal from the policy rate cut, many of the big banks have reduced their benchmark prime lending rates Bank credit has expanded too, but slower than the last year.

Some Policy Issues

This author is of the considered view that no further easing or fiscal stimulus is needed to combat the crisis. The banks have already given thrust to financing of Micro Small and medium Enterprises. Special training programmes are being organized by the nationalized banks so as to ensure that the credit needs of MSMEs are adequately and promptly met with. In the wake of failure of few internationally reputed banks coupled with the failure of several cooperative banks particularly in the state of Maharashtra, the author is of the view to increase the present insurance cover of Rs. 5.00 lakhs to Rs. 10.00 lakhs provided by the deposit insurance and credit Guarantee Corporation. This will certainly benefit in boosting the depositors confidence. There seem to be no change in the present credit monitoring system by the Reserve Bank of India.

Future Scenarios

The economic downturn which began in 2007 and will continue through 2009 is expected by many analysts to be amongst the most severe in the past 100 years. While the scale of the downturn remains uncertain, the full impact on the real economy has not yet been felt. Although a global rebound is expected in 2010, even emerging economies have proven considerably more vulnerable than previously believed, demonstrating the integrated nature of global financial and credit markets.

The longer term trend in key developing markets such as China or India will be a gradual slowdown in growth over the same period. Inflation forecasts are clouded with uncertainty and commodity prices—especially those of oil-will play a key role in determining the growth outlook for most countries.

So far as Indian economy is concerned that its growth rate will considerably fall down during the current year on account of failure of the monsoon over a large area. It is feared that the dual effect of the economic crisis coupled with the failure of the monsoon will severally affect the Indian economy and will require sizable period for its turn around.

The Government of India is seriously concerned over this current state of affair, and has initiated several measures to tame down the impact of this natural calamity on the common masses.

References

EAC (Economic Advisory Council to the Prime Minister): Review of the Economy, 2008-09, January 2009.

Lahiri, A. (16th January 2009): "Indian Financial Reforms: National Priorities Amidst an International Crisis", Sir Purushotamdas Thakurdas Memorial Lecture, Mumbai.

Nachane, D.M. (2007): "Liberalization of the Capital Account: Perils and Possible Safeguards", *Economic and Political Weekly*, Vol. XLII, No. 36, Sept. 8-14.

National Commission for Enterprises in the Unorganized Sector (NCEUS) (Nov. 2008): The Global Economic Crisis and the Informal Economy in India, Govt. of India.

The Economist (6th March 2008): "The Decoupling Debate".

The Global Economic Crisis and the Impact of the Indian Job Market

KISHORE KUMAR ROY CHOUDHURY

INTRODUCTION

Global Economic crisis in Indian job market is the product of Globalization. Naturally effects of global crisis reflected Indian Economy particularly in the job market. It can generally be deserved that globalization is one aspect of the evolutionary process of history. Globalization has been propelling the advancement in the field of science and technology; bent the ongoing globalization has not been on the stream of history, rather it has been imported in the global economy. Known to be as Neo-liberal globalization, this theory stands on eight economic Principles;

1. Prime responsibility is to bestowed on the marketing system,
2. Personal ownership can always bring forth the skill par excellence,
3. As regards management private enterprise is always more efficient than the public enterprise,

4. Each individual has to spend money to meet up demands of everyday life, and there will be no subsidy,
5. Country will have to settle up complexities, if there be any, arising out of inequalities,
6. Individual freedom will be of prime significance in the society,
7. Individual interest will have to be given the primary importance, and
8. Unrestricted competition will have to be ensured.

SOME POINTS ARE EXPLICIT FROM THIS NEO-LIBERAL GLOBALIZATION

1. Private ownership is dominating factor under this system,
2. Object like the collective welfare may be neglected, and
3. Principle of maximization of profit will be operative. Consequently enterprises incurring social welfare with less profit may be neglected and, as a result, important issues may be set aside whereas only some specific items of socio-economic fields will achieve greater importance. A kind of inequality will evidently come. Some features of the socio-economic inequality arising out of the globalization in India are being discussed onwards.

STRUCTURAL CRISIS

According to the projection of United Nations Population Division, the world is very close to reach the peak of historically highest youth population. One of the critical issues at present is to make a better supply side of employment in world and India also. Demand of skilled workers in the knowledge economy has hindered the progress of a large portion of world youth, especially in the developing countries. Sufficient value addition enhancing employability in the new age labour marked has not been realized, although the youth of today find for the first time the emergence of an era when purely economic value of higher education has assumed an unprecedented magnitude.

A significant portion of the world's total youth population lives in India. It is seen from survey that largest percentage of unemployed population in India is education youth. This is due to rapid expansion of IT sector and vast pool of English speaking, science educated skilled labour force. In India organized job sector is appallingly low at less than 5-6%. Almost 95% of newly created jobare still in unorganized sectors. Undoubtedly, with the outset of the liberalization process, Indian economy is growing fast and employment opportunities are increasing. Clearly, the aspiration of half billion youth for better living standard and higher income jobs cannot be engineered by agricultural sector which accounts for 54% labour market but only 22% of GDP contribution keeping pace with the fast moving globalized economy Indian youth needs to be enriched with such value based education including necessary employment skills.

As per 2001 census, 61.6% labour force in engaged in agriculture as compared to 17.2% in industry and 21.2% in services. There are some continual changes with slowly increasing labour participation rate in services and decreasing share of agricultural with industry labour share remaining almost constant.

From different survey we are getting the following result:

(i) Unemployment rates in India are continuously rising since 1990; and

(ii) Unemployment rates in 2004-05 are highest since 1972-73.

Table 1 reveals the work participation rates (WPR) for males and females, Table 2 gives the labour force participation rates. Finally Table 3 reveals the unemployment rate. It is seen from the tables that the work force participation rates for females are significantly lower than that of males in rural areas. While more than half of all the rural males reported themselves as workers.

On a longer than basis would suggest that there is tendency for WPR to fall for rural areas. In urban areas, the trend suggests greater stability in WPR for both males and females.

Table 4 gives the percentage distribution of workers in

TABLE I

Workforce Participation Rates (WPR) from NSS

	Rural Male				*Rural Female*			
NSS ROUND	*PS*	*PS+SS*	*CWS*	*CDS*	*PS*	*PS+SS*	*CWS*	*CDS*
27 (July'72 June'73	54.5		53.0	50.3	31.8		27.7	23.1
32 (July'77-June'78)	53.7	55.2	51.9	48.8	24.8	33.1	23.2	19.4
38 (Jan-Dec'83)	52.8	54.7	51.1	48.2	24.8	34.0	22.7	19.8
43 (July'87-June'88)	51.7	53.9	50.4	50.1(48.2)	24.5	32.3	22.0	20.7(19.6)
50 (July'93-June 94)	53.8	55.3	53.1	50.4	23.4	32.8	26.7	22.0
55 (July'99-June'00)	52.2	53.1	51.0	47.8	23.1	29.9	25.3	20.4
61 (July'04-June'05)	53.5	54.6	52.4	48.8	24.2	32.7	27.5	21.6
	Urban Male				*Urban Female*			
NSS ROUND	*PS*	*PS+SS*	*CWS*	*CDS*	*PS*	*PS+SS*	*CWS*	*CDS*
27 (July'72-June'73	50.1		49.1	47.7	13.4		12.3	10.8
32 (July'77-June'78)	49.7	50.8	49.0	47.2	12.3	15.6	12.5	10.9
38 (Jan-Dec'83)	50.0	51.2	49.2	47.3	12.0	15.1	11.8	10.6
43 (July'87-June'88)	49.6	50.6	49.2	47.7	11.8	15.2	11.9	11.0
50 (July'93-June 94)	51.3	52.1	51.1	49.8	12.1	15.5	13.9	12.0
55 (July'99-June'00)	51.3	51.8	50.9	49.0	11.7	13.9	12.8	11.1
61 (July'04-June'05)	54.1	54.9	53.7	51.9	13.5	16.6	15.2	13.1

Note: PS: Principal Status, PS+SS: principal and Subsidiary Status, CES: Weekly Status, CDS: Daily Status, Figures in parenthesis for the 43rd round daily status are estimate obtained from unit records.

different sectors of Indian economy from 1961 to 2001. It is seen that there exists dominance of the primary sector in providing employment over time. It become below 60 percent for the first time in respect of main workers in 2001. Among the males there has been a faster decline in proportion of workers in the primary sector, especially between 1991-2001. It is basically the agricultural sector that has registered this decline. There is also a decline in proportion of both the cultivators and the agricultural labours between 1991 and 2001.

EFFECTS ON EMPLOYMENT

If we have a look at the composition of GDP and its growth, it is clearly indicated that globalization has practically little role in GDP growth. Rather globalization has played a negative role in the growth of agriculture, as it has been

TABLE 2

Labour Force Participation Rates (WPR) from NSS

	Rural Male				*Rural Female*			
NSS ROUND	PS	PS+SS	CWS	CDS	PS	PS+SS	CWS	CDS
27 (July'72 June'73	55.2		54.6	54.0	32.0		29.3	26.0
32 (July'77-June'78)	54.9	55.9	53.8	52.5	26.2	33.8	24.2	21.4
38 (Jan-Dec'83)	54.0	55.5	53.1	52.1	25.2	34.2	23.7	21.8
43 (July'87-June'88)	53.2	54.9	52.6	52.5(52.1)	25.4	33.1	23.0	22.2(21.5)
50 (July'93-June 94)	54.9	56.1	54.8	53.4	23.7	33.1	27.5	23.3
55 (July'99-June'00)	53.3	54.0	53.1	51.5	23.5	30.2	26.3	21.9
61 (July'04-June'05)	54.9	55.5	54.5	53.0	25.0	33.3	28.7	23.7
	Urban Male				*Urban Female*			
NSS ROUND	PS	PS+SS	CWS	CDS	PS	PS+SS	CWS	CDS
27 (July'72-June'73	52.6		52.2	51.8	14.3		13.5	12.5
32 (July'77-June'78)	53.2	53.7	52.7	52.1	15.0	17.8	14.0	12.7
38 (Jan-Dec'83)	53.1	54.0	52.7	52.1	12.9	15.9	12.8	11.9
43 (July'87-June'88)	52.8	53.4	52.7	52.3	12.9	16.2	13.1	12.5
50 (July'93-June 94)	54.2	54.3	53.9	53.4	13.2	16.5	15.1	13.4
55 (July'99-June'00)	23.9	54.2	53.9	52.9	12.6	14.7	13.8	12.3
61 (July'04-June'05)	56.6	57.1	56.6	56.1	14.9	17.8	16.7	15.0

Note: PS: Principal Status, PS+SS: Principal and Subsidiary Status, CES: Weekly Status, CDS: Daily Status, Figures in parenthesis for the 43rd round daily status are estimate obtained from unit records.

TABLE 2 *(Contd.)*

Census	*Rural Male*	*Rural Female*	*Urban Male*	*Urban Female*
1971	53.6	15.5	48.8	6.7
1981	53.8	23.2	49.1	8.3
1991	52.4	26.7	48.9	9.2
2001	52.4	31.0	50.9	11.6

Notes: WPR reported above includes main and marginal workers.

completely neglected under the influence of foreign investment. Budgetary allocation for agriculture has been reduced from 27 percent in the pre-globalization era to only 6 percent as recorded in the year 2007 contribution of agriculture has come down from more than 25 percent to less than 20 percent. Sector which has

TABLE 3

Unemployment Rate

	Rural Male				*Rural Female*			
NSS ROUND	*PS*	*PS+SS*	*CWS*	*CDS*	*PS*	*PS+SS*	*CWS*	*CDS*
27 (July'72-June'73	1.2		3	6.8	0.5		5.5	11.2
32 (July'77-June'78)	2.2	1.3	3.6	7.1	5.5	2.0	4.1	9.2
38 (Jan-Dec'83)	2.1	1.4	3.7	7.5	1.4	0.7	4.3	9.0
43 (July'87-June'88)	2.8	1.8	4.2	4.6(7.4)	3.5	2.4	4.4	6.7(8.6)
50 (July'93-June 94)	2.0	1.4	3.1	5.6	1.3	0.9	2.9	5.6
55 (July'99-June'00)	2.1	1.7	3.9	7.2	1.5	1.0	3.7	7.0
61 (July'04-June'05)	2.1	1.6	3.8	8	3.1	1.8	4.2	
	Urban Male				*Urban Female*			
NSS ROUND	*PS*	*PS+SS*	*CWS*	*CDS*	*PS*	*PS+SS*	*CWS*	*CDS*
27 (July'72-June'73	4.8		6.0	8.0	6.0		9.2	13.7
32 (July'77-June'78)	6.5	5.4	7.1	9.4	17.8	12.4	10.9	14.5
38 (Jan-Dec'83)	5.9	5.1	6.7	9.2	6.9	4.9	7.5	11.0
43 (July'87-June'88)	6.1	5.2	6.6	8.8	8.5	6.2	9.2	12.0
50 (July'93-June 94)	5.4	4.1	5.2	6.7	8.3	6.1	7.9	10.4
55 (July'99-June'00)	4.8	4.5	5.6	7.3	7.1	5.7	7.3	9.4
61 (July'04-June'05)	4.4	3.8	5.2	7.5	9.1	6.9	9.0	11.6

Note: Figures in parenthesis for the 43rd round daily status are estimates from unit records

TABLE 4

Percentage Distribution of Workers by Sectors of Employment India, 1961-2001

Year	*Primary*			*Secondary*			*Tertiary*		
1961	73.4	69.2	82.6	10.6	11.5	8.6	16.0	19.3	8.8
1971	72.6	70.4	83.0	10.7	11.3	7.7	16.8	18.3	9.4
1981*	69.4	66.3	81.6	13.0	14.0	9.1	17.7	19.8	9.4
1991*	67.4	63.4	81.1	12.1	13.3	8.1	20.5	23.3	10.8
2001*	57.2	53.0	71.0	17.1	18.0	13.9	25.8	29.0	15.2
2001*	62.0	55.2	76.8	16.2	17.8	12.8	21.7	27.0	10.4

* This row for 2001 gives the distribution of main workers into primary, secondary and tertiary categories. Therefore, the figures for 1971, 1981 and 2001 are comparable.

* Figures in this row include both main and marginal workers.

Note: Figures exclude Assam and Jammu and Kashmir. Like 1971, 1981 and 1991 distribution of workers into three categories relates to main workers only.

Sources: Premi (2003: 104); Census of India 1991 (1993); Census of India 2001.

grown fastest, that is service sector, is mainly due to growth in IT, BPO sector, etc. This can be attributed to technological factors. India has emerged a hub for medical tourism it is because of the excellent human resources in the field of medicine and surgery.

According to a recently published survey, the interstate pattern of human development in India is full of much strileing contrast and there are dangers inherent in several patterns. In one survey it is found that in the year 2000 the developing countries unitedly imported foodstuff worth 225 billion US dollar. In comparison to that in 1988 the growth of this imported value is 62 percent. In competition with the agriculture and foodstuff commodities as nursed by the national subsidy and other internal sources these all in the agriculture market of the developing countries lag far behind. One thing is clear in recent times that the local diversity and environment in the agricultural, field will suffer a lot on the way of globalization the agricultural tradition of the country too will suffer. It is found in a survey that the number of the petty and marginal peasants in India in 2000 and 2001 year had been 76% of the total number of cultivators. In 2003 that number increased at the rate of 8.5 per cent. National investment has been reducing in the agriculture field. Consequently, productivity in the agricultural field is poor. In the first five year plan 37 percent of the total expenditure had been invested in the agricultural field. In the tenth plan this rate become 19.8 percent. When investment reduces, the rate of agricultural development too will reduce. Survey of 2002-03 reveals that only 41.2 percent of the total cultivated land came under the irrigation system. Yet now almost 59% net cultivated land depends on rainfall for cultivation. Agricultural development in India is not growing in harmony with globalization. An uneven growth is noticeable. It is found that during the ninth plan, that is in 1997-2002, the production of food grain lags far behind the target of 21.2 crore ton. Dreams of foreign investment which the advocate of globalization had delineated, did not come true in every industry. What happened in fact was de-globalization. During 1998-2001 scanty foreign capital has been invested in this country, and that too has been utilized for purchase of the local shares of their own foreign companies. The private banking companies including the foreign banks started entry in the Indian banking business. As a result, an imbalance developed. The private banks concentrated only on corporate demands and on the cities and metropolitan fields, as a result of which the backward fields receded farther back. The gap between the towns and villages widened more and more. The technological advancement of the villages remained steadily furthering back from the technological advancement of the cities and towns. And as such the small scale enterprises are faced with disadvantages. The first large scum happened in connection with the share market. Survey shows that progressive countries have increases export, but the process of commodities production in the workshops has not increased income in that proportion. In progressive countries labour intensive procedure is closely related to the commodity production process in the factories. Therefore in this case, it can be presumed that the intermediaries class emerges.

Another impact of Globalization is visible in India. Recently 158 year old America investment bank Leman brothers has become bankrupt. The greatest insurance company A.I.G was almost on the point of becoming bankrupt. This depression is all due to the home loon crisis that in the U.S.A some years ago. The small banks cropped up of that country started sanctioning home loans to the borrowers at rates lower than the usual ones. As the borrowers did not pay back loan money these banks grew to be bankrupts. Impact of depression in the market of U.S.A was tangible in the Indian market too. Sensex smashed in India.

CONCLUSION

From census report it is seen that the total population in India was 84.6 crores in the year 1991 and it rose to 112.4 crore in 2006. The rate of growth of population was 1.96 percent from 1991 to 2001. The rate of growth of rural male unemployment in the year 2004 was 9 percent (5.6 percent in the year 1993-94) and it was 8.1 percent (6.7 percent in the year 1993-94) in urban area. This figure in established in the regular basis. The figure in the sphere of female was 9.3 percent (5.6 percent in 1993-94) and 11.7 percent (10.5 percent in the year 1993-94). It is also seen in another survey that the rate of growth of employment in the public sector was declining in the year 1998 and 1999. And it was negative figure in the year 2002. Again in the private sector the rate of growth of employment in the year 2001 was 0.1 percent. The rate of growth of employment in both public and private sector in the year from 1991 to 2000 was.64 percent. Again the rate of growth of employment in public sector in the year 2000-2003 was negative (-0.80) and in the same year this rate in the private sector was 0.61 percent. It can be said the motive of investors in the era of Globalization is profit gaining. That is the miserable employment growth in going on. It is not the way of long run socio economic welfare. Inequality growth both in rural and urban sector. Poor area growing poorer.

It is seen that interstate disparities in the growth of gross state domestic product (G.S.D.P) have increased in the post reform period. In general richer states have grown faster than the poorer states. There is a large potential for growth which needs to be exploited for sustaining development in the country over a long period. This is necessary for improving regional and social equity for strengthening national integration.

Although disparities have accentuated in the post reform period, they have been building up in the pre-reform period itself for example, in the early 1960's the per capita GSDP of the richer states like Panjab, Maharastra and Gujarat was, on average, about 80 percent higher than the bottom four states, viz. Bihar, Uttar Pradesh, Orissa and Madhya Pradesh. The disparity increased to 125 percent by early 1970's and it escalated steeply to 200 percent towards the end of the nineties. New investment in the private sector has a tendency to concentrate in an already well developed area. Since well developed area offers private investors certain basic advantages, viz. labour, infrastructure facilities, transport, market and other external economic facilities.

References

Debes Mukherjee: *Ibid.*, p. 53 and Economic Survey, 05-2006, p. 2008.

Debes Mukherjee: *Samakalin Bharatiya Arthanity* (Bengali): New Centrel Book Agency (Pvt.) Ltd., Kolkata, January 2008, p. 123.

Dhirendranath Konar: The Scenario of Population Growth in India, Akamsha Publishing House, New Delhi: First edition, p. 179.

Himanshu: Preliminary draft of paper presented at conference on Sustainable Development and Livelihood: Delhi School of Economic, February 6th 2007: Title: Employment Trends in India: A Fresh Look at Post-trends and Recent Evidence.

Mahindra, K. Premi: Population of India: In the New Millennium: Census 2001, National Book Trust: India, p. 248.

Swadeshi, op. cit., p. 7, *Patrika*: Vol. 3 (Article Dipankar Mukherjee, p. 7).

The Indian Economic Journal, Vol. 54, Number : April-June 2006.

Tirthajyoti Sarkar, Ph.D. Student, University of Illinois at Chicago: 2007 CIPE International Essay Competition: Higher Educational Reforms for Enhancing Youth Employment Opportunity in India.

Viswayan: Bhabna, Durbhabna: A Collection of Essays on Globalization in Bangla) : Chairman of the Editorial Board: Amiya Kumar Bahchi; NBA Private Ltd., Kolkata, Vol. 1. (Article Dipankar Mukherjee), p. 198.

Viswayan: Bhabne, Durbhabna: (Vol. II): *op. cit.*, pp. 80-81.

The Global Economic Crisis and the Indian Economy

KAMNA

It is enough to mention the commercial crises that, by periodical returns, puts the existence of the entire bourgeois society on its trial, each time more threateningly. In these crises there breaks out an epidemic that, in all earlier epochs, have seemed an absurdity, the epidemic of overproduction. Society suddenly finds itself put back into a state of momentary barbarism. And why ? Because there is too much civilization, too much means of subsistence, too much industry and too much commerce. And how does the bourgeoisie get over these crises ? On the one hand, by enforcing destruction of a mass productive forces; on the other by conquest of new markets and by the more thorough exploitation of the older ones. That is to say, by paving the way for more extensive and more destructive crises and by diminishing the means where by crises are prevented.

Paul Samuelsson observes aptly about the present global crisis or meltdown that this debacle is to capitalism what the fall of the U.S.S.R. was to communism. The shocking events that attract the attention of the world are well known. So are the immediate origin of the meltdown in factors like the sub-prime crisis and the "greedy and irresponsible" business practices of Wall Street bankers. But there are deeper causes much like Tsunami, the full extent of which it is too easy to measure.

The unprecedented financial catastrophe happened and American administration had to abandon the gospel truth of non-intervention in an almost unthinkable manner because global capitalism's strategic of 1970s after about three response to the crisis. There is a financial decades of partial success failed, aristocracy in the shape of promoters, speculators and nominal directors, a whole system of swindling and cheating by means of corporation promotion, stock insurance and stock speculation and of fictitious capital interest bearing paper which is enormously reduced in times of crisis.[1]

In a system of production, where entire continuity of the production process rests upon credit, a crisis must obviously occur a tremendous rush for means of payment, when credit suddenly ceases and only cash payments have validity. At first glance, therefore, the whole crisis seems to be merely a credit and money crisis.

However, it was only the advent of modern imperialism marked by new features like all-round monopolization export of capital outweighing export of commodities like rise of financial oligarchy, etc. that money capital metamorphosed into financial capital and attained a much more influential say dominant position.

The supremacy of finance capital over all other forms of capital means the predominance of the rentier and of the financial oligarchy. It means that a small number of financially powerful states stand out among all the rest. Thus twentieth century marks a turning point from old capitalism to the new, from the domination of capital in general to the domination of finance capital.[2]

The Wallstreet debacle that swallowed firms like Bear Stearms and Lehman Brothers and impeilled the insurance giant American Interntional Group (AIG) has been driven by the fact that they and their customers were linked to one another by derivatives.

The case of Lehman Brothers graphically illustrates what a transition to super speculation can lead to. Before this September the 158 years old organization survived the American civil war, the two world wars, the great Depression, the September 11 terrorist attacks and one takeover attempt. Why did this meet with the calamitous collapse this time round. The answer lies when International Financing Review announced its report in 2005 :

> "Today the credit system acts like a king of central nervous system through which the overall circulation of money capital, to and from activities, farms, sectors, regions and countries is coordinated. It is but natural that the world economy is behaving like a person who has just received severe head-*cum*-spinal injuries."[3]

This crisis originated from United states and affected severely European and others Asian and African countries. World Economy has been integrated through globalization, liberalization and privatization. Hence shock of this crisis is to be felt by major nations to a lesser or greater extent depending upon the integration of the country with global market.

In the beginning the government of India declared that Indian economy is insulated from the present crisis. Then, they come out with the admission that the global financial crisis will not affect us much. Manmohan singh along with his finance minister had to reluctantly admit that no developing economy could possibly remain immune to the global crisis. The global crisis of such historic proportion where the total bailout packages by all the countries workout to some $ 3 trillion but still there is uncertainly whether the system can be salvaged. Bush administration alone has announced bailout package to the tune of over $990 billion apart from injecting fresh investment worth $ 200 billion in banks and private financial institution to recover the shock. The contagion is truly global in a globalised world. How can the high priests of globalization in India expect to insulate the economy from all pervasive crisis. Already the financial crash is having its impact on trade, FDI, exchange rates, remittances, BOP, forex reserve and above all, on the macro-economy in India. Goodbye to the rosy stories of double digit growth miracles, it is now an impending debacle that stares economic analyst in the face.

The possible social impact is mindboggling. The new

middle class in India is witnessing its first financial meltdown and a possible recession. The IT-BPO myth would soon be blown. Anyway if the job losses are already running into lakhs in the U.S. one can well imagine how much political pressure will build up there against outsourcing. If such leading names like Morgan Stanley, Merrill Lynch, J.P. Morgan, Goldman sachs and Lehman Brothers start biting dust and their brightest kids are given unceremonious marching order India is surely for a bad time. All booms in India based primarily on foreign money will soon go bust. The surpluses of neo-rich in India would find a greener pasture in greater acquisition abroad than investing a new in the dwindling economy at home.[4] Immediate impact of meltdown on Indian economy are varied and diversified. It has embraced stock markets where investor's wealth worth Rs. 2,50,000 corers was wiped out on the bourses on a single day on 10th October 2008. The SNNSEX fell by 1000 points before recovering some 200 points and intraday drop of some 800 points.

Indian bankers are safe, reassured the Governor of the R.B.I. Indian banks exposures to international markets is relatively small at 6% of their total assets, the rating agency Crisil said adding that even lenders with large international operations have less than 11% of their assets overseas. Liquidity position in India is comfortable. The banks and financial institutions might be slush with funds once again but the interest rates ruling high there is no pick up in the credit off take by small and medium enterprises. They are the main employment providers in the industrial sector. The employment in this sector has already taken a heavy toll. A deep and prolonged recession in the West might result in unemployment for millions of these workers. The R.B.I. hurried to cut CRR by 150 basis points to 7.5%, releasing more than $ 12 billion fresh liquidity into banking system. But experience of the Great Depression shows that all monetary and fiscal measures failed to recover the depression during 1930s in the west.[5]

Amartya sen said Global meltdown has been created by financial mismanagement and solution lies in restoration of the confidence of the investors and people at large It implies economic crises may be eased on account of psychological confidence. Impact of meltdown was noticed in the field of exchange rate. From unprecedented appreciation earlier a few months back, the rupee fell to record low reaching Rs. 49 and odd per dollar at some points. During the preceding period of the rupee appreciated by around 18%, now it has depreciated by around 19% during January-September 2008.the exporters were crying earlier are happy but it now the turn of importers to come to grief.[6]

The trade deficit is reaching alarming proportions. If exports are growing, imports are growing even more. Thanks to the workers remittances NRI deposits, FIIF investment and so on; the current account deficit at around $ 10 billion does not look so threatening. But for some reasons if the remittances dry up and FIIs funds take flight, it will be repetition of 1991 after a few years if forex reserves get depleted and trade deficits keep increasing at the present rate. Unprecedented high forex reserves were becoming a burden as most of these funds were in dollars, the government had parked most of them in U.S. treasury bonds or invested them in securities and bonds in foreign banks.[7]

AN INDIAN RECESSION

It may be a slowdown in India till now but a recession can not be ruled out in the medium term. Finance minister is claiming 7.5-8% growth this year. ADB has predicted 7% growth. Many rating agencies have put it at 6.5% from around 11-12% in 2006-07. Agriculture would be the saving grace due to a good monsoon. The long-term sustainability of the existing pattern of FDI flow is a guess in the midst of the global liquidity .... well, if high growth is to be driven primarily by foreign capital assisted by government land grab, tax waivers, assured returns guarantee for infrastructure investment and fabulous BOT terms and so on. The ratio of saving and investment to the GDP reportedly remains high at 35% still there is a slow down in Indian economy. The core sector growth is down to less than 4%. All the vital productive sectors are on a slow down. With such a structural background if and when the Indian economy slips into a recession, it will be protracted and there will not be a quick revival.[8]

Many approved SEZs are in doldrums as they are not getting any units and this whole thing is a massive real estate speculation of gigantic proportion. Despite RBIs reservations, the banks were competing to lend to SEZs promoters there is virtual absence of national land use policy. The urban planning and improvement legislation did not have a peasantry orientation to begin with. The result has been that market forces continued dispossession of peasantry of its land through means fair or foul. The comparative statistics provided by the 43rd and 59th round of NSS in regard to ownership of agricultural land by rural households is noteworthy. As many as ten million hectares of agricultural land has passed out of the hands of the rural households between 1992 and 2003 during the first decade of economic reform.

In other words, the pro-poor shift in the ownership of land attempted by the decades of land reforms has been totally swamped by the dispossession effected by market. The SEZs the legally sanctified source of new zamindari and rightly the eye of the storm of peasants protests all over India is only the highly visible tip of the iceberg formed by the market forces.[9]

Creation of exploitative employment opportunities and working conditions resulting from nullification of labour protection laws. Harsh condition of workers in existing SEZs in India and China are well known. The Development Commissioner may declare SEZs as "public utility services under the Industrial Dispute Act, implying workers will have no right to strike. One estimate indicates that 1.14 lacs farming households and an additional 82,000 farm workers have been displaced without jobs and shelters.

Apart from these aspects financial implications are mindboggling. Revenue losses due to unnecessary tax concessions comes cumulative to SEZs over the period 2004-05 to 2009-10 of Rs. 1,75,487 crores. Annually this is equivalent to about 6-7% of the central government's receipts during 2005-06. The foregone tax revenue is four times the annual allocation for NREGS and can feed 50 million hungry people every day.[10]

SOCIAL IMPACT

Suicide after market crash is an urban trend. Whether it is a seemingly well to do U.S. resident of Indian origin wiping out his entire family of middle aged brother-sister killing their parents and then committing suicide, the financial crisis has hit everyone and has hit them hard. At least farmers go alone leaving their family members in the lurch. The middle class boom might be glamorous but the depression in incomes and lossess in the markets are far more agonizing. The job losses due to recession in the west as well as a slowdown in India would far outweigh such outsourcing gains. The Indian BPO sector derives 40% of its revenues from the financial sector of the developed countries. The IT-BPO sector in India accounts for 5.5% of the GDP but 30% of export and a very high share of service sector employment. The impact on working class by means of wage compression and work loads, illegal retrenchment and worsening of job security and working conditions, etc. would be onerous.[11]

NREGS was thought to be the most effective and efficacious programme for poverty alleviation and employment generation which became the victim of lack of political will and apathy on the one hand and bureaucratic inefficiency, corruption and procrastination on the other, it is neither implemented with a mission, now proper assets are created.

Dr. Suvharao, Governor, R.B.I. in his J.R.D. Tata Memorial lecture on July 31, 2009, said that global imbalances along with development in the financial markets were the two root causes of the crisis. There were large and persistent current account surpluses in Asian economies and correspondingly current account deficits in advanced countries. Central Banks in Asian countries invested their large reserves in government bonds of the advanced countries. This drove down risk free interest rates to historically low levels caused an unprecedented credit expansion, lowered credit standard, eroded credit quality and encouraged the search for yield at all costs. All these have been the factors responsible for the crisis.

Although India did not contribute to global imbalance, it remained affected by the crisis principally because of its integration, through trade and financial market, with the rest of the world over the last two decades. Global imbalances can never be eliminated but they have to be managed in such a way that they do not reach destabilizing levels. Globally credit revival was felt necessary with huge fiscal packages to stimulate demand. They had to recapitalize their banks.

In India too, there have been tension between monetary and fiscal policies. RBI is fully cooperative with the government for crisis management. The government and RBI needs to strike a balance between short-term compulsion and medium-term sustainability with great care and judgment. High fiscal deficits show the seeds of next inflationary cycle which is equally alarming. Well accepted policy of the Central bank is to promise stable growth, low inflation and low unemployment.

In India there are a number of reasons why inflation targeting is neither desirable nor practicable.

(i) The Central bank of a large economy will have to be guided by a number of objectives at the same time-price stability, financial stability and growth.
(ii) Food items have a large weight in the various consumer price indices. They are susceptible to supply side specially due to vagaries of the monsoon.
(iii) There are several inflation indices.
(iv) Monetary transmission in India is impeded by large fiscal deficits.
(v) In the context of volatile capital flow, a single point monetary policy loses much of its appeal.

Turning to the interplay between the real and financial sectors, the financial sector had no standing of its own. It derives strength and resilience from the real economy. It is the real sector that should drive the financial sector, not the other way around.

Although the Indian economy is very large, its growth over the last two decades was largely confined to only a small fraction of the population, catering roughly 23% of the people. It has bypassed 77% of the population. The rapid economic growth had trickled down to them only partially. This 23% has provided a market larger than most other economies and attracted world investors and traders. In industry there are 58 million enterprises providing employment to 104 million workers. They are working in the units with an investment of less than Rs. 5 lakh, yet they contribute 31% of the G.D.P. spread over the whole of India.

We must increase the finance and credit to the 54 million tiny, non-farm units but they get only 2.2% of the net bank credit extended in the country. Remaining 4 million units with an investment up to Rs. 25 lakh get hardly 4% of the net bank credit. Even 1% increase in credit to them will increase employment by roughly 10 million and output by 0.4% of G.D.P.

The Price-rise-due-to-drought warning is a fraud. Of course, of a drought and major crop failure will push up prices further. But prices were steadily rising for five years since the 2004 election, long before a drought. Take the years between 2004 and 2008 when you had some good monsoon. And more than one year in which we claimed "record production" of food grain. The price of rice went up 46 per cent, of wheat by over 62 per cent, atta 55 per cent, salt 42 per cent and more. By march 2008, the average increase in the prices of such items was already well over 40 per cent. Then, they rose again till a little before the 2009 polls. And have risen dramatically in the past three months.[12]

The Agriculture Minister appears to have figured out that the stunning rise in the price of pulses may have little to do with drought. "There is no reason," he finds, "for prices to rise in this fashion merely on a supply-demand gap." He then goes on to find a valid reason : black-marketing or hoarding, but remains silent on forward trading in agricultural commodities. Many senior Ministers have long maintained that "there is no evidence" that speculation related to forward trading has had any impact on food prices.[13]

The price rise since 2004 could be the highest for any period in the country barring perhaps the pre-Emergency period. For the media, of course, July was far more interesting for the political parties in parliament over the gas war between the Ambani brothers. When these two barons brawl, governments can fall. Also, how could atta be more interesting than airline tickets (the prices of which fell dramatically over several years)? Food prices might have gone up but airline travel costs went down and those are the prices that mattered.[14]

So the price of aviation turbine fuel became a far more to-be-covered thing as private airlines threatened a strike demanding public money bailouts. At the time of writing, it appears the government will try and make things cheaper for them. These airline owners include some associated with the IPL, which got crores of rupees worth of tax write-offs last year. Maharashtra waived entertainment tax on the IPL and with so many games held in Mumbai that proved a bonanza for the barons paid for by the public.

There's always money for the Big Guys. Take a look at the budget and the "Revenues foregone under the central tax system." The estimate of revenues foregone from corporate revenues in 2008-09 is Rs. 68,914 corers.[15] By contrast,, the NREGS covering tens of millions of impoverished human beings gets Rs. 39,100 corer in the 2009-10 budget.

Remember the great loan waiver of 2008, that historic write-off of the loans of indebted farmers? Recall the editorials whining about 'rascal imprudence? That was a one-time, one-off waiver covering countless millions of farmers and was claimed to touch Rs. 70,000 corer. But over Rs. 130,000 corer (indirect taxes) has been doled out in concessions in just two budgets to a tiny group of merchants hogging at the public trough. Without a whimper of protest in the media. Imagine what budgets giveaway to corporate since 1991 would total. We'd be talking trillions of rupees.

Imagine if we were able to calculate what the corporate mob has gained in terms of revenue foregone in indirect taxes. Those would be much higher and would mostly swell the corporate kitty for the simple reason that producers rarely pass on these gains to consumers. Let's take only what the budged of 2009-10 tells us. Income foregone in 2007-08 due to direct tax concession was Rs. 62,199 crores. That foregone on excise duly was Rs. 87,468 crores. And on customs duty Rs. 1,53,593 crores. That adds up to Rs. 3,03,260 crores. Even if we drop export credit from this, it comes to well over Rs. 200,000 crores. For 2008-09, that figure would be over Rs. 300,000 crores That is a very conservative estimate. It does not include all manner of subsidies and rate cuts and other freebies to the corporate sector. But it's big enough.[16] Simply put, the corporate world has grabbed concessions in just two years that total more than seven times the 'fiscally imprudent' farm loan waiver. In fact, it means that on average we have been feeding the corporate world close to Rs. 700 crores every day in those two years. Imagine calculating what this figure would be, in total since 1991. Ask for an expansion of the NREGS, seek universal access to the PDS, plead for more spending on public health and education—and there's no money. Yet, there's enough to give away nearly Rs. 30 crores an hour to the corporate world in concessions.

If Indian corporate saw their net profits rise in April-June this year, despite gloom and doom around them, there's a reason. All that feeding frenzy at the public trough. The same quarter saw 1.7 lakh organized sector jobs lost is the very modest estimate of the Labour Ministery. That's not counting the 15 lakh jobs said to have been lost in just the export sector between September and April by the then commerce secretary.

And now comes the drought. A convenient villain to hang all our man-made distress on – and sure to oblige by adding greatly to that distress. A huge fall in farm incomes is in the offing. If the government wants to act on a war footing, it could start with a serious expansion of the NREGS.

It could launch, among many other things, the pond-in-every-farm programme. It could restructure farm loan schedules. It could start getting the idea of monsoon management into its thinking. It could curb forward trading-linked speculation that was driving one of our worst price rises in history long before the drought was on the horizon. And it could declare universal access to the PDS. That cost could probably be easily covered by, say, canceling the dessert from the menu of the unending corporate free lying in this country.

In place of adopting above mentioned measures Mammohan Singh is suggesting the states to limit in the BPL beneficiaries while he is also expressing the confidence that no body will go hungry in the country. This is being done in the light of the National food security bill that is in the process. The Union government wants to limits the targeted BPL beneficiaries to 5.91 crores as per 2009 population estimates of present 6.52 crores. Majority of the states disputes the center's poverty estimates. They also do not want the present monthly entitlement of 35 kg of subsidized food grain per BPL cardholder reduced. It seems that nor only entitlement is truncated but even the number of beneficiaries is going to be reduced.

Politician are men of promises and Manmohan Singh is not an exception. In one breath he talks of inclusive growth and declares no body will die for want of food and when he announces to truncate the number of persons of BPL and reduces the quantum of food grain for the Antyodya scheme to be reduced in the future, this appears to be irreconcilable. Hence, it is resulting in bailout packages for industrialist, it amounts to marching order for the poor who need bailout most.[17]

Notes and References

1 Arindan Sen, Finacial Tsunami in USA, Invetigating the Root causes and Broader Implications, *Liberation*, November 2008.

2. Arjun Sengupta, Planning for Inclusive development. *Janta*, Vol. 63, No. 47, 14.12.2008.

3. B. Sivaraman, Impact of U.S. Meltdown on Indian Economy, *Liberation*, November 2008.

4. Banbari Lal Sharma, National Conveyor Campaign Against SEZ and Land Displacement, *Janta*, Vol. 64, No. 9, May 3, 2009.

5. *Ibid*.

6. C.R.L Nursimhan: A Succinct Exposition of the Global Economic Crisis, *The Hindu*, 17/08/2009.

7. Communist Manifesto.

8. Government of India. Budget 2009-10.

9. Ibid., p. 10.

10. Ibid., p. 12.

11. Ibid., p. 9.

12. *International Financing Review*, 2005.

13. *Manmohan Singh, Prime Minister. The Hindu*, 31.8.2009, Delhi.

14. P. Sainath, Drought of Justice, Flood of Funds, *The Hindu*, Saturday, August 15.2009.

15. P. Sainath, *Op. cit*.

16. S.P. Shukla, Globalizations: Life and Livelihoods, *Janata*, Vol. 63, No. 11, April 6, 2001

17. S.P. Shukla, *Op. cit*.

Tackling Unemployment Problem under Global Recession: Can Self-Help Groups be the Solution?

REKHA RAMESH GAONKAR AND ELIZABETH JOEY HENRIQUES

BACKGROUND OF THE STUDY

The industrialized economies of the world witnessed large scale economic crisis. The economic upheaval triggered chiefly by the sub-prime mortgage bust in the United States has had a cascading effect on the global economy. The crumbling of large global institutions, the loss of their credibility and the consequent liquidity freeze wrecked havoc across nations. While major economies of the world—the US, the European countries, Japan went into a state of recession, growth in Asian countries has slowed down.

The Indian economy has not remained isolated from the fallout and implications of the global recession. India's growth rate in 2008-09 was 6.7% as compared to 9% in the previous year. The findings of a first of its kind survey conducted by the Labour Bureau of the Ministry of Labour and Employment to find out the impact of the economic slowdown on employment in India revealed that 5 lakh people were rendered jobless in a period of two months between October and December 2008.

As Sudha Pilla, Secretary of the Ministry of Labour and Employment noted 'The Ministry of Labour and Employment took serious note of the economic slowdown and it felt the need to have an assessment of its impact on employment to enable the Government to take preventive and ameliorative measures to arrest the decelerating employment in the country.' The Government has been sensitive to the fallout of the recession on the domestic economy. The monetary and fiscal policies of the Government have reflected the need for crises management. India has been experiencing a chronic unemployment problem for years. The displacement of many skilled and unskilled workers due to the recession has compounded the problem. Under such circumstances micro-credit and Self Help Groups would help to create some modest employment opportunities if not high paid jobs.

The implications and consequences of the recession on employment call for a rethink and revaluation of the very perception of growth and development and the strategies adopted to achieve the same. To quote Albert Einstein, "We can't solve problems by using the same kind of thinking we used to create them." The Keynesian philosophy of 'pump priming' and 'compensatory finance' has not lost its relevance. The rationale behind advocacy of government spending and largesse in times of recession is the need to augment purchasing power and the propensities to consume in the economy. Augmentation of income in the hands of citizens would serve as the requisite catalyst to kick start the economic engine. For this, however, the problem of employment generation will have to be addressed. The government needs to step in and tackle the issue of unemployment by initiating various preventive and ameliorative measures.

This paper is an attempt to explore the possibility and potential of the SHG-Bank programme as an effective tool of employment generation in both normal and recessionary times. In a country like India characterized by a 'rural-urban' and 'rich-poor' divide, the SHGs have emerged as a ray of hope for employment creation and poverty alleviation. The researchers have relied on their findings based on field data collected to conclude and confirm the significance and relevance of Micro Credit and SHGs in the task of addressing the problem of unemployment.

LITERATURE REVIEW

In recent times micro-credit and SHGs have come to be looked upon as a 'magic bullet' for many economic problems experienced by the marginalized sections of society. The SHGs function as the core of the micro-credit programmes. Governments have been using SHGs as a via media to generate employment opportunities. Self Help Groups are voluntary associations of people, generally women who share a homogenous and common socio-economic background. A single group consists of 10-20 members and may or may not be registered. SHGs constitute the core of the micro-credit programme. The micro credit being disbursed both from the thrift fund as also from the formal credit delivery system to the poor through the SHGs has enabled them not just to satisfy their immediate consumption needs but also in the longer run to set-up small micro-level enterprises and build sustainable livelihoods.

Several researchers and academicians have studied the impact of micro-credit and SHGs. Zaman, H. (2001) asserts in his impact study of micro credit in Bangladesh (A case Study of BRAC) that Self Help Groups have played a valuable role in reducing the vulnerability of the poor through asset creation, income and consumption smoothing, provision of emergency assistance and empowering and emboldening women by giving them control over assets and increased self-esteem and knowledge. Puhazhendi and K.J.S Satyasai (2001) who assessed the performance of SHGs located in 11 states in India by undertaking a pre and post-SHG situation study of different economic and social variables, found that membership of the SHG has succeeded in cultivating the habit of thrift among members, has brought about an improvement in asset ownership, savings, etc. Khandker's (2003) study found that those who are poor in landholdings and formal education generally participate in micro-finance programmes. The study also reveals that the micro-finance programme has benefited the extremely poor sections of society and has also resulted in reducing the extent of poverty at the village level with its spillover effects.

The impact of micro-credit on employment has been specifically studied by several researchers. Husain (2002) in his study based on women borrowers of the Grameen Bank in Bangladesh observed that more than 80% of the women had no productive occupations before joining the SHG. The bank had generated new employment for the women SHG members thereby increasing the labour force participation rates. Prasad (2000) noted in his study that SHGs had facilitated the increase in the number of man-days of employment. The income generating activities taken up by SHG members is generally at a micro level and is informal in nature. Most of the members are involved in agro-based activities. Snehalatha (1994) reported that SHG members were involved in activities such as dairy farming, sericulture, vegetable cultivation and micro business. Hommes (1997) whose study on SHGs in Vietnam revealed that animal breeding and fruit crop raising were the common micro-enterprises undertaken. As pointed out by Jerinabi (2002), micro-credit programmes extend small loans to the poor people for self-employment projects that generate income, allowing them to care for themselves and their families.

OBJECTIVES OF THE STUDY

1. To throw light on the employment status of the SHG members 'before' and 'after' joining the SHG.
2. To detail the type of employment that the SHG programme has generated.
3. To examine whether the SHG programme has brought about a substantial change in employment generation.
4. To find out if there is any difference in the size of impact on employment in SHGs formed by NGOs and SHGs formed by the Government under the Swarnjayanti Gram Swarozgar Yojana.

METHODOLOGY

The State of Goa comprises of two districts – the North Goa District and the South Goa District. For the purpose of the present study, a total of 100 SHGs were randomly selected. Fifty SHGs were randomly selected from each of the two districts. Of the 100 SHGs selected, 50 have been formed by different NGOs operational in the State while the other 50 have been promoted by the State Government under the Swarnjayanti Gram Swarojgar Yojana. While the latter respondents belong to the Below Poverty Line (BPL) population, membership of SHGs formed by NGOs by and large is Non-BPL. The SHGs selected have been in operation for a period of three years and above. Structured interview schedules were administered to five members of each of these 100 SHGs. A total of 500 SHG members were interviewed. The findings of the paper are based on the responses of these respondents. In order to assess the impact of the SHGs on the SHG members a 'before SHG' and 'after SHG' approach has been adopted. Besides the primary data collected, secondary sources of data viz. journals, newspapers, books and the internet have also been employed. Simple statistical tools such as percentage as also the 'paired *t*-test' have been utilised to analyse the data. Data analysis has been done using the SPSS package. The field data for the present study was collected during the period September 2007 to March 2008.

MAIN FINDINGS OF THE STUDY

Employment Status Pre- and Post-SHG Membership

Several factors motivate the entry of individuals into SHGs. While some individuals seek membership of SHGs so as to avail of credit and enhance their savings, there are others who view the SHG as a via media to self-employment. Earlier studies highlight the positive impact that SHGs have had on employment generation. It is through the SHG that the members can avail of credit with the help of which they can initiate some income generating activity or micro-entreprise. Table 1 throws light on the employment status of the respondents 'before' and 'after' joining the SHG.

TABLE 1.1

Employment Status of Respondents Pre- and Post-SHG Membership

Employment Status	*Pre-SHG Membership*		*Post-SHG* Membership	
	Frequency	*Percent*	*Frequency*	*Percent*
No	299	59.88	75	15.00
Yes	201	40.20	425	85.00
Total	500	100.00	500	100.00

Source: Field data.

From the data in Table 1 it is clear that there has been a significant change in the employment status of the respondents after joining the SHG. While 299 (59.88%) respondents were not engaged in any economic activity prior to SHG membership, post SHG membership, the number of respondents who continued to remain unemployed was 75(15%). On the other hand, the SHGs facilitated in the creation of 224 additional employment opportunities.

Nature of Employment Generated Through SHGs

Table 2 details the sector-wise employment of the respondents before and after joining the SHG. It can be inferred from the data that the maximum employment has been generated in the trade/secondary sector.

Majority of the respondents (47.8%) are engaged in small business and retail trade. Women have a tendency to take up informal activities such as preparation of sweets, pickles, papads and other edible food items which don't have much of a market. Furthermore, it has been observed that these income generating activities are replicated by many members of the SHG who reside in the same locality leading to unhealthy competition and conflicts of interest between group members. Not much attention is paid to the packaging of the product or its pricing. The study findings indicate that while just 34 of the respondents were employed in the secondary sector prior to joining the SHG, the number swelled to 239 post-SHG membership. Additional employment generated in the primary sector was comparatively

TABLE 2

Sector-wise Employment Status of Respondents Pre- and Post-SHG Membership

Sector	*Nature of Economic Activity*	*Pre-SHG Memberhip*		*Post-SHG Membership*		*% Change*
		No.	*%*	*No.*	*%*	
Primary Sector	Agriculture, horticulture, dairy, fishing	131	25.2	132	26.4	1.2
Trade	Grocery and general stores, Sale of readymade garments, retail trade–sale of milk, vegetables, fruits, handicrafts, pickles, papads,sweetmeats and other eatables.	34	6.8	239	47.8	41.0
Services	Catering, mid-day meals, tailoring, tuitions.	17	3.4	35	7.0	3.6
Employed	Government and Private sector	19	3.8	19	3.8	0.0
No Activity	Housewife/unemployed	299	59.8	75	15.0	44.8
TOTAL		500	100.0	500	100.0	

Source: Field data.

negligible (1.2%). Just 7% of the respondents are engaged in activities associated with the services sector. The study findings also indicate that employed individuals have also become members of the SHGs. A total of 19 respondents are salaried public and private sector employees. It has however been observed that those involved in preparation of sweets and other edible items of food do not have regular employment as the number of days they are employed is conditioned by the demand for their products which by and large is not consistent.

IMPACT ON EMPLOYMENT GENERATION

An attempt has been made to analyse whether SHGs have significantly impacted employment generation. The paired *t*-test has been used to test the hypothesis. In order to examine the impact of SHGs on employment, the number of days that the respondents have been employed 'before' and 'after' joining the SHG has been considered.

Hypothesis

H_0: SHGs have not had any significant impact on employment generation.

Testing of Hypothesis using Paired t-test

H_0: SHGs have not had any significant impact on employment generation

H_1: SHGs have significantly impacted employment.

TABLE 3A

Paired Samples Statistics

	Mean	*N*	*Std. Deviation*	*Std. Error* Mean
Number of Days Employed After Joining SHG	127.91	500	110.266	4.931
Number of Days Employed Before Joining SHG	67.78	500	107.005	4.785

TABLE 3B

Paired Samples Correlation

	N	*Correlation*	*Sig.*
Number of Days Employed After Joining SHG & Number of Days Employed Before Joining SHG	500	.688	.000

TABLE 3C

Paired Samples Test

	Paired Differences							
				95% Confidence Interval of the Difference				
	Mean	*Std. Deviation*	*Std. Error Mean*	*Lower*	*Upper*	*t*	*df*	*Sig. (2-tailed)*
Number of Days Employed After Joining SHG - Number of Days Employed Before Joining SHG	60.122	85.817	3.838	52.582	67.662	15.666	499	.000

Computed from Field Data.

Table 3a provides descriptive statistics related to the before and after periods with regards to mean, number of respondents, standard deviation and standard error of mean. While the mean number of days employed per annum before joining the SHG is 67.78, the mean number of days employed per annum after joining the SHG is 127.91. The correlation Coefficient for the 500 pairs of observations is 0.688 with a significance value of 0.000. Furthermore the mean difference between the two pairs of observations is 60.122. This implies that the number of days the respondents were employed before joining the SHG is lower than the number of days employed after joining the SHG. The test results show a *t*-statistic of 15.666 with 499 degrees of freedom. The two-tailed *p*-value is 0.000 which is less than the 5% level of significance. Thus it is proved the SHGs have positively impacted employment. The average number of man-days of employment in the two periods viz. 'before' and 'after' joining the SHG is significantly different from each other.

The null hypothesis is therefore rejected at 5% level of significance which implies that the SHGs have indeed positively and significantly impacted employment.

The results of the study are consistent with the view that micro-credit programmes and SHGs help in enhancing employment.

An attempt has also been made to find out the **impact size** based on the formula used by Rosenthal (1991) Rosnow and Rosenthal (2005) and Field, A. (2005)

Calculation of Effect Size

$$r = \sqrt{t^2 / t^2 + df}$$

$$= \sqrt{15.666^2 / 15.666^2 + 499}$$

$$= \sqrt{245.42 / 245.42 + 499}$$

$$= \sqrt{245.42 / 744.42}$$

$$r = 0.57$$

wherein,

r = Effect Size
t = Paired t statistic
df = Degrees of freedom

It can be inferred from the analysis that the impact on employment is considerable as 0.5 is considered the threshold of a large impact size. Thus, on an average, the number of man-days employed before joining the SHG is significantly less (M = 67.78, SE = 4.785) than the number of man-days employed after joining the SHG. (M =127.91, SE = 4.931, t (499) = 15.666, $p < 0.5$, r = 0.57)

Employment Generation in SHGs Formed by NGOs and SHGs Formed by the Government

In the present study an attempt has also been made to examine the efficiency of the Self Help Group Promoting Institutions in generating additional employment (SHGPIs). Two SHGPIs have been taken into consideration – the NGOs and the Government which through its District Rural Development Agencies is actively involved in the promotion of SHGs under the Swarnjayanti Gram Swarozgar Yojana (SGSY) in the State. Table 4 reveals the additional job creation in SHGs formed by these two promoting agencies.

It is evident from the data presented in Table 5 that the impact on employment has been positive irrespective of the agency which has promoted the SHGs. However it can be inferred from the data that the NGOs have been more successful in generating additional employment as compared to the Government. While in the case of the former, 138 respondents were gainfully employed post SHG membership, in the case of the latter, 86 respondents took up income generating activities after joining the SHG. This disparity in employment generation can be attributed to the fact that while the focus of the government agencies *vis-à-vis* SHG formation is target-oriented, the NGOs take upon the task of SHG promotion as a mission towards realizing the goal of a better and more progressive society. This finding is echoed in the study by Choudhury and Mohan (2001) who mention that NGOs are better equipped for Capacity building of SHGs and promotion of micro-enterprises.

TABLE 4

Employment Status Pre- and Post-SHG Membership—Promoter-wise

Sr. No.	Promoter	Employment Status				Additional Employment Generated	
		Pre-SHG Membership		Post-SHG Membership		Nos.	Percentage
		Unemployed	Employed	Unemployed	Employed		
1.	NGO	173	77	35	215	138	27.6
2.	Government	126	124	40	210	86	17.2
3.	TOTAL	299	201	75	425	224	44.8

Source: Computed from field data. Figures in brackets indicate percentages.

CONCLUSION AND SUGGESTIONS

It is quite evident that SHGs in the State of Goa have contributed to generation of additional employment opportunities. The study findings indicate that a large proportion of these jobs created have been in the informal sector. The paired *t*-test testifies to the positive impact that SHGs and microcredit have had on employment generation. Furthermore, employment generation is more in the NGO promoted SHGs compared to the Government promoted groups. The basic reason for this anomaly is the role played by the various SHGPIs. NGOs are found to be more active. Besides, as SHGPI's, the performance of the DRDAs has been found wanting. On the other hand, it has been observed that the mobilisers and field staff employed by other SHGPIs like the NGOs, Co-operatives, Voluntary Agencies and Social Workers restrict their activities not just to promoting SHGs but are also continuously monitoring the activities of the SHGs, arranging for training programmes, imparting skills to SHG members, interacting, guiding and motivating them to participate in productive economic activities. The philosophy of these organizations is based on the realm of people-centered development. However, there are certain areas of concern. It has been observed that the respondents take up income generating activities that don't necessarily have long-term sustainability. Lack of marketing linkages for the products is a severe handicap to the women entrepreneurs. Members also lack entrepreneurial abilities and are not equipped with the requisite skills and training to pursue and make their business a success. To address the challenge of employment promotion among the SHG members, capacity building, skill development, development of appropriate marketing strategies, planning and cost-benefit analysis is necessary. The different SHGPIs operating in the State need to look into these issues.

On a larger perspective, taking the economy as a whole into consideration, the fact that the SHG-Bank linkage programme can effectively address and ameliorate the problem of unemployment particularly among the poor and marginalized sections of society cannot be ignored. The SHG programme already has State patronage. The programme has proved that the poor are 'bankable'. The high repayment rates and the negligible rates of default certify that this segment of society whose credit requirements were otherwise bypassed by the formal banking system can be relied upon as 'credit worthy' customers. The SHG programme already enjoys State patronage. Its potential as an employment generator however needs to be recognized and acted upon. The SHG movement needs more momentum and coverage so as to bring into its fold a larger segment of society it caters to. There is also a need for an effective regulatory mechanism to ensure that the Micro Finance Institutions do not aggrandize their own profits at the expense of the poor and that the benefits of the programme percolate to those for whom it is intended.

However, it is to be noted that the job opportunities SHGs offer might solve the problems of semi-skilled and unskilled unemployed workers. As far as job creation for skilled workers is concerned, the Government will have to take up some concrete and effective steps by way of deliberate and appropriate fiscal and monetary measures.

References

Business Standard, October 13, 2009.

Choudhuary R.C. and N. Mohan (2001), Micro Entreprises Development and SHGs, Micro Credit for Micro Entreprises, Hyderabad: National Institute of Rural Development, p. 403.

Field, A.. (2005), Discovering Statistics Using SPSS (2nd Edition), Sage Publications.

Hommes, T.D. (1997), Self Help Groups in Vietnam, Development and Co-operation, Vol. 5, pp. 25-26.

Jerinabi, U. (2002), Microcredit Management by Women's Self Help Groups, New Delhi, Discovery Publishing House, p. 7.

Khandker R Shahidur (2003), Micro-finance and Poverty: Evidence Using Panel Data from Bangladesh, World Bank Policy Research Working Paper, 2945.

Prasad, V. (2000), Self-Employment-women Set to Change Face of Kolar, *The Indian Express*, May 21, 2000, p. 9.

Puhazhendhi, V. and Satyasai, K.J.S. (2002), Economic and Social Empowerment of Rural Poor through Self Help Groups, *Indian Journal of Agricultural Economics*, July-Sept. 2002, Vol. 57, No. 3.

Rosenthal, R. (1991), Meta-analytic procedures for social research (revised) Newbury Park, CA, Sage Publications.

Rosnow, R.L. and Rosenthal. (2005), Beginning behavioral researcah: A conceptual primer (5th Edition), Englewood Cliffs, NJ: Pearson/Prentice Hall.

Snehalatha, M. (1994), A Study on the impact of thrift and credit groups in improving the status of rural women, M.Sc. Thesis, Andhra Pradesh Agricultural University, Hyderabad.

http://www.nabard.org

http://www.wikepedia.com

Zaman, H. (2001), Assessing the poverty and vulnerability impact of micro credit in Bangladesh: A case study of BRAC, Unpublished background paper for World Bank, World Development Report, 2000-01, Washington.

Can the Present Post-Crisis Recovery be Sustained?

SAROJ SINHA AND C.K. SHAHI

India, the countries within the country, 1.14 billion diversities, 21 languages, the world's greatest problems and the million opportunities to solve them, the 'system' and the systematic, the leaders and the politicians, booker prizes and thumb impressions, the who-you-know and the what-you-know, high tea and hunger, yoga and traffic jams, khajuraho and moral police, arranged marriages and happily-ever-afters, gold medals and red tape, yesterday and tomorrow—all exist in perfect harmony. A management miracle, as some would call it. May be that's why the world thinks the Indians are the best guys to well manage the world.

Planning Commission deputy chairman Montek Singh Ahluwalia has said India's economic scenario may be grimmer in 2009 compared to 2008. The IMF, Asian Development Bank and other institutions each of this, seeing India's growth rate falling to 5 per cent or below. There may be ground to brace for a deeper downturn but India's growth, even revised downwards, would remain relatively healthy. In last year's final quarter, the US economy contracted by an annualised rate of 6.2

per cent and Japan's economy by 12.7 per cent. India's estimated growth rate was 5.3 per cent during the same period. The comparison speaks for itself.

India needs effective firefighting but some jolts are beyond anyone's control. Exports, for instance, plunged 21.7 per cent in February, thanks to a global demand slump, making even the revised 2008-09 export target of $170-175 billion look like a tall order. While a narrower trade deficit is good news, the fall in non-oil imports indicated poor domestic demand for capital goods and raw materials, suggesting stalled expansion by industry. So, India must focus on domestic economic activity to shore up growth. The Planning Commission, for instance, says 2009-10 could clock 7.4 per cent growth with boosted public investment in construction.

Signs of healing are apparent in sectors like auto, or steel and cement thanks to construction in rural and semi-urban sectors. If urban middle-class consumption is down, rural demand is buoyant. There has been record capital outflow but FIIs seem to be coming back. Equally heartening is that the Committee on Financial Sector Assessment, analysing the results of bank stress-testing, has found Indian banks in relative clover in terms of cost-to-income ratio or capital adequacy. Though its report did not consider the post-crisis period, its reference to India's financial sector resilience stands, even accounting for global turmoil. Regulatory grip on public sector banks would, however, require easing in future given the financial sector's need to expand, innovate and modernise in a heavily underbanked country.

Inflation last week was expected to go below zero but the 0.31 per cent figure bucked in nine-week declining trend. While low inflation stimulates spending, there has been concern over whether it reflects sluggish demand. The last thing a slowing economy needs is to go into a deflationary tailspin, with consumption withheld on expectations of a persisting price slide. Whether such anxieties will be further assuaged this week remains to be seen. To boost demand, the RBI must boldly use its considerable legroom on monetary policy at a time the combination of massive debt and falling tax receipts makes it imperative for the government to balance fiscal expansion and consolidation.

The latest cuts in overnight interest rates for banks are accompanied with the now-customary exhortation that they should, in turn, bring down the cost of credit for the economy at large. The central bank's admonitions have been largely ignored through the five reductions in its policy rate to 5 per cent from 9 per cent from October 2008. State-owned banks are lending to their prime customers at around 12 per cent and private banks charge up to 4 percentage points more, not significantly less than a year ago. Partly because banks don't seem able to shake-off their aversion to risk and partly because the government's humungous borrowing programme is overwhelming the money market.

Of the Rs. 390,000 crore the Reserve Bank has pushed into the system since the global credit market seized up, the government would have moped up Rs. 326,512 crore in the year to March 2009. Next year, the government intends to borrow another Rs. 332,835 crore. Add to this the leeway states have been given to borrow in excess of their medium-term targets. Financing the Centre's fiscal deficit—optimistically projected at 5.5 per cent of the GDP—is crowding out lending to other sections of the economy, explaining the downward stickiness of interest rates. As the central bank nears the end of its rate—easing cycle—and that does not appear too far off—interest rates will face mounting pressure to climb. Beyond a point, the pressure will also be felt on the price line.

Which is altogether not a bad thing. A combined central and state deficit of 11 per cent and a tax-to-GDP ratio of 12 percent mean the government is spending every fourth rupee in India. Bumping this up to take the slack in the economy is a copybook response. The tricky bits are the quality of government spending and the long tail in scaling it back. Deficit financing is self-limiting if the government's working expenses edge out investment by companies, as is happening at this point. If we are to come out of this mess not too badly bruised, focused spending—and not merely more spending—is key. When it comes to governments, bigger is not necessarily better.

The world is in its worst economic shape since the Great Depression. While it's easy to lay the blame on Gordon Gekko-types, the meltdown is a bit larger than Wall Street. It's now clear the past two decades of boom hid a Giant Global Imbalance two ends of whom were the US and China. It toppled over last year and the consequences continue today. A short, imbalanced history is put forth below.

Let us first of all discuss the American Excess whose Problem : It all starts with the end of Yakee frugality. Ove a 20-year period, Americans gradually stopped saving. By 2006, the US's balance books were redder than a Trotskyite. Americans were pulling in about $800 billion a year from overseas to pay for their consumption which resulted in imbalance. Normally, this would have led the rest of the world to shy away from the dollar, thus forcing up US interest rates and curtailing American excess. It didn't happen. The reason is China which may be dubbed as Sino-surplus. There the problem is that like other East Asian tigers, China has been exporting like crazy and making its people save like crazy. When Singapore does this, it's a drop in the bucket. When a billion people do it, it generates an ocean of capital looking for places to invest. This also lead to an imbalance. All this capital should have driven up the renminbi's value and helped reduce exports. Beijing didn't allow. It hoarded the dollars, creating a foreign exchange mountain. Some of the dollars, mixed with Chinese savings, were directed into infrastructure and factories. Combined with an artificially low currency, this meant even more exports and more dollars. This Ponzi Cycle further created a problem. What to do with a trillion-plus dollars in reserves ? China financed US government debt. This kept US interest rates low and encouraged American extravagance. This became a vicious cycle. More US spending meant more Chinese exports which meant more US debt buying, which meant more US spending. This, in turn, created a further imbalance. So long Chinese lending matched US spending, this system—sometimes called Bretton Woods II—might have gone on for years. But a US-China imbalance became global and US spending became speculative.

The above narrated situation created a Global Divide which created a fresh Problem. The US wasn't alone in overconsuming. China wasn't alone in oversaving. Britain was an economic microcosm of the US. Oil-rich Gulf states, Germany and most emerging economies did some variation of China's dollar-sucking. By 2008 emerging economies had a capital surplus of about $900 billion, well ahead of the US capital deficit.

This added to the existing imbalance. The world was financially divided. One half let its credit markets finance spending gone mad. The other half fiddled their currencies or suppressed consumption to ensure dollars kept coming in. India did a bit of both and on a smaller scale, making it a bit more sure-footed than most.

Let us now consider what might have been the outcome. It aggravated the ongoing problem. As The Economist wrote, if all this capital had been invested in new technology this could have had a fairytale ending. But the dotcom bust put tech in the doghouse. Washingtonians focussed on using its share of the capital to pay for two wars, New York City focussed on real estate speculation. To top it all, central banker to the World Alan Greenspan believed markets would self-correct. But China wasn't acting like a market economy. Its action had to be compensated by US regulatory action—and Greenspan didn't act.

Consequently, a new Imbalance cropped up further. Cheap capital began flowing into US real estate. It mated with a belief that new derivative instruments meant risk could be spread around the world and reduced to zero. This begat the subprime monster. As a senior IMF official said, "Subprime offered high returns, no risk. Amazingly, educated people fell for this." By 2007, over $400 billion worth of US home buying was purely speculative. Owning two or three houses made Americans fell even richer, so they bought even more geegaws made in China.

The future, thus, appears to be imperfect under all the present turmoil, the world economy may actually be rebalancing. The average American is spending less, saving more. China's exports are crashing and Beijing is trying to stimulate domestic demand. The readjustment is, therefore, proving painful. Industries that did well out of US spending are sinking. Commodity economies like the Gulf states and Russia who boomed because of China's export machine are in free fall.

Will a Great Global Balance emerge when the dust settles? Yes, but it won't be easy. The US economy is 3.3 times larger than China's, notes Michael Pettis of Peking University, so China would have to increase consumption by an impossible 40 per cent to balance the present US savings rate of 6 per cent of GDP.

China, like most emerging economies, sees dollar reserves as family silver and won't sacrifice them without a fight.

Looked at this way, the US's attempt to hold up spending through stimuli and China's determination to export are silly as both shore up the Great Global Imbalance. The truth is that it can't be saved. All this stuff only softens the landing. The market will dictate a rebalance. It may be for the better. As economist Ed Yardeni of Yardeni Research argues, recessions are essential to a capitalist economy because they "purge the economy of speculative excesses".

Warning : Even with the meltdown, the world is and will still be flush with capital. Post-World War II, only the US generated wealth. Today, there are a dozen centres of wealth creation. It seems strange to say so now, but the world had better start thinking of how to use all this excess money two years hence. What we don't want is Uncle Sam pulling out his credit cards again. What we do what is capital into emerging economy infrastructure and new technology.

Have stimulus packages brought the world's traumatised economies back to life? Or have they set the scene for inflation and big future debt burdens? The answer is that they may have done both. The key question now concerns the order in which these outcomes occur. The theory behind the massive economic stimulus efforts that may governments have undertaken rests on the nation of the 'output gap'. This is the difference between an economy's actual output and its potential output. If actual output is below potential output, this means that total spending is insufficient to buy what the economy can produce.

A stimulus is a government-engineered boost to total spending. Government can either spend more money itself, or try to stimulate private spending by cutting taxes or lowering interest rates. This will raise actual output to the level of potential output, thereby closing the output gap.

But the stimulus effect of quantitative easing is far less certain than even that of fiscal stimulus. While the policy caused credit spreads to narrow and bond market liquidity to improve, many banks have been using the extra money to rebuild their balance sheets (the equivalent of increased household savings) rather than lending it to businesses and individuals. Several conclusions can be drawn from what admittedly are back of the envelope calculations. The first is that stimulus packages around the world arrested the slide into depression, and may have started a modest recovery.

Second, it is too early to scale down the stimulus, as Japan and the US seem ready to do. As one British official said ahead of the G-20 summit in Italy in July, "We should start to prepare exit strategies, but we should start implementing them only when [we] are sure [we] have got a recovery that is entrenched and self-sustaining, and I don't think anyone is saying we are at that point yet".

Third, existing policy, even if maintained, will not produce self-sustaining recovery. At best, it offers the prospect of several years more of sub-normal activity. A double round of stimulus packages is needed to counteract the real prospect of a double-dip recession.

The time to start worrying about inflation is when the recovery is entrenched. To pay back the debt without strain, we need a booming economy. Talk of government spending cuts is premature. "A boom, not a slump, is the right time for austerity at the Treasury", said Keynes who was ever right.

The International Monetary Fund's (IMF) latest outlook for the world economy has a lot of hope pinned on Asia, particularly India and China which it sees growing at 5.4 per cent and 8.5 per cent, respectively, in 2009. The swift turnaround in the rest of Asia's export-oriented economies is also 'remarkable'. But it is a rebound fed by temporary factors like fiscal and monetary easing, resumption of capital flows, and inventory adjustment. "These forces may not be able to bring about a self-sustaining recovery if activity does not strengthen in other regions," The IMF warns. "The challenge is to determine when and how to withdraw policy support while ensuring a successful transition to more balanced medium-term growth."

The US and Europe are in for protracted adjustments as they repair their financial systems and households that suffered asset price bubbles busts rebuild their savings. The IMF estimates potential growth in the US will remain below 2 per cent for a considerable time on permanent output losses relative to pre-crisis trends. As a corollary, Asia will have to tweak its demand to rely less on exports. The structural shift requires wider social security to discourage precautionary Asian savings, more robust financial markets to lessen the dependence on foreign capital and flexible exchange rates to restore the global trade balance. For the immediate future, the IMF flags double-dip recession. "Is a renewed recession in the offing over the next year as expansionary monetary and fiscal policies loss impetus and private demand fails to gain momentum in the face of limited credit?" The answer : there is recovery, but it will be weak by historical standards.

India's aggressive fiscal expansion has put it at the forefront of this recovery. Its stock market has climbed a staggering 110 per cent from its post-crash low and its factories are restocking inventories furiously. Historically, India has trailed most of Asia in exports, so the dependence on the West for demand revival is low and the need for medium-term restructuring will be less onerous. The principal area of concern is the timing of the exit strategy. Being among the first to recover, India will have to unwind its fiscal and monetary stance at a time when most of the world will be pursuing it vigorously. A small price to pay for standing out in a crowed.

The world is stepping out of the deepest recession since World War II within a year of being plunged into it, thanks to the largest coordinated bailout in history. The International Monetary Fund (IMF) said Asia is pulling for ahead of the rest, but its assessment of India's economy appears understated. The IMF retained its projection for Indian economic growth at 5.4 per cent in 2009. This implies that growth would be slower during July to December. Gross domestic product (GDP) for April to June quarter grew 6.1 per cent, up from 5.8 per cent in the previous quarter.

For IMF's projections to come true, India's GDP would have to grow at an average of 4.85 per cent during July to December—an unlikely scenario given recent macro-economic data that mirrored signs of a recovery.

Industrial output rose by 6.8 per cent in July, with manufacturing, which accounts for 80 per cent of overall industrial output, growing by 6.8 per cent. But the real story lay in the consumer durables sector that galloped ahead at a healthy 19.8 per cent—implying private consumer demand is reviving growth through increased purchases of refrigerators and televisions. "Indian think-tanks including National Council for

Applied Economic Research (NCAER) have always been optimistic about growth here", said Suman Berry, director general, NCAER. "Investment seems to be reviving and that is a positive sign." The RBI, whose projections are considered to be the most conservative, has maintained an overall growth of more than 6 per cent, while the finance ministry has been consistent with a 6 per cent plus forecast. Professional forecasters and think thanks have projected a growth rate of about 6.5 per cent.

Major Asian economies achieved a remarkable rebound from the global financial crisis, but it is not certain the recovery can be sustained. China and India would lead Asia's expansion in 2010, growing at rates of 9 and 6.4 per cent, respectively. Japan will grow 1.7 per cent in 2010.

Export-dependent China, Japan and smaller neighbours faced slumping demand for their manufactured goods and a decline in investment after the collapse of Lehman Brothers last year. Their outlook improved during the first half of 2009. The recent, swift turnaround of economic fortunes is remarkable. Questions remain about whether the rebound can become a self-sustaining recovery – ahead of a stronger growth pick-up in the rest of the world.

China, which along with Indonesia and India was the only Asian economy to escape severe recession, achieved a growth of 7.1 per cent in the first half of 2009, fuelled by a huge domestic stimulus plan. That helped a region-wide recovery.

Asia's intensifying rebound was driven by expansionary fiscal and monetary policies, a recovery in financial markets and capital inflows, as well as the build-up of depleted inventory. Despite these positive signs a sustained turnaround is not assured.

References

Bhagwati, J., "Anti-globalisation : Why?", *Journal of Policy Modeling*, 26.

Business Week, "Look who's sweating now", *Business Week*, 42.

Fortune, "The Merger mania countinues", *Fortune*, 132.

Gordon, J., "Is Globalisation a myth or a fact?", [Online]. Available : http://www.jakeg.co.uk/essay/globalisation.htm.

Harrison, B., Lean and Mean: The Changing Landscape of Corporate Power in the Age of Flexibility, New York: Basic Books.

Klein, N., No Logo: No Space, No Choice, No Job, London: Flamingo.

Krugman, P., Pop Internationalism, Cambridge MA: The MIT Press.

Lang, T. and C. Hines, The New Protectionism: Protecting the Future against Free Trade, London: Earthscan.

Maddison, A., Monitoring the World Economy, Paris: Organisation for Economic Cooperation and Development.

Martin, H.P. and H. Schumann, The Global Trap: Globalization and the Assault on Prosperity and Democracy Pretoria: HSRC.

Matthews, R., "The myth of global competition and the nature of work", *Journal of Organisational Change Management*.

McMichael, P., Development and Social Change: A Global Perspective, London: Sage.

Shah, A., WTO Doha "Development" Trade Round Collapse. [Online]. Available: http://w.w.w.globalissues.org/TradeRelated/FreeTrade/Dohacollapse.asp.

Ukpere, W.I., "The functional relationship between globalisation, internationalisation, human resources and industrial democracy". (Ph.D. Thesis). Cape Town: Cape Peninsula University of Technology.

World Federation of Exchange, Derivative Market Survey, Paris: WFE/IOCA.

Index